In memory of Mary Appleton, my maternal grandmother, and Mr Tibbs, so much more than just a feline companion over the past fifteen years of my writing life.

POSTCARDS FROM SANTIAGO

ALSO BY SPENCER VIGNES

The Server

A Few Good Men: The Brighton & Hove Albion Dream Team

The Wimbledon Miscellany

Lost in France: The Remarkable Life and Death of Leigh Roose,
Football's First Superstar

The Train Kept A-Rollin': How the Train Song
Changed the Face of Popular Music

Bloody Southerners: Clough and Taylor's Brighton & Hove Odyssey

Eric & Dave: A Lifetime of Football and Friendship

THE GEORGE ROBLEDO STORY

POSTCARDS FROM SANTIAGO

THE FIRST OVERSEAS STAR OF ENGLISH FOOTBALL

SPENCER VIGNES

Biteback Publishing

First published in Great Britain in 2025 by
Biteback Publishing Ltd, London
Copyright © Spencer Vignes 2025

978-1-78590-974-0

10 9 8 7 6 5 4 3 2 1

A CIP catalogue record for this book is available from the British Library.

Set in Minion Pro and Gotham

Printed and bound in Great Britain by
CPI Group (UK) Ltd, Croydon CR0 4YY

FSC
www.fsc.org
MIX
Paper | Supporting
responsible forestry
FSC® C013604

'To travel is to live.'

HANS CHRISTIAN ANDERSEN

CONTENTS

AUTHOR'S NOTE

Several of those who kindly agreed to be interviewed for this book consider English to be their second language. Rather than reworking or 'polishing' quotes so the sentence construction seems less Spanish and more English, their words have been left pretty much as said. If someone's speech pattern appears a little unorthodox or quirky, then that's probably why.

Prior to 1992, the four main professional football leagues in England and Wales were known as the First Division, Second Division, Third Division and Fourth Division. The First Division is now the Premier League, the Second Division is currently the Championship, the Third Division is League One, and the Fourth Division is League Two.

INTRODUCTION

It was a question that had everyone in the room stumped almost to the point of silence.

'Who holds the record for the most league goals scored by an overseas player in the top flight of English football in a single season?'

I felt as if I should know the answer, having written about sport for the vast majority of my adult life. But I didn't. There I was, appearing as a guest at the Brighton branch of Sporting Memories, a UK charity which encourages older people to meet and reminisce through talking about sport, and I'd seemingly been exposed as a total fraud.

A few educated guesses had been made initially by the twenty or so members who'd gathered to hear me talk about my latest book before getting down to the far more serious business of their weekly Monday morning quiz.

Thierry Henry?

Cristiano Ronaldo?

Jürgen Klinsmann?

What about Dennis Bergkamp? Or Luis Suárez?

One by one, our quizmaster, the former England rugby union international, cricketer and BBC broadcaster Alastair Hignell, batted away each incorrect answer, including my own shot at restoring some professional pride (Mohamed Salah, just in case you were wondering).

Gradually, the suggestions became little more than shots in the dark. Robin van Persie? Gianfranco Zola? Osvaldo Ardiles? Not Ricky Villa, surely? Robert Pires? Until, in David Ginola's wake, the well of potential candidates ran dry and an air of befuddlement fell across the group.

Maybe it was the presence of the former Wales and Newcastle United goalkeeper Dave Hollins in the room that did it, but out of the blue, someone came up with a name, the correct name at that – George Robledo.

George Robledo! Yes, YES!

…and it all came flooding back.

Some twenty or so years previously, I'd covered a Newcastle United game at St James' Park during the managerial reign of Bobby Robson, often cited as one of the nicest guys to walk the Earth, let alone work in football. The post-match press conference had ended, but Robson continued talking to some of us hacks who weren't on a deadline about his heroes, the ones he'd watched playing for Newcastle while growing up in north-east England in the years immediately after the Second World War. He mentioned Jackie Milburn – I knew about him. He mentioned Joe Harvey – I knew about him too. He mentioned Bobby Mitchell – I'd sort of heard of him. But then

Robson said another name, which meant absolutely nothing to me. That name was George Robledo.

Clocking a couple of blank expressions in our midst, Robson gave us George Robledo in a nutshell. I wasn't taking notes, just listening intently, but this much I do recall – he'd come as a boy from Chile to Yorkshire, worked as a miner prior to becoming a professional footballer (Robson had also served underground as a trainee electrician at a colliery in County Durham) and scored lots of goals for several clubs. I also recollect Robson saying he saw plenty of George Robledo in Alan Shearer. Praise indeed, as anyone who might remember Alan Shearer in his 1990s pomp would acknowledge.

On the long drive back home, I thought a lot about George. Here was someone who scored thirty-three league goals for Newcastle United in the First Division (or the Premier League in today's money) during the 1951–52 Football League season. No other overseas registered, foreign-born player had reached that number before and no other overseas registered, foreign-born player has reached that number since (although as I write, Mohamed Salah of Liverpool is indeed doing his level best to change that). At the time of my visit to Brighton (January 2023), Manchester City's Norwegian international striker Erling Haaland was on course to break George's record, a feat Planet Football has since decreed he achieved. But then, as one extremely clued-up member of that Sporting Memories group had pointed out, Haaland was actually born in Leeds. As in Leeds, England, where his father once played football. Going by the rules of geography, George is, as I write, still the record holder. Splitting hairs? Maybe, maybe not. It all depends how accurate or perhaps pedantic you want to be.

Either way, there were two undeniable truths about George Robledo. One, he'd clearly been a phenomenal football player. And two, his remarkable achievements seemed to have been almost completely forgotten about in his adopted country. Over the course of writing and researching this book, I've learned a little about how this has been allowed to happen.

The British Isles (and as a sports writer, this is something of a bugbear of mine) has morphed into the undisputed global leader for airbrushing large chunks of its football history from the public consciousness. If it occurred before 1992, when football was rebranded rather than reinvented with the arrival of the English Premier League, then it's almost as if it never happened. Forget about Stanley Matthews. Forget about Tom Finney and John Charles. Forget about Nat Lofthouse, Jimmy Greaves and Denis Law. Forget 'em all, because they played a long time ago when the world was black and white and their achievements don't really count anymore – or so the brainwashers would have you think. This doesn't happen in Italy. It doesn't happen in Spain. It doesn't happen in Brazil, Argentina or any of the game's other traditional bastions. It doesn't happen in George's native Chile. And yet, when it comes to the British Isles (and I say the British Isles as the gravitational pull of England's top football clubs has long been particularly felt in Ireland and Wales), the delete button has been pushed on huge swathes of what went before, burying the treasure instead of celebrating and preserving it.

On reaching Cardiff, I fired up my laptop to see if a book had ever been written about George, partly because I wanted to read one and partly (the greater part, admittedly) because I'd felt a sudden calling and fancied having a go myself.

No such book existed.

So I went for it, blind at that stage to what exactly I was taking on but determined to unearth the treasure that was, and indeed remains, George Robledo. The catch about unearthing something long hidden is that besides all the 'wonderful things', as Howard Carter described the contents of Tutankhamun's tomb on first sight, you can also chance upon plenty of heartache. And so it would prove with George. To paraphrase Gordon Sumner, aka Sting, born a modest walk from St James' Park when George was at his zenith as a player, love can mend lives, but it can also break hearts.

Then again, George Robledo's generation were masters in the art of triumphing over adversity. Which, from where I'm sitting, is another reason why the British Isles should strive to be more Italian, more Spanish, more Brazilian, more Argentinean and more Chilean in terms of remembering those footballing greats once familiar to millions. It's not as if they haven't got astonishing stories to tell, even if they do come at you from beyond the grave.

Spencer Vignes
Cardiff, Wales
March 2025

1

ALL THOSE YEARS AGO

'We shall go on to the end.'
– WINSTON CHURCHILL

George Robledo saw the ball coming late, almost too late to do anything about it. Under normal circumstances, he would draw his head back before bringing it forward sharply to meet the heavy brown leather orb, much as a cobra attacks its prey. Doing it that way, he found, put more pace on the ball, and more pace on the ball meant the goalkeeper was less likely to react in time to make a save.

But these weren't exactly normal circumstances.

Six minutes remained in the 1952 FA Cup final, the last six minutes of what had been a long, demanding season, consisting of forty-two league games and half-a-dozen FA Cup fixtures. In the league George had notched thirty-three goals for Newcastle United, topping the First Division scoring charts in the process. Another five had followed in the FA Cup, taking his overall tally for the campaign to a thumping thirty-eight.

Now, in game seven of Newcastle's FA Cup run, beneath the twin towers of Wembley Stadium, with Winston Churchill – *the* Winston Churchill – on hand to present the trophy to the winning team, George was feeling tired and frustrated. Of all the opportunities that had presented themselves in his dreams to score goal number thirty-nine, only one had materialised in reality (and he'd blasted that high over Arsenal's crossbar just after half-time). Usually George would be confident that, even at this late stage, one more chance would present itself. Today, he wasn't so sure. Even if it did, would 'Pancho', as his teammates called George on account of his Chilean heritage, have the required stamina and composure to break the stalemate and score the winner?

Bobby Mitchell, Newcastle's mesmeric left-winger, reckoned he knew the answer. Tall, thin and blessed with a deceptively lazy stride that fooled many an opponent, the Glaswegian was determined to set George up with that one last chance. Sure, Mitchell could see his teammate was flagging mentally as well as physically. All the more reason to plant the ball right on George's head so he barely had to move for it.

As Arsenal's defenders closed in, Mitchell steadied himself before crossing towards the far post, where George, during a conversation in the dressing room at half-time, had told him he would be waiting should such a scenario present itself.

And he was.

That was the good news. The not so good news was the ball came towards George at speed through a crowded penalty area. With little time to react, he instinctively let it glance off his brow towards the near post, the one place he knew George Swindin in the Arsenal goal might struggle to cover. At which point, the entire stadium and everyone inside it – the players, the spectators, the officials, the press men, the photographers around the touchline, even old Winston himself – seemed to freeze. Or at least they did to George. It was as if, he would recall many years later, Wembley Stadium was a record player and some giant hand had reached down and lifted the needle, cutting the sound as well as the action in an instant.

Would the ball end up in the net to register the only goal of the game?

Would Swindin scramble across in time to make the save?

Would the ball hit the post and come back into play or go out for a goal kick to Arsenal?

…or would he faint right there and then through sheer exhaustion before discovering the answer to any of the above (more than a possibility, so his ailing body told him)?

All of this was being played out in mere seconds, which, to George, felt like an eternity.

When the giant hand eventually returned the needle to the record, it came accompanied by a roar from the Newcastle supporters among the 100,000-strong crowd. George's header had struck the inside of Swindin's left-hand post on its way into the back of Arsenal's net. For the second year running, Newcastle United had won the FA Cup and Tyneside was going to party like it was 1945. As were parts of Yorkshire, Chile and just about anywhere else connected to the Robledo family and their remarkable story.

He considered himself to be a calm, rational soul, did George. War tends to shape you that way, as does a depression, post-war frugality and thirteen months working down a coal mine. The perfect recipe, without a doubt, for a grounded personality.

And yet scoring the winner in an FA Cup final can do funny things to a person.

Did George celebrate his goal by careering around the field like a speedboat without a driver, despite his aching limbs? Yes, he did. Did he jump partially clothed into the swimming pool at the team hotel later that evening? That would also be a yes. Did he amble up and down the corridors of the train carrying the team back to Newcastle, singing songs and handing out cigarettes to strangers? Yes, yes, he did that as well. All totally out of character. But then how often does a player get to score more league goals in a single season than anybody else *and* the winner in a cup final? If you can't let your hair down then (and George did indeed have a lovely head of jet-black hair to go with his film star looks), when can you?

He knew what this would all mean, of course. For more than three years, ever since George had started scoring goals for Newcastle United and especially since starring for Chile in the 1950 World Cup, the lucrative offers to go and play abroad – where footballers weren't constrained by a maximum wage and could virtually name their price – had flooded in. Now there would, inevitably, be more. It was a nice problem to have and George certainly wasn't complaining. Except that moving overseas would involve uprooting the whole Robledo family – himself, his mother and his two brothers – yet again. Wherever one went, the others followed. That was the rule. All for one and one for all. George loved Newcastle and its people, just as he'd loved Yorkshire on arriving in England from Chile as a child. Leaving certainly wouldn't be easy. On the flip side, going abroad equalled financial security. The itch he'd developed to travel and experience different cultures would get scratched.

4

As long as he kept scoring goals for Newcastle, the dilemma over whether or not to leave England wasn't about to go away.

Right now, however, George resolved to live life in the moment and enjoy himself for a few precious days. He had an FA Cup winner's medal in his back pocket, as did his brother Ted, a fellow member of Newcastle's victorious Wembley team. The fact they'd shared in the experience, having literally come so far together in their relatively young lives, made it all the more special for the pair of them. Ted had even played a part in the winning goal by passing the ball to Bobby Mitchell, stationed on United's left flank.

Part of living in the moment involved returning to the pile of newspapers that his mother had bought after the final. You know, just to make sure Swindin hadn't in fact saved his header. In particular, George found himself drawn to a black and white photograph that captured the exact point in time when the needle had returned to the record. There was teammate Jackie Milburn on the right, with his back to the camera. There was George tussling with Arsenal defender Lionel Smith, both men looking towards the goal, one in hope, the other in despair. And there, oh joy of joys, was the ball on its way over the line, the beaten Swindin helplessly observing its passage.

'As the press cameras caught it!' screamed the headline on page six of *The Journal*, Newcastle upon Tyne's daily newspaper. 'George Robledo has done the damage. The ball, headed in, has just struck the inside of the Arsenal goalpost and is on its way into and across the goal.'

The Journal wasn't the only newspaper which featured the photograph. Most of the UK nationals carried it, as indeed did many of the other big regional titles such as the *Birmingham Post* and *Liverpool Echo*, which, like *The Journal*, doubled up as national papers, bringing important domestic and world news to the doorsteps of local readers.

And so it came to pass that the photograph was spotted by an eleven-year-old pupil at Dovedale Road Primary School in Liverpool called John Lennon. So taken with the photograph was Lennon, despite not really liking football, that he painted a picture of it. The only difference, besides the addition of some colour to Wembley's turf and the players' kits, was the ball hadn't yet crossed Arsenal's goal line in Lennon's picture. Instead, it hung tantalisingly in mid-air, with Swindin seemingly poised to make the save. At the top he'd scribbled 'John Lennon, June 1952, AGE 11', accompanied at the bottom by just one word – 'football'.

In the years that followed, John Lennon would become one of the twentieth century's most celebrated songwriters, both as one-quarter of a certain rock and pop combo called the Beatles and a solo artist. When the time came to choose the artwork for his 1974 album *Walls and Bridges*, Lennon reached for a selection of paintings and drawings dating back to his final term at Dovedale Road. Among them was his recreation of George Robledo's winning goal in the 1952 FA Cup final, which ended up being reproduced on the front cover.

George had felt tired. He'd felt frustrated. It had, up to the point when he scored the winning goal, been George's worst performance of the entire 1951–52 season. John Lennon didn't know any of that. The eleven-year-old future Beatle simply recognised the photograph for what it was – a knockout action shot of a football player scoring a goal. A football player who, ironically, had taken his first steps on British soil in Lennon's home city of Liverpool. A football player who, like Lennon, lacked a father figure. A football player raised by a strong, independent, uncompromising matriarch, also like Lennon.

'The worst pain is that of not being wanted, of realising your parents do not need you in the way you need them,' Lennon would declare in a 1971 interview. George Robledo knew that pain. It was, in part, what spurred him on to such greatness in his chosen sport. But then he also had Elsie Robledo, his mother, to fall back on. Those record-breaking thirty-three goals in the league during the 1951–52 campaign, plus the six in the FA Cup, belonged as much to her as they did to him.

Little could George have imagined that his record, the one for the most league goals scored by an overseas player in the top flight of English football in a single season, would stand for such an extraordinarily long time.

2

TOMORROW NEVER KNOWS

'Fear is petrol.'

– JUDI DENCH

She weighed almost 18,000 tonnes, measured 551 feet in length and spent the vast majority of her working life ploughing backwards and forwards between her home port of Liverpool and Valparaíso in Chile. That was the MV *Reina del Pacifico*, Spanish for 'Queen of the Pacific', launched in Belfast in 1931 and regarded as something of a jinx by those who served aboard her. There was the time when she ran aground on a sandbank off Bermuda with over 400 passengers on board, remaining beached for three days until being successfully refloated. There was the time a crankcase in her engine room exploded during trials in the Irish Sea, killing twenty-eight crew members and technical staff employed by her owners, the Pacific Steam Navigation Company. Perhaps most famous of all, there was the time when former UK Prime Minister Ramsay MacDonald died on board as she made her way across the Atlantic Ocean. The old man's health had been failing and he'd been greatly affected by the recent death of King George V, who he counted as a good friend. A holiday in South America, it was felt, would do him wonders. The *Reina* and her dark reputation soon put the kibosh on that.

Then there were the multitude of other less newsworthy dramas that play out when you throw hundreds of people together at sea for days or even weeks on end – such as the one that befell Elsie Robledo and her three sons one March morning in 1932.

Born in the terraced house that was 3 York Street, West Melton, Yorkshire, on 27 October 1895, Elsie Oliver – as she started out in life – had not long turned twenty-three when she took up a job in Argentina as personal assistant to the wife of George Ellis, a well-to-do chemical engineer employed in the mining industry. In 1924, Mr and Mrs Ellis relocated to Oficina Alianza in Chile, a rough and ready outpost in the Atacama Desert renowned for its large deposits of sodium nitrate (sometimes known as Chile saltpetre), used in the production of explosives and fertiliser as well as preserving meat. Elsie went with them, and it was in Oficina Alianza that she met Arístides Robledo, the twinkly eyed company accountant at the mine where Ellis worked.

Arístides and Elsie married, settled down and had three children. There was George, born on 14 April 1926. There was Edward, better known as Ted, born on 26 July 1928. Then there was Walter, born on 8 December 1931, by which time Mr and Mrs Ellis were on the point of cashing in their chips and returning to the UK. A military coup led by General Luis Altamirano had tipped Chile into a period of political instability, with no fewer than ten governments holding power between 1924 and 1932. Throw in the effects of the Great

Depression, along with the bell beginning to toll on Chile's saltpetre mining industry, and the ties that once bound the couple to South America were fraying.

And so George Ellis booked passage on the *Reina del Pacifico* for all five of the Robledos. Elsie's South American odyssey was at an end. Though both her parents had died since she'd left West Melton, returning to the relative security of Yorkshire, with its familiar faces and steadier employment prospects, made perfect sense. When the day came, the Robledos made their way to Iquique to meet the ship, bound for Liverpool, on its first scheduled stop out of Valparaíso. Up the gangway on the port side they went, at which point the *Reina* started casting its witchy spells.

'They were there with their bags, ready to depart, at which point my grandfather, Arístides, said he was going back to buy cigarettes for the journey', says Elizabeth Robledo, the only child of George Robledo.

And he never returned. Everyone was looking for him all over the boat. It even waited long past its departure time while the search went on. In the end they couldn't hold it any longer, so they pulled up the gangway and the boat left without him, but with my father and the rest of his family on board.

Why did Arístides do it? That, in the Robledo family, was always the million-dollar question. Maybe he couldn't face the prospect of leaving his homeland? Maybe his marriage to Elsie was disintegrating? Perhaps, as his youngest son Walter always suspected, Arístides was having an affair and abandoned ship to be with his secret love?

'Anything is possible,' says Elizabeth Robledo.

What we do know is that he vanished. Apparently, he turned up in his home city months later. They say he was very, very embarrassed about what he had done and that he just couldn't leave his relatives behind in Chile. But who knows what else was going on with him? I don't know and I'm not sure whether my father ever did either. He never talked to me about what happened that day. I heard it mentioned in conversations, but they were never very long conversations because I don't think there was much to talk about.

At six years old, a child can show empathy, tell right from wrong and distinguish between fantasy and reality. Touch wood, they will have learned to count on the unconditional love and support of both parents. Despite the importance of school, family will still be the overriding influence on their development. Walter Robledo was only three months old when the *Reina* set sail from Chile without his father on board. Ted was three years old. George, however, was just one month shy of his sixth birthday. He might not have understood the reasons why his father had suddenly walked out of their lives, but he would have known that's exactly what he'd done. Without any explanation, without any goodbye, without so much as a backwards glance.

Antofagasta. Callao. Mollendo. Paita. Balboa. Cristóbal. Kingston. Havana. Bermuda. Vigo. A Coruña. Santander. One by one, the *Reina* ticked off its various ports of call en route from a Chilean autumn to a European spring, twenty-four days at sea in no-frills, third-class accommodation. Twenty-four days for a young boy to keep himself occupied, having explored every deck, corridor and lounge within hours of leaving Iquique.

Twenty-four days for a young boy to think, 'What happened back there?'

Finally, on Saturday 2 April 1932, Liverpool loomed out of the haze, with its bustling quaysides and scuttling Mersey ferries. Back down the *Reina*'s stairs went the Robledos, minus Arístides, to be processed by customs and immigration before embarking on the final leg of their mammoth journey, this time by train through the Pennine hills to Elsie's native Yorkshire. What questions she must have faced on setting foot in West Melton for the first time in fourteen years can only be imagined. Elsie, though, was made of stern stuff ('formidable' appears to be the word most commonly used to describe her). We know not, all these years later, whether she ever expected or indeed wanted to see Arístides again. What we can say is that the Elsie Robledo who arrived in West Melton in 1932 was determined to make a fresh start for her children as much as herself. An estimated 9 million people left Liverpool during its heyday as a port to pursue new beginnings in the New World. Mrs Robledo and her three sons bucked the trend by sailing the other way, yet her desire to create a new life for them in her old world burned just as fiercely.

Soon after arriving, the Robledos moved into 97 Barnsley Road, West Melton, living above a corner shop which had, up until then, been run by one of her uncles. The shop was called Oliver's and it was known for selling hardware and timber, but Elsie turned it into a general store providing all and sundry.

As for George, he started attending the nearby Brampton Ellis Infant School before graduating to Brampton Ellis Juniors. Despite his reserved nature, making friends came relatively easy. It helped that English was his first language, courtesy of Elsie. Communicating with other children was not a problem. But he also excelled at ball games, particularly football and tennis. For any child or young person parachuted into a new environment, sport can be a great leveller. Being good at it gets you popular quickly. The fact that George was modest and not at all big-headed about his talents made him even more appealing to his classmates, girls as well as boys.

The hand that life had dealt him meant George grew up fast during those early weeks, months and indeed years in West Melton. 'I look at pictures of him at that time and he seems very mature compared to the other boys his age,' says Elizabeth Robledo.

That's because he assumed the responsibility of being a dad for his two brothers. He took over the role of being their father. I don't know how it affected him. He just did it, without ever saying anything bad about my grandfather. He probably suffered on the inside, and there would have been things he had to sacrifice to be there for his brothers, but he never expressed any regret about it. He loved his mother, he loved his two brothers and he was always looking after them. That never changed, even when he became a man. He was also very lucky because of the school he went to. The values he learned at Brampton Ellis – be brave, be strong, be polite, be honest, be humble – helped him deal with the situation he found himself in. He grew up quickly, but those values meant he grew up to be a wonderful person. He, and our family, have so much to thank that school for that it makes me cry just thinking about it.

In a working-class area dominated by coal mining and without a man's salary to support the family, money could often be tight in the Robledo home, despite Elsie's best efforts behind the counter and the support of relatives. David Kitchen, born and raised in the area around West Melton, recalls the time his grandfather, Lawrence Kitchen, first spotted the young George Robledo playing football on a piece of common land. He was good, anybody could see that, but what really caught Lawrence Kitchen's eye was that George wasn't wearing football boots. 'People were poor then,' says David Kitchen.

As the old saying goes, folk left their doors open because they had nothing to steal. George was playing in an old pair of shoes because he had no boots. So, my grandfather went and bought him a pair. I'm pretty sure they were only second-hand, but at least he now had some boots. I think they were the first football boots George ever had.

How poor were the people of West Melton and the surrounding towns and villages of the Dearne Valley in the 1930s? Among the poorest, if not the poorest, in the UK is the simple answer. The majority of households lacked a fixed bath. One in four people had access to their own toilet. Barnsley, situated five miles to the north-west, suffered the highest infant mortality rate in Britain. The mines kept the local (not to mention the national) economy going, but with them came the ever-present spectre of pit disasters and industrial diseases brought on by exposure to coal dust. The arrival of hire purchasing towards the end of the decade brought prosperity for some. However, for the majority, a combination of squalor, misery, darkness and filth prevailed.

'The fathers worked the pits. The mothers held down domestic jobs and also brought up the children. And the children became a reflection of their parents. Some fathers would gamble too much or drink too much, and the children would suffer.' So wrote the former Sheffield United, Sunderland and Leeds outside-left Colin Grainger, born in nearby Havercroft and seven years George's junior, in his autobiography *The Singing Winger*. In reality, the qualities that existed in the mining communities of Yorkshire tended to transcend the often grim realities of life. The spirit of the people and their resolve was immeasurable. Folk really did look out for each other, something that proved invaluable in times of war and industrial dispute. For all its ills, there were worse places to spend your formative years. George Robledo eventually left West Melton, but West Melton and what it stood for never really left him.

And in football circles, he was far from alone in that department. Tommy Taylor. David Pegg. Kevin Keegan. David Seaman. Ron Flowers. Joe Harvey. Alan Sunderland. Karen Walker. Mick McCarthy. John Stones. The list of footballers, some better known than others, raised in or around George and Ted's adopted corner of Yorkshire is both long and impressive. The vast majority, once they'd gone out into the world, spoke warmly of the values instilled in them at a young age by their communities. They might not necessarily have wanted to move back in a hurry, but they remembered those places fondly. And that feeling was, by and large, reciprocated.

'The one thing they celebrate in the Dearne Valley and many of the smaller communities across South Yorkshire is when their local heroes go on to do great things,' says journalist Ashley Ball of the *Barnsley Chronicle*.

That was certainly the case when I was growing up in the 1990s, when you would still hear talk of the Robledo brothers and what they had achieved. It's a bit more tribal now in terms of which team you support. But to me, it doesn't matter if someone turns out for Sheffield Wednesday, Sheffield United, Barnsley, Manchester City or whoever – if they're local, then I'll celebrate that. And it doesn't matter in what sport either. We've produced talented rugby players and cyclists, but historically, what our region has really excelled in is footballers and boxers. To see them doing well brings joy to what is a tough area. George had a tough upbringing and people still have tough upbringings now. There's not a lot of money around in the Dearne Valley. There never has been. The way we can level the playing field and do our bit is in sport. That's where we can get our joy.

'If my memories appear to be those of somebody observing his past through rose-tinted spectacles, consider how many great and good footballers in post-war Britain emerged from mining communities,' continued Colin Grainger in his autobiography.

Our world was a football training ground, an academy, and although not everybody came out of the experience having flourished, those austere streets were a space in which enchantment became possible. We did not even need a football. A tennis ball would do. And, of course, four coats for goalposts. At virtually no cost, we had a game that could occupy and stimulate every boy in the village, week in week out, throughout our adolescence.

Through his own adolescence, George created goals and he scored goals – 129 of them in four seasons for Brampton Ellis Senior School, to be exact. This included four against Thurnscoe Hill in the final of the 1938–39 Totty Cup, a competition for schools in the Don and Dearne areas of Yorkshire.

'George was always remembered as being a head above everyone else in the school team, not in stature but in skill,' says the renowned British music and sports writer Richard Williams, whose grandfather, Harold Steer, was headmaster at Brampton Ellis Senior School during the period when all three of the Robledo boys were pupils.

Of course, Ted also made a living from the game, but he was always more of a journeyman player, whereas George was the genuine article. He was an outstanding figure, he really was, and it was no surprise that he went on to achieve what he did. Funnily enough, my grandfather used to say young Walter would have been the best footballer out of the three of them had he not worn spectacles, but Walter always pooh-poohed that idea and said it was nonsense. Either way, they clearly made a formidable trio.

'Back in 1973 or 1974, when I was about eight years old, one of the teachers asked me to help carry a few boxes upstairs to a store room,' says former Brampton Ellis pupil David Wood, now Barnsley FC's official club historian, who grew up in West Melton.

> I distinctly remember him unlocking the door and indicating where the boxes should go, and I noticed that the room was full of old pictures from years gone by. One was of a school production with pupils dressed in what seemed to be Robin Hood attire. And there, in the middle of them all, was a picture of a football team proudly displaying their newly won trophies. Straight away, my eyes went to the boy sat front and centre – George Robledo. Before I could say anything, the teacher chimed up: 'There will never be a school team to match those boys.' There is something about the way George looks in that picture which sets him apart. He looks older, more mature. He'd travelled outside Yorkshire for a start, which the other kids in the photograph probably wouldn't have done. Besides, perhaps, from going on holiday to Blackpool. He'd seen things that the others hadn't.

In all likelihood, George would have created and scored plenty more goals at schoolboy level had he been living in normal times. At the start of his final year of formal mainstream education, 1939–40, the uneasy peace that had existed across most of Europe for some considerable time was finally broken. In the early hours of Monday 4 September, barely a day after the UK had declared war on Germany following the latter's invasion of Poland, the air raid sirens rang out in anger for the first time across the Dearne Valley. It proved to be a false alarm – the aeroplane buzzing around was, in fact, an Allied one – but the tone was set. After months of rumour, speculation, public awareness campaigns and trial blackouts, everybody's worst fears had been realised.

Despite their mining heritage, the Dearne Valley and the surrounding areas were not considered to be an immediate or high-risk target during the Second World War. And so it proved, as Germany, in the wake of the eight-month 'phoney war' that marked the start of hostilities, focused its wrath mainly on Yorkshire's major industrial cities and conurbations, with Sheffield and Hull suffering devastating attacks in December 1940 and May 1941 respectively.

Nevertheless, the Dearne Valley was most certainly affected by the war as, for the second time in twenty-five years, a significant proportion of the area's young men took up arms. Many of them would never return, with several local footballers listed among the dead, including former Barnsley forward Fred Fisher, killed in July 1944 when his Lancaster bomber was shot down over France while on a bombing raid to Stuttgart.

For the Robledo family, the war could potentially have ripped the carpet from under their existence only a matter of years after arriving in England. 'Foreigners' or indeed anyone with what appeared to be an exotic surname were often subjected to suspicion, tipping into outright hostility or even internment, something Italian communities across the UK discovered after Italy chose to nail its colours to Germany's mast. Fortunately, Elsie's local roots cushioned the family from any animosity that they might otherwise have experienced. It helped as well that George and the more outgoing Ted were popular sporty figures who, if push came to shove, could look after themselves. Fortunately, the need to watch one another's backs in wartime never materialised.

On leaving Brampton Ellis Senior School aged fourteen in 1940, fresh from scoring another five goals in the final of that year's Totty Cup (a 2–2 draw against Bolton Modern followed by a 4–0 win in the replay), George started attending Barnsley Mining and Technical College, with a view to getting a trade under his belt. That, pretty much up until the arrival of the Premier League and its riches in the 1990s, was the way it went for the majority of budding footballers, just in case the playing career fell through or to have something to fall back on in later life. Making a living from the game was always George's holy grail, but the uncertainty brought on by war added an extra dimension to keeping one's options open.

Football. Tennis. Table tennis. College. Fulfilling his duties as secretary of the local Brampton Youth Group. Keeping an eye on his mum and two younger brothers. That was George Robledo in his mid-teens, as war raged around the globe. But increasingly, football was beginning to govern his waking hours. Within days of Germany invading Poland, a decision had been taken to abandon the Football League fixture programme on the premise that large groups of people gathering together in the same place probably wasn't a good idea. However, after a few weeks the government chose to permit the playing of friendly matches, with the Football Association establishing a regional Wartime League in order to cut down on non-essential travel. With many sportsmen either on active service or performing other vital duties, a special 'guest player' system was established where a club could field any team member, registered or not, providing they could get to and from the ground on the day of the game. Football, in other words, kept ticking over. Not only that, but some clubs continued to actively pursue young talent, much as they would have done in peacetime. Which is how George, having excelled at schoolboy level, came to the attention of both Barnsley and Huddersfield Town.

It was at Belle Vue, home of Doncaster Rovers, in May 1942 that George made what can loosely be described as his first appearance for a professional football club, representing Barnsley against a Northern Command side made up of footballers serving with regiments based in the north of England. He scored twice, something which only seems to have piqued Huddersfield Town's interest.

The following season, 1942–43, George signed on as an amateur with Huddersfield, playing just the once during Ted Magner's relatively brief tenure as manager, in a 3–3 draw at Bradford City. That in itself appears to have made Barnsley manager Angus Seed (wryly described as 'a sober man in a grey overcoat' by the one-time *Barnsley Chronicle* journalist turned television presenter Michael Parkinson) all the more determined to nab George and tie him down to something more substantial. On 22 July 1943 he did just that, signing the rookie to a one-year professional contract worth £2 per match under the watchful eye of George's uncle Frank Oliver, who acted as a co-signature due to his nephew still being seventeen.

'He is one of the finest lads I have seen and I predict a great future for him,' Seed, with great perception, told the *Barnsley Chronicle* reporter covering the story of George's signing. As Parkinson also wrote of Seed, 'What he lacked in personality he made up for in an ability to spot rare talent, which kept him in the job for nearly twenty years.' George, as it turned out, would prove to be one of his greatest finds, if not the greatest. And there were more than a few – Danny Blanchflower and Tommy Taylor, to name just two.

He was young. He was confident. He was strong. He was, as they say, fit as a butcher's dog. And now George was officially a professional football player, ready to face the somewhat make-do-and-mend world of the Wartime League.

At which point the war itself – or to be more precise, Ernest Bevin – intervened.

3

WORKING CLASS HERO

'The machines that keep us alive and the machines that make machines are all directly or indirectly dependent on coal. In the metabolism of the Western world, the coal miner is second in importance only to the man who ploughs the soil.'

– GEORGE ORWELL

On Tuesday 12 October 1943, Gwilym Lloyd George, Minister of Fuel and Power in Britain's wartime coalition government, announced in the House of Commons that some conscripts, instead of going to fight, would in future be directed to the mines. At the start of the war, the powers that be at Westminster rather short-sightedly sent thousands of young coal miners into the armed forces. These miners, by and large, weren't replaced because the men who might otherwise have filled their shoes were also conscripted into the forces. By the autumn of 1943, supplies of coal to fuel the war effort and heat domestic homes during the impending winter were running horribly low – this at a time when the UK also depended on coal to power its ships and trains. Throw in a combination of poor industrial relations, discontent over wages and absenteeism (often down to sickness, the burden of the work underground having fallen to older miners) and Britain was at the point where something had to give.

Three months later, on 2 December, Ernest Bevin, Minister of Labour and National Service, came to Parliament to put some flesh on the bones of the policy. Over the next five months, 30,000 men aged from eighteen to twenty-five would be redirected to what became known in some quarters as the 'underground front'. In practice, this meant one in ten young men called up were, as of immediate effect, going to work in the mines. They were chosen by lot. If your registration number came out, then you were a 'Bevin Boy' destined for a mine. This was not up for debate. If you didn't go, prison beckoned.

Throughout the remainder of the war, Bevin Boys were often targets of abuse, regarded by some as cowards or draft dodgers. The police frequently stopped them as possible deserters. Once hostilities were over, the Bevin Boys received no medals for their contribution to the war effort, with official recognition being conferred by the British government as late as 1995. It's fair to say dogs have been treated better.

On 14 April 1944, George Robledo turned eighteen years old. Despite wanting to further his fledgling career as a football player, he was also keen to do his bit by fighting for his adopted country. Ernest Bevin had other ideas. Out came George's registration number in the lot. Whether he liked it or not, he was heading for the mines.

The first Bevin Boys from outside the Dearne Valley arrived in the area at the start of 1944, being billeted in the town of Wombwell. George, needless to say, didn't have quite so far to travel. The miners of West Melton, and there were plenty of them, tended to work at one of three pits – Wath Main Colliery, Manvers Main Colliery or Cortonwood (the proposed closure of which proved to be the spark that ignited the long and bitter miners' strike of 1984–85). George landed Wath Main.

And so began thirteen months juggling professional football and mining. It started with six weeks' training, four spent in a classroom in Doncaster followed by two at Wath Main itself. Next came four weeks of supervised work below ground alongside an experienced miner. Eventually, George was let loose on the coalface itself, working what was known as the Silkstone Seam, renowned for its high-quality coal that gave off considerable heat and left little ash after burning.

George wore his helmet and his steel-capped safety boots – and he needed to. At that point in time, coal mining was regarded as the most dangerous job in the UK. Thousands of men (some of them barely men at that) were killed or seriously injured while doing it, with many more contracting industrial diseases. The danger came from the difficult working conditions and the gases that were released through the extraction of coal. At least fifty-nine men perished at Wath Main during its 112-year existence, including seven in one go on 24 February 1930, killed when firedamp (the term used for flammable gas found in a coal mine) was ignited by, irony of ironies, a safety lamp. Thirteen men had died as recently as February 1942 in an explosion at the nearby Barnsley Main Colliery, a number that still pales in comparison to the 361 miners and rescuers who lost their lives in the very same neighbourhood following a series of blasts at Oaks Colliery on 12 December 1866.

Nevertheless, coal mining remained a proud career choice. Those who did it derived satisfaction from their craft and the contribution they made to the national economy. George, born and raised in mining communities on opposite sides of the world, got that and so fitted in well in the dark and dangerous world below. He was productive in terms of digging out coal, once being told to 'slow up' by a laconic older miner charged with filling the wagons waiting to transport the black stuff to the surface. That, along with his burgeoning reputation as a footballer, meant he was spared the unfair flak directed at many Bevin Boys.

It also helped that George understood the concept of teamwork. As far as he was concerned, being a miner was very much like playing football in that you had to have complete trust in those around you. Except, of course, there was far more at stake down there. Lives, which could get taken at any moment by explosions, gas, fire or inrushes of water, were on the line. Down there, if you didn't work together you and everyone else might never see daylight again.

Besides trust and teamwork, there were other similarities between mining and football that George warmed to. The sense of humour, camaraderie and spirit that abounded at Wath Main really wasn't so different to what he experienced in the dressing room at Oakwell, home to Barnsley Football Club since 1887.

'We will build a soccer team that the rugbyites will not crush,' the Reverend Tiverton Preedy, founder of what was initially called Barnsley St Peter's FC, had declared on the club's inception, keen to instil some good Christian values into what had until then been very much a rugby town. George rarely went to church (and despite being a sucker for ball games, never took to rugby). That didn't stop him finding sanctuary at Oakwell, where, despite the world being in turmoil, five-figure crowd numbers continued to gather to watch their team play in the Wartime League. He scored on his debut in a 3–1 win over Sheffield Wednesday. He scored in the 2–2 draw against, of all clubs, Huddersfield Town. A week later, as if to emphasise the point, he scored against Huddersfield again. All told, George played twenty-one times for Barnsley during the 1943/44 campaign despite doubling up as a miner towards the end of the season, scoring seven goals in the process. Somewhere along the line he even found time to turn out for Lincoln City against Bradford City under the special 'guest player' system. It was nothing spectacular, but having only just turned eighteen, George had made a mark.

Angus Seed, however, wasn't content with mere marks. Barnsley's manager could see that George had all the ingredients to be a good attacking player, maybe even a great one – speed, strength, vision, awareness, courage, a fierce shot in either boot, outstanding in the air despite his 5ft 9in. frame. Seed also recognised there was far more to George's game than scoring goals. He was a great passer of the ball and, aged eighteen, a natural when it came to creating space in the opposing team's half of the field. In fact, George wasn't so much a striker as an 'inside-forward', the term used in the 1940s and '50s for creative players who not only scored goals but supported the centre-forward, occupying something like the second striker or 'hole' position of more modern times.

Through 1944 into 1945, Seed set about converting George from the spearhead position he'd inhabited throughout his youth into this deeper attacking role. When Barnsley weren't in action, and even occasionally when they were, Seed would send George to watch proven centre-forwards and inside-forwards playing in other fixtures, just so the teenager could see how the two positions dovetailed. Back then there was no *Match of the Day*. There was no Sky TV. There was no YouTube. If you wanted to see a player in action, other than catching snippets of newsreel at the cinema, you had to be there in the flesh. On one occasion, George's 'homework' involved attending an England versus Scotland international at Villa Park, Birmingham, to observe rival centre-forwards Tommy Lawton and Jock Dodds, both considered by Barnsley's manager to be about as good as it got in front of goal. Seed's reasoning went something like this – sooner or later the war would be over, after which society and hopefully football would return to normal. He wanted George to be ready for when normality came.

In the meantime, life continued to be thoroughly abnormal. The latter part of 1944 saw more men from the Dearne Valley and Barnsley areas killed than at any other time during the war, largely as a consequence of hostilities intensifying in mainland Europe following the Normandy landings that summer. Fred Fisher's death in the skies over France in July wasn't the only fatality to affect those connected with the town's football club. Winger George Bullock had been a major cog in the Barnsley side that won promotion to the Second Division, or what is now the Championship, in 1939. The 27-year-old, while serving as a naval airman in the Fleet Air Arm, was returning from a dance to his base in Cheshire when he was killed in a car crash.

Through it all, the humble, inestimable Seed did his level best to keep the flame burning in whatever way he could, including organising benefit matches for the bereaved. George's twenty-three goals in thirty-eight appearances during the 1944–45 season in no way made up for the tragic loss of Fisher and Bullock, not to mention those supporters killed or injured while on active service, but at least they served as crumbs of comfort.

Over the course of 1944 and 1945, George noticed for the first time that people were starting to behave differently around him. They said hello on the bus when he was travelling to Oakwell, followed him in the street on his way to Wath Main and, much to Elsie's bemusement, dropped by Oliver's under the pretence of buying something to see if he was at home. When Wath Wanderers took on Denaby United in the replay of the local Montagu Cup final in 1944, over 5,000 people packed into Mexborough's pint-sized Hampden Road ground in the knowledge that George would be guesting for Wath. Strictly speaking, they weren't all there to see him – 'the Mont', as it's more commonly known, often featured current and former professional players. However, there was no doubt who the star of the show was, as that year's attendance remains a record for the competition, which still takes place annually between amateur teams from the Barnsley, Doncaster and Rotherham areas. A letter which arrived at Oakwell addressed to George thanked him for 'raising our spirts at this darkest of times with your exciting play'. It wasn't the kind of adulation that can trick a person into forgetting who they are, but it was most definitely in the local hero ballpark.

On Monday 30 April 1945, as Allied forces surrounded Berlin, Adolf Hitler committed suicide. On Friday 4 May, with the last pockets of German resistance quashed, British Field Marshal Bernard

Montgomery accepted the unconditional surrender of German forces in the Netherlands, Denmark and north-west Germany. On Monday 7 May, Supreme Allied Commander General Dwight D. Eisenhower accepted the unconditional surrender of all German forces, news of which was broadcast over the radio to the British people later the same day. And on Tuesday 8 May, George and his Barnsley teammates lost 4–2 at home to Huddersfield Town. Only 527 people were there to see the match because, it being Victory in Europe Day, most right-minded souls were either in the pub or at a street party. There was jubilation, there was thanksgiving and, despite some thunderous storms across parts of Yorkshire, there were bonfires topped by effigies of the Nazi dictator. Regardless of Huddersfield putting one over their neighbours, it was a good day to be alive in and around West Melton.

For George, the icing on the cake came with the news that Ernest Bevin would no longer be requiring his services down the mines. As of Friday 11 May, he was being released from service. It wasn't that George couldn't wait to see the back of Wath Main. On the contrary, in fact. But now he could return to football full time. He'd always known going underground would be temporary. To spend the whole of one's working life among the dirt, the noise, the danger… well, that took a special kind of human being. The respect George gained for the men of Wath Main and their kind would remain with him the rest of his life. As Elizabeth Robledo recalls, 'It was some-thing he was always immensely proud of, the part that he played in the mines during the war.'

The Second World War may have officially ended that summer with the surrender of Japan but football in the UK, for the time being at least, was in no fit state to return to its pre-war league format. George might have grown muscles where thirteen months previously there had been no muscles, but other players returned to their clubs from service either out of condition or unlikely ever to withstand the rigours of professional football again. Some grounds remained either wholly or partially out of action due to bomb damage, while petrol rationing continued to restrict travel. Rather than resuming half-cocked, the Football Association took the sensible decision to continue with the Wartime League for another season. The FA Cup, though, would return for the 1945–46 campaign, giving fans the chance to watch some competitive football, with clubs playing each other over two legs (instead of the traditional one game) up to and including the quarter-final stage.

On Saturday 5 January 1946, George made his first 'official' appearance as a professional footballer playing for Barnsley at St James' Park in the third round of the FA Cup against Newcastle United – the very same Newcastle United that would tempt him away from his adopted Yorkshire three years later. Over 60,000 people were there to see it, by far the biggest crowd George had ever set eyes on, let alone performed in front of. In common with many other clubs, the Newcastle team of 1946 bore little resemblance to the 1939 version. But that's not to say they weren't a force to be reckoned with, scoring goals aplenty throughout the season including nine in one match against a Stoke City side featuring Stanley Matthews. On the final whistle, Matthews had made a beeline for one member of Newcastle's team, a raw 21-year-old centre-forward who'd caught his eye. 'I think you have a bright future if you continue to play like that,' he told him.

The centre-forward's name?

That would be Jackie Milburn.

In the not-too-distant future, George Robledo and Jackie Milburn would strike up a fearsome partnership, leading to a friendship that would last them the rest of their days. This, however, was the beginning of 1946 – at which point, they'd never heard of each other. Although Barnsley scored twice through Gordon Pallister and an own goal by United captain Joe Harvey, Newcastle dominated for long periods and replied with four goals of their own, Milburn grabbing two. Newcastle, so the general consensus went, already had one foot in the fourth round.

Nevertheless, interest in the second leg at Oakwell, to be played on the afternoon of Wednesday 9 January (the concept of floodlights having not yet touched down in English football), remained high. One local colliery, ahead of the anticipated mass bunk-off, even had the foresight to put up a tongue-in-cheek notice for its workers to read: 'In order that the management may have knowledge of the number intending to be absent on Wednesday afternoon, will those whose relatives are to be buried on that day please apply by Tuesday for permission to attend'.

In pouring rain and with 27,000 spectators packed inside Oakwell, Barnsley's players set about Newcastle as if their lives depended on it. Joe Wilson, nicknamed 'Farmer' due to his immense frame and the fact he'd once been an agricultural labourer in north-east England, made it 1–0 to Barnsley on the day before Gavin Smith squared things at 4–4 on aggregate. When George set up Jimmy Baxter to make it 3–0 the turnaround was complete, with Barnsley even being afforded the luxury of a missed penalty.

'There had been many tremendous fightbacks before in the club's history and indeed there has been many since, but none surely have bettered the display that Wednesday afternoon,' wrote local author and Barnsley fan Grenville Firth of what remains one of the standout results in the club's history. If Jackie Milburn and Newcastle United hadn't heard of George beforehand, they certainly knew about him now. 'The man behind the win was George Robledo,' United's manager Stan Seymour later confided to one journalist. 'It was the first time I had ever seen him and I was greatly impressed.'

Seventeen days later, George's first official goal arrived in the first leg of the fourth round at home to Rotherham United. There were, in hindsight, way too many people in the ground that day for the conditions to be anything like safe. But this being a local derby, and with Barnsley having played so well against Newcastle United, wild horses weren't going to stop anyone who wanted to be there from getting inside. Take the official attendance of 37,100 then add another couple of thousand, so those who were there reckoned. Once again Barnsley triumphed 3–0, with George sealing a wonderful individual and team performance by scoring the third goal, ultimately prevailing 4–2 on aggregate. He scored again in the fifth round as well, a piledriver in the first minute of the second leg away to Bradford Park Avenue, although that couldn't prevent Barnsley from losing 2–1 over both matches.

Still, any lingering despondency at taking leave of the FA Cup was offset by the team's form in general, allied with that of their Chilean Yorkshireman who notched a further fifteen goals in the Wartime League during the 1945–46 season. It may only have been a friendly, but the way Barnsley's new-look post-war side set about dismantling Everton towards the end of April 1946, winning 4–0 at Goodison Park (with George creating two and claiming one for himself), didn't half bode well for the future.

• • •

There's a theory among those in the know that goes something like this – at times of social and economic advance, Barnsley Football Club tends to do alright. In 1912, during the high-water mark of industrial unionism in the UK, 'Battling Barnsley', as they were dubbed, went all the way to the final of the FA Cup, beating West Bromwich Albion 1–0 in a replay after the first match finished goalless. In the late 1970s, when you still couldn't move for collieries in the area, it was Allan 'Sniffer' Clarke, once of Leeds United's front line, whose appointment as manager laid the foundations for the club's rise from the fourth to the second tier of English football. In 1997, with regeneration in the air and plans afoot to transform the town into some kind of Tuscan hill settlement (yes, really), it was Danny Wilson who led Barnsley into the promised land of the top flight for the first time in the club's history. And in the mid-to-late 1940s and early 1950s, it was Angus Seed whose team, a cocktail of brute force and no little amount of skill, did so much to banish the Second World War blues. Without, it should be said, actually achieving anything other than putting smiles on faces.

The half-a-dozen or so years that followed the war were bumper times for British football. Starved of entertainment throughout the hostilities, hundreds of thousands of demobbed men with gratuities to burn made for their local clubs once regular fixtures resumed in the FA Cup and, as of the 1946–47 season, the league. Indeed, the 1946–47 campaign saw attendance figures for Football League matches hit a record 35 million spectators, rising to in excess of 40 million for each of the three seasons spanning 1947–50. At a time of austerity, drabness, rationing and mourning, football's golden years, as they became known, did more perhaps than anything else to raise morale from Aberdeen to Exeter.

'The impact of economic conditions on sport was perhaps clearest in the late 1940s and early 1950s,' writes Martin Johnes, professor of modern history at Swansea University.

> Full employment and a desire to forget the horrors of war created a high demand for entertainment, but material shortages and the government's need to export manufactured goods meant there was little for people to actually spend their money on. Spectator sport, however, was both cheap and easily accessible and attendances thus reached an all-time high in this period.

Although Barnsley's attendances in the league failed to match those witnessed during their memorable mini-FA Cup run of early 1946, they were still more than healthy, averaging over 19,000 at home during the 1946–47 campaign and rising to 21,050 the season afterwards. But maybe that league versus cup crowd disparity was, in hindsight, no bad thing. Had Barnsley prevailed against Bradford Park Avenue, there is a fair chance they could have faced Bolton Wanderers in the next round. Instead, Bolton found themselves paired against Stoke. On 9 March 1946, thirty-three people were crushed to death and over 500 injured when the two sides met in the second leg of their quarter-final at Burnden Park, Bolton's home until 1997. With rationing still in force, police became preoccupied guarding food in one of the stands instead of preventing gatecrashers climbing over turnstiles in another part of the ground. The Home Office inquiry into the subsequent crush called for stricter safety standards at UK grounds – recommendations which were, needless to say, largely ignored. Given the colossal attendances of the time, it's a minor miracle that the tragic events of Burnden Park weren't repeated on other occasions across the land.

The post-war football boom benefitted Barnsley and their manager Angus Seed immeasurably. As Anthony Clavane, in his excellent 2016 book *Moving the Goalposts*, writes, 'Seed's team were infused with the optimism and idealism of an era that created the modern welfare state, achieved full employment and nationalised hundreds of privately owned mines.' On 1 January 1947, all the rights, assets and liabilities of the coal mining industry were transferred from the coal owners to the new National Coal Board, established by the Labour government under the Coal Industry Nationalisation Act of the previous year. Mining communities such as West Melton had waited a long time for this moment. They saw it as a time of liberation, an end to the days of working for a pittance and the dawning of a new, fairer, safer age in which people, not profits, would come first.

And to an extent, and for a while, they did.

The irony was that Barnsley's players, most of whom lived in the community, weren't much better off financially than the miners who came to watch them. Some, in fact, were worse off. In 1947, following prolonged arbitration, the wage for the best players in the

First Division increased to a maximum of £12 per week during the playing season, falling to £10 per week during the summer close season. Those plying their trade in the English Second, Third and Fourth Divisions would have earned considerably less. At Barnsley, as was the standard practice throughout the land, if you weren't in the first team then your wage automatically dropped further, something that could cause resentment between men competing for the same positions. In addition, players weren't automatically allowed to move clubs when their contracts expired, an anomaly that potentially tied them to one employer for life. It was, in short, an archaic system, one that amounted to a colossal restraint of trade. Small wonder George returned to Barnsley Mining and Technical College after the war as a part-time student. It didn't matter that he'd started scoring goals aplenty for his local club. In his head (and his mother's, more of which to come) he needed a safety net.

Why didn't the players rebel against this godawful state of affairs, not just at Barnsley but throughout the land? Put simply, they knew no different.

In time, things would change. In January 1961, the Professional Footballers' Association (PFA), the union that serves to protect, improve and negotiate the conditions, rights and status of professional players in England and Wales, succeeded under its chairman Jimmy Hill in having the maximum wage abolished. Even then the Football League initially refused to budge on the wider issue of contracts that, in effect, tied footballers to one club for life, only climbing down after the PFA declared strike action.

This, though, was the late 1940s. The cards remained stacked in the clubs' favour and there seemed diddly-squat the players could do about it. All they could hope was that their respective clubs and managers were of the more enlightened variety. And that's where George and his Barnsley teammates landed on their feet.

Angus Seed knew there were more attractive ports of call within spitting distance of Barnsley – the likes of Sheffield Wednesday and Sheffield United to the south, Leeds United to the north and the Manchester clubs just over the Pennine uplands to the west. He also knew those clubs and others further afield would eventually come calling for his brightest young stars. When that happened, he resolved not to stand in a player's way but to help secure the best possible deal for them. The striplings in the squad grew to understand and appreciate this, while the older seasoned pros respected Seed for his knowledge, judgement, honesty and sense of fairness. He ran a happy ship, in other words.

Whether apocryphal or not, there's a story about Seed that sums up both the man and his qualities. During a poor run of results, the manager received several complaints from supporters. Did he know many of his players were spending their afternoons playing snooker in a local hall? Why were they there when they could be practising their football? This piece of news didn't vex Seed in the slightest. It meant the players were spending valuable time together: laughing, bonding, relaxing, sharing stories. To shield them from further scrutiny, he told his potters to spend a few afternoons at the ground instead. There they could play snooker to their hearts' content, away from prying eyes.

You can't turn back time, so they say. Except that in August 1946, you could. Seven years before, on Sunday 3 September 1939, the 1939–40 Football League season had been abandoned after just eight days (in Barnsley's case, three fixtures) following Germany's invasion of Poland and Britain's subsequent declaration of war on Germany. When the Football League finally resumed, the fixtures for the 1946–47 season were a replica of those published for the 1939–40 campaign. Just as they had done on Saturday 26 August 1939, so Nottingham Forest travelled to Barnsley on Saturday 31 August 1946 for what would be George's long-awaited Football League debut. He'd made a splash in the Wartime League. He'd made a splash in the 1945–46 FA Cup. Now George went and did it again, scoring a hat-trick in a 3–2 win to send Oakwell into a state of euphoria.

Just how pivotal a moment that was, not only for George or Barnsley but domestic football in general, would only become apparent over time. In the summer of 1946, the game was facing the same kind of issues as society in general. On the one hand, the country needed to rebuild. On the other, there wasn't enough manpower to carry out all the work that had to be done. People from across Europe, often refugees displaced by the war, offered an instant solution (over 18,000 Poles, Italians and Hungarians came to work in British coal mines, many of them settling in Yorkshire), as did immigrants from the West Indies, Africa and other imperial colonies. Almost inevitably, some of these economic migrants played football to a pretty decent standard.

'The league soon featured firsts from, among other places, Bermuda, Jamaica, Hungary, Italy, Iceland, Latvia, Norway, Poland, Sweden, Spain and Switzerland,' wrote Nick Harris in his book *England, Their England*, which charts the history of foreign footballers in the English game. 'Some of this new wave were refugees, others civil servants or students or servicemen or businessmen. Some were professionals, others amateur. Some stayed a few games, others for decades. What George Robledo did, on Saturday 31 August 1946, was announce their arrival in emphatic fashion.'

Three days later, George scored twice as Barnsley bulldozed their way past Sheffield Wednesday at Hillsborough, winning 4–2. The following week they battered Wednesday again, George grabbing one and creating two in a 4–1 victory. 'Impressions gained when one is young frequently have a lasting effect, which is probably why, apart from St James' Park [in Newcastle], the ground I most prefer to play on is that of the Sheffield Wednesday club at Hillsborough,' George declared some years later in a magazine article.

It was here that I saw my first ever professional soccer match when a schoolboy. The vastness of Hillsborough, the tremendous and good-humoured crowd, and the thrill of seeing star players in action made this a memorable day for me, and even now I feel something whenever I visit Hillsborough that I rarely experience on any other ground. The pitch, also, is always in first class condition throughout the season. The Hillsborough spectators are a good sporting lot who really appreciate good football and readily recognise its finer points. Another thing that endears the Wednesday's ground to me is the fact that when I played there for Barnsley I rarely failed to score, so that most of my memories of it are associated with at least a reasonable amount of success.

By the end of September Barnsley sat top of the Second Division table, having won six and drawn one of their opening seven league games, scoring twenty-one goals in the process. It was, in the words of one local journalist, 'champagne stuff', with George creating and finishing opportunities seemingly at will.

Alas, keeping them out at the other end would, as autumn made way for winter, prove to be Barnsley's undoing. And then there was the winter itself to contend with.

On Wednesday 22 January 1947, following what had been an un-seasonably mild spell, the temperature across the UK dropped like a stone. Down came the snow for fifty-five days on end, drifting up to seven metres deep in parts of Yorkshire. Everything ground to a halt. Animals perished. People perished. Schools closed. Rivers froze. Energy supplies to homes, offices and factories were dis-rupted. When warmer air finally arrived in mid-March, the snow melted, causing widespread flooding across lowland areas. Between 25 January and 22 March, Barnsley played just three matches, all of them away from the icy clutches of Oakwell (including one in rela-tively temperate Plymouth). Yet with people's lives and livelihoods on the line, sport didn't really matter one iota. Football's place in the grand scheme of things became, quite literally, crystal clear.

The colossal fixture backlog caused by the freeze of 1947 meant Barnsley kept on playing football right the way into June, rediscov-ering their swagger during the closing weeks of the season with a string of impressive high-scoring wins. All told, the team scored eighty-four goals over the course of forty-two league games, an average of exactly two per fixture. The catch was that they con-ceded a whopping eighty-six to finish a disappointing tenth in the table.

'On reflection it must appear that a great chance had been lost in gaining admission to the First Division,' wrote Grenville Firth in his official history of Barnsley FC.

> If only the club had used a little foresight and strengthened the weak positions a little earlier with two or three experienced quality players, then the chance may not have been lost. One must have felt sorry for the Robledos, [Johnny] Kellys and [Jimmy] Baxters who were really First Division players, having to perform their skills at an inferior level. In fact Robledo had scored twenty-five goals in first team matches and was becoming another target for the big clubs.

From that point on, every game George Robledo played for Barnsley became a farewell. Whether he wanted to or not, he was always going to leave. He was simply too good for that level of professional football. It was just of case of when and where George would be going. The only surprise was the farewell lasted so long.

4

GETTING BETTER

'Football is a simple game. The hard part is making it look simple.'
– RON GREENWOOD

Tottenham Hotspur wanted him.

Sheffield Wednesday wanted him.

Newcastle United wanted him.

Sheffield United wanted him.

There were, apparently, other suitors. But those four clubs were at the front of the queue, the most persistent enquirers, the ones Angus Seed had deemed worthy of George Robledo's signature.

What Tottenham Hotspur, Sheffield Wednesday and Sheffield United didn't know was that Newcastle were always the favourites to land George. Why? Because Seed was from Lanchester, a village in County Durham where everyone supported either Newcastle United or Sunderland. In the absence of any interest from Sunderland, Newcastle occupied pole position. It really was that straightforward.

The first communication from Newcastle had come early in 1947

45

in the shape of a telegram sent by Stan Seymour, United's manager. (Besides once playing for Newcastle, Seymour was at various stages also vice-chairman and a director of the club, hence his nickname 'Mr Newcastle United'.) Would Barnsley be prepared to part with their prolific inside-forward? Seed put the question to George who, in turn, consulted his mother. At that point, Elsie Robledo had no desire to leave West Melton and as George was happy at Barnsley, Newcastle's advance was politely declined. Still, Seed promised Seymour that should the situation change, Newcastle could have first refusal.

Seed had a reputation within the game for being a man of his word and it was a promise he would ultimately keep. In the meantime, Newcastle just had to be patient and hope George didn't get injured, a perpetual risk in the hurly-burly world of post-war professional football where protection from referees was scarce and treatment equalled little more than the ubiquitous bucket and sponge administered by a trainer with scant medical know-how.

Aside from the goals, the craic of a good dressing room and Seed's almost paternal role in his development both as a player and a man, there was another reason why George didn't want to jump ship quite yet. In 1947, Ted Robledo had joined him on the payroll at Oakwell. Ted had potential but was less of a natural footballer than his older brother. He was also still in his teens and, as the old saying goes, a bit green. What harm would it possibly do, thought George, to stay at Oakwell for another season or two to be at Ted's side, especially after all they had been through together since leaving Chile?

'Another good strong player, no mug,' recalled the former Barnsley inside-forward Johnny Steele many years later of Ted, before adding a slight caveat. 'You could tell he'd lacked a father. He used to follow me around and wait outside the ground for me. Sometimes I couldn't get rid of the boy! I felt like a father to him. But fortune didn't smile on them, did it?'

Much as they had during the 1946–47 season, Barnsley continued scoring and conceding goals with abandon throughout the 1947–48 campaign. The holes in the back line meant George increasingly found himself playing deeper, foraging to break down the opposition and, wherever possible, launch attacks. It was exhausting work, carried out more often than not on muddy pitches bearing little resemblance to the lush, green carpets of today. Consequently, George scored only nine goals that season, though he created plenty more.

On their day, Barnsley shone like few other sides outside English football's top flight. Take, for example, the 3–0 away win against Tottenham Hotspur in March 1948 when George and Jimmy Baxter, his fellow inside-forward, tore into the Londoners from kick-off, scoring a goal apiece. Yet there were also times when their cavalier approach as a team bordered on naivety, such as the back-to-back 4–1 and 5–2 defeats at Leeds United and Sheffield Wednesday respectively during September 1947. Somehow Barnsley managed to fuse frustration and entertainment, which perversely only seemed to endear them even more to their supporters.

'In many ways these were amongst the most exciting years to be a Barnsley fan,' wrote Brian Dennis, John Daylin and Derek Hyde in *Barnsley Football Club The Official History, 1887–1998*, published in 1998.

Although the club had no real success, the years after the war were enjoyed as a honeymoon between club and town as once again the country tried to return to normal after the war. Football was a familiar and comforting ritual which provided a sense of fun and hopefulness after the despair of recent years. Fans flocked to enjoy themselves. The Barnsley players they watched were the last bloom of the rose, and the fans revelled in the glory of their play and the richness of their characters. Without team success, it was an era in which the players themselves were definitely the main attraction. [Danny] Blanchflower, [Johnny] Kelly, Robledo, Baxter and [Cecil] McCormack, every supporter had his favourite and every game was an adventure. Packed tightly around Oakwell, supporters could call out to players on the field as if they were hailing them across the street. They bantered freely and humorously with each other on the terraces, ooohed and aaahed at every play, and clapped fiercely to applaud good play by both teams.

In *The Singing Winger*, Colin Grainger, a regular at Oakwell as a boy, paints a fascinating picture of what it was like watching games at that time:

Attending football matches in the mid-to-late 40s was a strange if exhilarating experience. There was uniformity about it all. People would wear suits in one of three colours – black, grey or brown. Flat caps proliferated. Behaviour was almost always good. Conversation rather than singing was rife. People used to just stand there and observe in a constant state of deference. To get a feel for how British society changed from the late-40s to the mid-60s, consider how the comportment of the football spectator changed. Within 12 or 15 years, every kind of fashion and every kind of song could be witnessed on the terraces.

Interestingly, given the health risks we are now aware of and the ridiculously high fitness levels of the modern professional footballer, Grainger also recalls that George 'was one of those players who always seemed to be sucking on a cigarette in the dressing room before the match or at half-time'. Not that it ever seemed to affect his performances. Then again, George was only twenty-two in 1948, the age when a man tends to think of himself as immortal. He, and the countless other professional footballers who enjoyed a cigarette back in the day, either wouldn't have been aware or necessarily have cared about the long-term effects of smoking. We know now that the nicotine and carbon monoxide from smoking makes blood 'sticky' and narrows the arteries. We know now that smoking increases the resting heart rate to dangerous levels where physical activity is concerned. We know now that smoking reduces a person's lung capacity. Lighting up even a few cigarettes a day can decrease the body's ability to use oxygen effectively. By the end of his life, George was a chain smoker, his lungs black through decades of dragging on cigarettes and puffing pipes. It was a habit that would bring his time on earth to a premature conclusion. Quite how he managed to do what he did on a football field, especially considering the amount of running that came with his position, is almost beyond comprehension.

Encouraged by Angus Seed not to drop so deep and to focus on doing his own job on the field rather than that of other players, George's goalscoring touch returned during the 1948–49 season, as Barnsley recovered from a slow start to climb the table. Once again, when they were in the zone as a team, as in the 4–0 demolition of Sheffield Wednesday at Oakwell in October, they were almost untouchable against second-tier opposition. By now George's modus operandi had become well established: make goals, score goals, always stay on the move, and do things simply, effectively and with the minimum of fuss. It was almost as if he operated in plain sight, hence his nickname of 'the shadow' among Barnsley fans.

The only downside to this style of play was that George's considerable contribution to the team could on occasion go overlooked, even by his teammates. 'There wasn't a lot of fancy stuff in his play, but he was good in the air and he was an effective finisher,' Johnny Steele once rather matter-of-factly remarked. Then again Steele, who died in 2008, was a proud Glaswegian and gushing praise isn't exactly a renowned Glaswegian trait.

Others, though, had no scruples about expressing their admiration for George. 'He brings the lithe, animal grace of the jungle into the rugged English football grounds,' wrote John E. Reynolds in his book *Stars of Soccer*, published in 1948.

His ball control is quick and easy. The twisting and swerving of his body are a delight to see. He brings the hot, exotic jungle rhythm to the football field. His football is born of the warm blood, the subtle poise and dignity of his people. Robledo moves like a Latin dancer, his feet nimble and expressive. He weaves the weird pattern of South American undergrowth into his dribbling. His headwork is as swift and deadly as a striking snake and he springs into the air with exultation whenever he flashes one past the goalkeeper.

His people were, of course, as much from South Yorkshire as South America, but why let the facts get in the way of a bit of literary panache? Either way, it was hard to disagree with Reynolds' assessment that, as an overseas-born player in what was still a relatively parochial sport, 'Robledo brings something rare and exotic to the game'.

Then there was the anonymous supporter who turned to verse to express his, or perhaps her, admiration for George, submitting a poem called 'Robledo, The Red Shadow' to the *Barnsley Chronicle*, which the newspaper subsequently published:

> Swooping down upon the foe
> The fearless shadow streaks
> The crucial moment is near
> The air is filled with shrieks
> The brave defenders bar the way
> Their hearts are true as steel
> But they are in the shadow's path
> His fury they must feel
> Relentless he surges on
> Intrepid, fearless, cool
> The foeman cannot stem the tide
> Engulfed in this whirlpool
> With desperation in their hearts
> They give a cry of pain
> Then – crash – the ball is in the net
> Robledo strikes again

'George Robledo was a revelation,' raved Dennis, Daylin and Hyde in their official club history.

At a time when foreigners were unheard of in the English game,

Robledo provided Barnsley fans with all the magic and enchantment that modern crowds expect from imported players, in the
dour and unlikely setting of post-war Oakwell. Not that George was
really all that foreign by this time, for he had lived in West Melton
since he was five, but his foreign birth gave him a little romance.

For all his exoticism, not to mention that splash of romance, George
cut a remarkably modest figure off the field. 'Unassuming' is the
word used to describe him by lifelong Barnsley supporter Don
Wearmouth, who as a young boy would wait outside Oakwell after
matches armed with his autograph book. Besides putting pen to
paper, George often went the extra mile by taking Don's book into
the changing rooms to get other players to add their signatures.
Once first-team training was over, he'd willingly stay behind to
work with younger players on their technique before catching the
bus back to West Melton – the very same bus that ferried him to and
from Oakwell on match days, breathing in the same smoky air as
the supporters who paid his wages. Nothing ever seemed to be too
much trouble for George and people loved him all the more for it.
Including, so it appears, the blazers within the corridors of power at
the Football Association.

Hard as it might be to believe for, say, anyone born since 1970, but
there was a time not so many decades ago when players at second-
or sometimes even third-tier clubs would get selected to play for
England. You didn't have to be a top-flight performer to receive the
call-up. If you were good enough, then you were in. At that point in
time, the English national team was in something of a transitional
phase as new faces, such as Jackie Milburn and Preston North End

winger Tom Finney, replaced those who had trodden the boards before the war, with the evergreen Stanley Matthews (who'd made his debut as far back as 1934) carrying on regardless. The World Cup of 1950 was on the horizon. England, for all sorts of nit-picky reasons which we'll arrive at in a couple of chapters, had never appeared at a World Cup before and were keen to recruit players who might impress on the global stage.

But there was a problem. The man who managed the national side did not actually get to select the team.

Yes, you read that correctly.

Appointed as England's first ever team manager in 1946, Walter Winterbottom was hobbled by a selection process that heaped all the responsibility for producing results on his shoulders, while leaving the power in the hands of the meddling elders who infested the FA. Selection of the international side was to all intents and purposes carried out by committee, with the fate of thoroughbreds such as Matthews, Nat Lofthouse, Len Shackleton and Stan Mortensen determined by a 'those in favour' and 'those against' voting system. All Winterbottom could do was hand over a list of recommended players to the FA chairman and hope. Small wonder, perhaps, that a country with such remarkable talents at its disposal as the aforementioned four – not to mention Milburn, Finney, forwards Tommy Lawton, Raich Carter and Wilf Mannion, defender Billy Wright and goalkeeper Frank Swift – went into decline during the 1950s rather than lording it on the world stage. Small wonder as well that silly mistakes could be, and often were, made.

Like, for instance, considering a Chilean national for England duty.

In September 1948, somebody at the FA contacted somebody

at Barnsley Football Club asking if George would come to a get-together in Manchester. The request, typical of the FA's haywire ways, was made at the very last minute, meaning there was little or no time to find out what exactly this get-together was all about. George took his boots and kicked a ball around for a couple of hours alongside Finney, Milburn and other luminaries, but at no point did anyone in charge explain to him that this was actually a pre-selection gathering ahead of England's forthcoming fixtures against Northern Ireland and Wales.

In the event, George was selected to play for an FA XI against an RAF XI in Huddersfield. The game was, in essence, an international trial match, but again, nobody mentioned this key piece of information to George, who ran amok, scoring no fewer than four goals. Only then, it appears, did the FA stop to ask whether a man called Robledo, who bore all the physical characteristics of someone from Chile, was even qualified to play for England.

'No,' came the most succinct of replies.

'Following the number of enquiries regarding my possibilities of playing for England, Sir Stanley Rous, then secretary of the Football Association, made an official statement to the press,' George recalled many years later in a letter to the Yorkshire-based author David Watson about the FA's subsequent attempt to save face. 'Unfortunately I am unable to lay my hands on it. However, it implied that whilst the FA were conscious of my merits, it was not possible for me to be considered for an England place due to the fact that I was born outside the Commonwealth.'

'I don't know whether England put any pressure on him to change his citizenship,' says Elizabeth Robledo.

What I am sure of is that he never wanted to change. He was determined to be Chilean, even though he didn't know one single word of Spanish at that time. He could have done it. He had, after all, been living in England for many years by then and his mother had been born in Yorkshire. But he didn't. Even with the 1950 World Cup coming up, he didn't want to switch. And I don't think that's something he ever came to regret.

If there was one thing the FA's bumbling ineptitude did achieve, it's that it helped clear the fog surrounding George's future. In December 1948, Newcastle United chose to be a little more proactive and make another enquiry about his availability. Angus Seed put it to George who, once again, consulted his mother. Elsie remained content in West Melton but appreciated what a huge opportunity this was for her eldest son.

There was also by now another sub-plot at work, one that touched on being a potential bargaining tool for the Robledo family. On the first Saturday of that month, Ted had made his first-team debut for Barnsley at left-half (or left-midfield in today's terminology) against West Bromwich Albion at Oakwell. George was adamant that he didn't want to leave Yorkshire without Ted alongside him or, preferably, the whole family in tow. And so he told Seed to inform Newcastle that he would sign for them – providing they also took his brother as part of the deal.

It was undoubtedly a risky ploy, not that George saw it that way. 'My dad took his brother everywhere,' adds Elizabeth Robledo. 'They were so close, he would never have moved without him.' In an interview given shortly before his death in 2022, younger brother

Walter Robledo concurred. 'George was the one who insisted that the two of them stick together,' he said. 'My mother wouldn't have let George move without us anyway, mind.'

Just how much of a say did Elsie have when it came to the future of her footballing sons? Plenty, if these words taken from an article published in the *Barnsley Chronicle* as early as September 1943 are anything to go by:

Two brilliant young Barnsley football brothers, well on their way to star careers, have a manager behind the scenes whom they consult in everything – their mother. And what she says goes. She is helping to mould their careers by seeing that they have trades at their fingers' ends apart from football. George Robledo, seventeen, a powerfully built centre-forward, is fast becoming one of the shining lights of the Barnsley first team. His brother Edward, only fifteen but also a strapping lad, made a hit with his initial display last weekend in the same position with the reserve team. Angus Seed, the manager, thinks a lot about them both. 'George has everything in his favour – size, speed and, what is more important, brains,' he said. The Robledo boys listen to what their mother has to say when thinking about their future. Since George was six, she has brought up her family of three lads single-handed. There is another brother, Walter, aged eleven, who is also a promising footballer. So when Mrs Robledo said 'Football or no football, the boys must have a trade,' George was apprenticed to a builder, and studies in his spare time at the local technical school, which Edward attends as a full-time pupil.

In a self-penned 1952 magazine article reflecting on his career so far, George wrote about Elsie's influence at that critical juncture in his teenage life.

> While I was still at school, Major Frank Buckley, who was then managing Wolverhampton Wanderers, approached my mother and suggested that I should sign for Wolves. As you doubtless know, manager Buckley is a remarkably shrewd judge of young footballers. He doesn't often go wrong in his appraisal of the possibilities of any 'raw' boy, such as I undoubtedly was in those days, and I regarded it as a remarkably pleasing compliment that the great Wolverhampton chief should think me good enough to join his 'nursery'. Mother, however, had other views. Wisely, she insisted that before ever I thought of the possibility of making my living at football, I should first complete my education. Though I was a little disappointed at the time, as any boy would be, I have realised fully since how right she was. So instead of going to Molineux, I went on to Barnsley Technical College and took up an engineering course.

The studies might have dried up well before the end of 1948, but Elsie's grip remained. George wasn't prepared to move to Newcastle without Ted, but neither of them would be going unless all four members of the family relocated to north-east England, as per Elsie's wishes.

In the meantime, football continued to come first. In the draw for the third round of the FA Cup, Barnsley had been paired against the formidable Blackpool side containing the two Stans – Matthews and Mortensen. The match was scheduled for Saturday 8 January 1949 at Oakwell, with police stipulating that it should be an all-ticket affair, the first of its kind at the ground, in order to manage the anticipated droves. Such was the interest in the tie, with every one of the 38,000 tickets sold well in advance, that Angus Seed asked Newcastle to hold back on the proposed transfer until the match had been played, a request United graciously agreed to.

On the day, Barnsley gave as good as they got despite Blackpool attempting, in the words of one reporter, to 'do a job' on George, allocating the task of marking him to the nearest player at any given time. It was a tactic that largely worked, albeit one that nullified the effectiveness of some of their own star names in the process. With sixty minutes on the clock, Matthews centred from Blackpool's right flank for Mortensen, who steered the ball past goalkeeper Pat Kelly, thus ending Barnsley's interest in the FA Cup for another year. On the final whistle, visiting captain Harry Johnston, one of the outstanding English defenders of his time, sought out George for a handshake and to offer some words of encouragement. 'I think you and I are going to be seeing a fair bit of each other soon,' declared Johnston. As it turned out, he couldn't have been more right.

Once the circus of the FA Cup had left town, so Barnsley resumed negotiations with Newcastle over George's transfer. United made it clear they were not in the slightest bit interested in taking Ted. However, if the only way to secure George's signature was to do some kind of a deal for the two brothers, then so be it.

On Saturday 22 January, George played and scored in what proved to be his final match for Barnsley, a 4–0 home win over

Queens Park Rangers. Five days later, on the morning of Thursday 27 January, Newcastle manager George Martin travelled south along with Stan Seymour (who, at that time, occupied what would now be regarded as a director of football position) to meet Barnsley officials and the Robledo family, with negotiations toing and froing between a backroom in a local hotel and 97 Barnsley Road, West Melton, where Elsie remained throughout.

At one point, as Walter Robledo recalled years later, proceedings began tipping into the surreal.

> I was in the room with George and Ted, and my mother said I was moving to Newcastle, too. So Seed said to Seymour, 'Will you pay this boy £3 a week until he gets a job?' Seymour said, 'Oh, don't worry, he'll get a job quickly.' But Seed wouldn't drop it. He said, 'This transfer isn't happening unless that lad gets £3 a week until he gets a job.' Eventually Seymour agreed, but the transfer almost fell through because of me!

For the record, Walter Robledo did eventually get a job, a highly skilled one at that, as an analytical chemist responsible for analysing the chemical structures of substances. And Newcastle, good as their word, delivered on that £3 a week. At least they did for a while.

The combined fee for both George and Ted was reported at the time as being between £25,000 and £26,000. In fact, the correct amount was £26,500, of which £23,000 went on George. Had those figures been made public at the time then it would have made him the most expensive British player ever, breaking the previous record transfer fee of £20,050 paid by Sunderland to Newcastle in February

1948 for Len Shackleton. 'The Shackleton record must stand,' George Martin was quoted as telling a reporter at the time. 'We made a joint bid for two players, not two separate bids.' If intended as a way of shielding George from any pressure to deliver while also maintaining Ted's dignity, then Newcastle's little white lie succeeded.

Right to the very end, hoping that everything would fall through, both Sheffield Wednesday and Sheffield United continued to lie in wait. Wednesday went as far as sending a delegation of their own to Barnsley on 27 January, with chairman William Fearnehough and two directors setting up residence in another of the town's hotels, just in case negotiations with Newcastle broke down. Despite the apparent best efforts of Walter Robledo, they didn't, leaving Wednesday, long-time admirers of George and so often the victims of his sharpshooting, disappointed.

'My association with the Barnsley club lasted until 1949, and was a very happy one throughout,' wrote George in the same 1952 magazine article in which he acknowledged his mother's conspicuous influence.

I like to think that I did well for them, but at the same time I am first to admit that I was fortunate to get such a good grounding in the game at so early an age. As the policy of Barnsley in the early post-war years was 'no sale of any players', I had come to look upon it as virtually certain that I should remain with the club a long time, perhaps to the end of my playing days. While it is easy to make resolutions not to yield to transfer suggestions, however, a club like Barnsley, which is not always supported as well as it might be, may sometimes find the temptation too much, especially when the gates have been declining and the exchequer is running low. Anyhow, whatever the cause, when Mr George Martin, who was then manager of Newcastle United, made an offer for my brother Ted and myself, the Barnsley board decided to accept it. Any player, of course, can decline to be transferred if he so wishes. In my case, however, and also in the case of Ted, although we were for many reasons sorry to leave the Yorkshire side, the opportunity of taking part in First Division football was most attractive and we had no objections.

Barnsley's gates hadn't been declining and their exchequer wasn't running low. Nevertheless, £26,500 was a colossal amount of money in 1949, enough to keep a lower league club in the black for a hefty chunk of an entire season. George did well for them, both on the field and at the bank.

All told, George made 114 first-team appearances for Barnsley, not including the wartime years, scoring forty-seven goals in the process. Ted, on the other hand, made just five, all of them in the weeks leading up to their transfer to Newcastle. As if in some kind of mourning, the wind seemed to go out of Barnsley's sails in the months and indeed years after George's departure. While cult heroes such as midfield hard man Sidney 'Skinner' Normanton remained, alongside the odd gem unearthed by Angus Seed (most notably centre-forward Tommy Taylor and midfielder Danny Blanchflower, who would later shine for Manchester United and Tottenham Hotspur respectively), so the likelihood of gaining promotion to the First Division gradually diminished.

The respectable ninth-place finish of the 1948–49 campaign made way for thirteenth in 1949–50, fifteenth in 1950–51, twentieth in 1951–52 and twenty-second in 1952–53, spelling relegation to Third Division North (consisting of twenty-four English and Welsh clubs located above an invisible line stretching roughly from The Wash to a point somewhere between Shrewsbury and Wrexham). Barnsley were by no means a one-man team with George in the side, but the hole created by his exit far exceeded that of his relatively diminutive stature.

'I'll let you into a little secret,' says Don Wearmouth. 'When I heard he was going, I cried. It meant such a lot at the time. He might have come from Chile, but he may as well have come from the Moon. You're going to miss someone like that, aren't you? And we really missed him.'

5

THE WORD

'Let me live, love, and say it well in good sentences.'
– Sylvia Plath

Thursday 27 January 1949 was, in rag trade parlance, a busy news day at Kemsley House on Westgate Road, Newcastle upon Tyne, home of the city's three main newspapers *The Journal*, the *Evening Chronicle* and the *Sunday Sun*. At Westminster, Members of Parliament for the north-east had been assured by the Admiralty that a number of Royal Navy ships due for repair would be heading for the Palmers Hebburn yard on the River Tyne, a prospective shot in the arm for the area's employment statistics. A few feet away in the main House of Commons Chamber, MPs from across the country continued to debate war in Palestine. Closer to home, efforts to refloat the 635-tonne coaster *St Abbs Head*, which had run aground in fog off the Northumberland coast the previous evening, proved successful. And 120 or so miles to the south, attempts by Newcastle United to sign George Robledo were, as we've seen, coming to the boil under the watchful eye of a team of reporters posted in Barnsley, at St James' Park and in the newsroom.

At around 11.15 p.m. the story, cobbled together from all the various sources, began taking shape, ready to hit the streets the following morning in *The Journal* under the headline 'Newcastle Beat Rivals For Robledo Signings':

At 11 o'clock last night, Newcastle United manager Mr George Martin signed George Robledo, 23-year-old centre or inside-forward, and Ted Robledo, wing-half, aged 20, Barnsley's Chilean-born brothers, at a joint fee of £25,000, mostly for the well-known forward. Sheffield Wednesday competed for George's signature. United beat keen competition, chiefly from Sheffield Wednesday and Sheffield United. Barnsley's biggest ever [transfer fee received] challenges in the case of George Robledo the £20,050 record paid by Sunderland to Newcastle for Len Shackleton. Yesterday Barnsley manager Mr Angus Seed contacted Newcastle in fulfilment of a promise made to Mr Stan Seymour two years ago, when the latter tried to sign George Robledo. At that time Mr Seed would not part. He considered Robledo one of the most rapidly advancing forwards in the game. He still does. But he promised that if, and when, Robledo wanted a move, Newcastle would have first notification. The Robledos, sons of a Chilean father and English mother, were brought to England when George was seven. He was a notable schools player who played for Barnsley A, then with a Huddersfield junior club, before returning to Barnsley as an amateur when sixteen. Mr Martin left Newcastle for Barnsley yesterday morning. In the afternoon he saw officials of the

Second Division club. Discussion was then adjourned until 8 p.m. Towards 9.30 p.m. the brothers Robledo left the hotel where the meeting was being held along with Mr Seed and Mr Martin for their home. Mr Seed and Mr Martin returned about 11 o'clock to the hotel and informed the Barnsley directors that the brothers had consulted their mother and agreed to go to Newcastle.

There's the odd inaccuracy in there, but then there usually is when a story comes together at speed on deadline from different places, so it's hard to fault the journalists responsible, who by and large did a good job. Alongside the words, a rather playful sub-editor inserted head-and-shoulder pictures of the brothers, both flashing smiles, under the headings 'Meet George' and 'Meet Ted'. And meet George and Ted the people of Newcastle and its environs most certainly did because, true to form in an area renowned for its obsession with football, all copies of *The Journal* had sold out by midday on Friday.

By that time, George – and only George, not Ted – was on board an express train heading from Yorkshire to Bristol where Newcastle United were scheduled to play Bristol Rovers in a friendly match the following day (both clubs having made early exits from the FA Cup, which had reached the fourth-round stage that weekend). In the evening, George was introduced to a fair chunk of Newcastle's squad at the team hotel, some United players having remained in the north-east rather than make the long journey to the West Country for what was, after all, only a friendly. This would prove a wise decision, as the match was abandoned in the sixty-fifth minute when the fog that had rolled in from the Bristol Channel became too dense for the crowd to see the players and vice versa. It was, as debuts go, the damp squib of damp squibs, but at least George had now met and kicked a ball around with some of his new teammates, even if he hadn't always been able to see them.

With that, George returned to West Melton to continue packing the family's possessions, ready to move to Newcastle.

• • •

The Newcastle upon Tyne that the Robledos first discovered in February 1949 was a far cry from the Newcastle of today, with its fancy restaurants, roaring nightlife and numerous tourist attractions. The shadow of the pre-war depression, when 200 men had marched from the once proud shipbuilding mecca of Jarrow to London to protest against the destruction of their communities and industries in what famously became known as the 'Jarrow Crusade' of autumn 1936, still hung over the city and its surrounding areas. 'A stranger from a distant civilisation observing the condition of the place and its people would have arrived at once at the conclusion that Jarrow had deeply offended some celestial empire of the island and was now being punished,' observed J. B. Priestley in his 1934 book *English Journey*. The same could be said in the late 1940s for umpteen towns and villages within Newcastle's orbit, which since anyone could remember had always relied on coal mining or shipbuilding to put bread on the table.

For the time being, the demand for coal, especially after six years of war, remained high. The railways, the power stations, the factories and almost all UK households still relied on it, keeping the colliery wheels of Northumberland and Durham turning. Even as late as 1948, 50 per cent of the world's shipbuilding orders came to the UK. Alas, new trades, new trade routes, new construction methods, the decline in ocean liner traffic and the rise of the jet airliner would all, in a very short time, conspire to send Britain tumbling down the world's shipbuilding league, bringing misery to those whose livelihoods once depended on it.

'The end of the Second World War saw the beginning of the long change in the industrial landscape of Tyneside,' write Alistair Moffat and George Rosie in their book *Tyneside: A History of Newcastle and Gateshead from Earliest Times*:

> It was slow, it was painful and it was sometimes heartbreaking, but it was inevitable. Quite simply the rest of the world was not prepared to let Britain's industrial centres – Birmingham and the Midlands, west central Scotland, South Wales, Teesside, Tyneside – to continue to operate as the planet's workshops. The days when Britain could rely on supplying much of the world's coal and most of the world's ships were gone, whether the people of Britain re-alised it or not.

Like Barnsley and the Dearne Valley, Tyneside had got off relatively lightly compared to other parts of the UK when it came to the havoc wreaked by aerial bombing. Again, as with Barnsley and the Dearne Valley, that's not to say Tyneside didn't go to war. The professional and territorial battalions of the Durham Light Infantry and the Royal Northumberland Fusiliers, Tyneside's most famous regiments, were involved in virtually every major campaign of the Second World War, from the home front to conflict with Japan in south-east Asia. Merchant seamen from the north-east found themselves in the thick of it as their vessels came under attack from German aircraft, submarines and shipping. Many a Tynesider laid down their life between 1939 and 1945 in the name of king, country and freedom. It's just that the vast majority of them did so on the ocean waves or foreign soil.

Set against such poverty, grief and economic turbulence, it sounds glib to talk about the cathartic power of football. And yet for millions of people the world over, that's exactly what it has. For all football's ability to divide and occasionally stir the wrong kind of emotions, it is also a sport, or rather a force, that can unite, inspire and help people forget their woes, for ninety minutes on any given day at least. That's certainly the case when it comes to the relationship between Newcastle United, its supporters, and the wider communities of Durham and Northumberland. Maybe, just maybe, it's something to do with the geographical position of St James' Park, located right at the centre of Newcastle upon Tyne, visible from every approach, the lord of all it surveys. Bobby Robson certainly thought so.

'The stadium has not always been so monumental or so majestic, certainly not when I was growing up, but it has expanded as the club has developed, and the team has always gripped the hearts and minds of fans who troop up in their tens of thousands to worship on match day,' the former Ipswich Town, England, Barcelona and, yes, Newcastle United manager wrote in 2008, the year before his death.

Supporters everywhere believe, quite rightly, that their own favourite club is special, but it is my firm contention that Newcastle has a history, culture and location that makes it wonderfully, beguilingly different. It is a single club city with a stadium at its heart, sitting flush among some architectural jewels in a region where a football result, good or bad, can affect productivity at work and shape the mood of a week.

And if you got to wear the famous black and white jersey, well that was something else altogether. As goalkeeper Jack Fairbrother once said, 'You weren't footballers when you played for Newcastle United in those days. You were gods.'

Gods they may have been, but that hadn't stopped successive Newcastle teams from underachieving in the years immediately before and after the Second World War. Relegated from the First Division in 1934, it wasn't until 1948 that the club regained its seat at English football's top table, sweeping to promotion on a tidal wave of colossal crowds drawn to the altar by men such as skipper Joe Harvey, centre-half Frank Brennan and top scorer Jackie Milburn.

Against all expectations, United then pushed hard for the Football League title throughout much of the 1948–49 season, going top of the table just before Christmas with a 1–0 win over Everton. Nevertheless, the need to strengthen the side was, according to Stan Seymour and manager George Martin, always there. They tried and failed to land the Hibernian and Scotland outside-right Gordon Smith. They tried and failed to sign winger Bobby Langton from Blackburn Rovers. They tried and succeeded in recruiting another winger in the shape of Bobby Mitchell. And some two years after first making eyes at Barnsley, they finally managed to prise George Robledo from Oakwell.

On Wednesday 2 February 1949, the Robledo family – George, Ted, Walter and mum Elsie – boarded a train at Doncaster bound for Newcastle Central, their possessions having been sent on ahead by road. It was a journey George had made several times before when playing for Barnsley at St James' Park. This time, probably because it represented a new beginning, he noticed things that he hadn't before – the billiard table expanse of the Vale of York, the magnificent view of the cathedral at Durham from the city's railway viaduct, the sweeping rows of terraced houses that carpeted the hills of Newcastle's southern suburbs. And there, at last, Newcastle upon Tyne itself, as seen from the King Edward Bridge looking down over the mucky old River Tyne. 'Barnsley with bridges,' George thought to himself. Barnsley, both then and now, as anyone with sight who has ever visited both places will testify, looks very little like Newcastle. But the sentiment was there. Already, he felt at home.

The semi-detached house which was to be the Robledos' actual home for the next four years was at 5 Ridgeway in Fenham, a quiet residential street to the west of the city centre. At that time, football clubs, or at least the better-off ones, kept what were known as 'club houses' for the use of staff or players from outside the area and this was one of around half-a-dozen owned by United.

It took half an hour to walk from Ridgeway to St James' Park, and that's what George, accompanied by Ted, did on Saturday 5 February ahead of his Newcastle league debut against Charlton Athletic, boots tucked under his arm, cigarette in mouth, coat collar turned up against the blast of a north-east winter. Over 56,000 people were there to see the first South American registered player ever to appear for Newcastle United, despite the sub-zero temperature. Barnsley's post-war attendances had been relatively impressive, but this was something else altogether.

Some Newcastle supporters, and members of the media, had been wondering whether United would field their new signing higher up the field at centre-forward, alongside Jackie Milburn, as opposed to his familiar inside-forward position, given George's ability to score as well as create goals. George Martin, perhaps sensibly, chose to keep him where he was more accustomed. George didn't find the net in what proved to be a comfortable 2–0 win but he did impress. 'I have rarely been so solidly pleased with such a [debut] performance,' wrote the correspondent from *The Journal*. 'His sturdy industry, prompt and unselfish disposal and quick positioning was most impressive on Saturday. If his fine soccer sense suggested tip top centre [forward] abilities, he did so well where he was that we need not quibble.'

Seven days later, George turned on the style away to Middlesbrough in what was admittedly only a friendly – not that you would have known by the size of the 36,000-strong crowd. In an entertaining 3–3 draw, he not only created United's first and third goals for George Stobbart but also scored the second himself, tapping home from close range. 'On this evidence, Newcastle appear to have hit the jackpot with Robledo, who harried throughout,' declared the reporter from the *Daily Express* who covered the match. 'He is a centre [forward] and an inside [forward] all in one and will surely help shoulder the burden for Milburn when it comes to the creating and scoring of goals.'

On the first Saturday in March, Newcastle went head to head with Sunderland at St James' Park in a match that, having lost 1–0 to Manchester City in the interim, they really needed to win to keep up the pressure on title rivals Portsmouth. For the uninitiated out there, Newcastle United and Sunderland don't get along. You might think, being separated by only a dozen or so miles and with fan bases built initially on the coal and shipbuilding industries, there would be common ground. You would be wrong. One club plays in black and white, while the other delight in red and white. One club plays its home games on Tyneside, the other on Wearside. One lot are Geordies while the other identify as Wearsiders (do not, under any circumstances, confuse the two). For all our earlier talk of football's cathartic powers, Newcastle United versus Sunderland divides like a blowtorch through butter.

Once again the conditions were shocking, but almost 60,000 people still passed through the turnstiles to witness the latest instalment of a rivalry dating back to Christmas Eve 1898. It blew a gale and it snowed, and Sunderland went in at half-time 1–0 to the good. Within a minute of the restart, Milburn had equalised. When Tommy Walker's cross was then spilled by Sunderland goalkeeper Johnny Mapson, George was on hand to smash the loose ball into the unguarded net for what proved to be the winner. Put simply, he could not have chosen a better time or place to score his first competitive Newcastle United goal. That night, for the first but certainly not the last time, George Robledo was the toast of Tyneside.

Throughout what remained of the 1948–49 campaign, George continued to shine with his conjuring and sharpshooting, scoring important goals against Arsenal, Blackpool, Bolton Wanderers and a brace at the expense of Derby County. 'He used to blast them in from all directions, and they went like a bullet,' another of the St James' Park new boys, Bobby Mitchell, observed of 'Pancho', as George affectionately became known in Newcastle's dressing room. Defender Charlie Crowe also noted the marked effect his arrival had on Milburn. 'Jackie was a better centre-forward when George Robledo came along,' he recalled. 'They were the perfect pair.'

George's outstanding form couldn't, however, prevent United from tiring at the finish line, trailing in fourth place some six points behind champions Portsmouth (under the old system of two points for a win, abolished in 1981). It had, nonetheless, been a hugely encouraging season for the Magpies, as they were and indeed are still known, given it was their first in the high life after fourteen years in the wilderness.

Anyone fortunate enough to meet George during his time at Newcastle, and indeed throughout his life, will have encountered someone who, for all his sporting prowess, remained a remarkably grounded man of relatively few words. At least verbally. On paper, it was quite a different story.

George loved writing letters, postcards and notes to people, something that only really came to light in the weeks and months after the Robledo family left Yorkshire. He wrote to all sorts – former mining pals, Barnsley supporters such as Don Wearmouth, people he'd known at Brampton Youth Group, even Harold Steer, his old headmaster. Wearmouth, for one, would send him copies of the *Green 'Un*, the Saturday evening sports paper published as part of *The Star* in Sheffield, in return. 'Am always interested in reading matter from the old district,' replied George to Wearmouth on headed notepaper bearing the Robledos' address and postcode. (5 Ridgeway, Fenham, Newcastle upon Tyne 4, as it was then). In the twenty-first century, professional footballers don't tend to correspond in reams with former work colleagues, supporters, old friends or mentors. Back then, in the pre-digital days when longhand prevailed, professional footballers still didn't tend to correspond in reams with former work colleagues, supporters, old friends or mentors.

'My dad was a quiet man, very much an introvert, which some people might find surprising,' says Elizabeth Robledo.

> So much of what he wanted to say or express, he did so in writing. He seemed to find it easier to communicate that way. And he really was an excellent writer, probably because he did so much of it. He loved writing letters and postcards and he loved receiving them as well, hearing people's news and finding out what they were doing in their lives. That's something that never left him.

In the spring of 1949, word of George's way with, er, words reached the offices of the *Barnsley Chronicle*, still in the market for news surrounding one of the area's favourite sons. That summer, rather than taking the well-earned break they so desperately needed as well as deserved, Newcastle United's first team were booked to go on a six-week tour of North America, taking in eleven games and 7,000-odd miles by railroad, stopping off in places many *Barnsley Chronicle* readers would never have heard of. How about George enlighten them by penning a series of articles from across the pond?

At noon on Friday 13 May, United's party of sixteen players and six officials left Southampton for New York City on board the *Queen Mary*, one of the most famous ocean liners in the world. Two weeks later, the first instalment of 'On Tour With George Robledo' appeared as the lead story on page seven of the *Barnsley Chronicle*, under the headline 'Cigarettes And Nylons Galore On Floating Village'. The crossing, or at least the first part of it, had been rough, leading to a bout of seasickness among many of the 400 passengers, but even that couldn't tarnish the novelty of travelling on a luxury liner, free from the confines of wartime rationing (which remained in force in the UK until the early 1950s).

'Everything on board was magnificent, the shops being full of practically everything,' wrote George.

> There is an unending supply of best quality chocolates, fresh fruit and cigarettes: every conceivable kind of British and American cigarettes – duty free. Twenty of the popular brands cost 9d, so everyone appeared to be smoking themselves to death. Nylons are also plentiful and food is the last word. The majority of dinner and luncheon menus have nine courses. One is free to go through the lot. No one accomplished this feat on our trip, though Frank Brennan [Newcastle's tough, no-nonsense centre-half], in a gallant effort, waded through eight courses!

Having docked in New York City on Wednesday 18 May, Newcastle's party spent a few hours in Manhattan before catching the overnight sleeper train to Montreal for the opening game of the tour the following day. 'To those of us here for the first time, it was an unforgettable sight,' George wrote of their arrival into New York Bay after five days at sea.

> Manhattan on the one side and New Jersey on the other and then the Statue of Liberty. It was nearly a case of men overboard as everyone rushed to the rails to take snaps. In the background were the inspiring skyscrapers with the Empire State Building

majestically standing out. In two hours we did a little sightseeing. First, Madison Square Gardens, then the Empire State Building, and finally the one and only Broadway. Every building was enveloped in a blaze of light. We read the latest news on an illuminated revolving tape. Traffic is far thicker than in London. What cars there are, streamlined and up-to-date. It's hard to tell whether they are coming or going!

Which, equally, was something you could say about Newcastle's overworked players. Once the magic of New York City had been left behind, it wasn't long before the reality of what lay ahead began to dawn on them. The itinerary was gruelling beyond belief, involving plenty of overlapping and reversing – New York City to Montreal, Montreal to Toronto, Toronto to Saskatoon, Saskatoon to Edmonton, Edmonton to Vancouver, Vancouver to Seattle, Seattle back to Vancouver, Vancouver to Winnipeg, Winnipeg to Toronto, Toronto to New York City, New York City back again to Montreal. Small wonder 'everyone in the party was keen to get home' as George tactfully put it in his final despatch, published in the *Barnsley Chronicle* on Saturday 16 July.

But along the way there were highlights. Oh, how there were highlights. And rather than churning out earnest match reports, George captured them all in his writing: the thrill of playing under floodlights for the first time, the novelty of using a white football instead of the standard British brown leather lead balloon, visiting Niagara Falls where 'the noise is terrific', watching the Rocky Mountains roll by through the windows of a railway observation car, facing a Saskatchewan XI featuring several indigenous Americans in front of 'a crowd of Indians in full traditional dress', going to see the New York Yankees play baseball, the lure of the Big Apple with its 'large number of all-night eating places' and cinemas that 'do not close until 4 a.m.' and enjoying a drink at the Broadway restaurant and bar owned by heavyweight boxing champion Jack Dempsey. For some members of the Newcastle United team it was all a little bit too off the wall, especially coming at the end of a long season. George, however, embraced the experience in body and mind as well as in print.

'I don't know who had the idea for him to produce those pieces, I'm just glad that they did,' says Ashley Ball of the modern-day *Barnsley Chronicle*.

They're beautifully written with great attention to detail, the kind that wouldn't disgrace any true journalist. You can imagine what people in, say, West Melton would have thought reading his words, discovering this other world where people went to the cinema in the middle of the night and watched sport under floodlights. How he got the articles back to England, I don't know. He can't have posted them because that would have taken too long, so my guess is via some kind of wire service which itself can't have been easy, given how hectic their schedule was. It's proper foreign correspondent stuff coming from a football player, and I'm sure our readers of the time must have loved it.

Like shooting fish in a barrel. That, in essence, is what Newcastle's North American tour of 1949 amounted to, at least on the field. Against second- or third-rate opposition, United plundered a grand

total of seventy-nine goals from ten wins (the eleventh and final fixture, scheduled to take place in Montreal, was cancelled due to fa-
tigue in Newcastle's ranks). Jackie Milburn alone scored thirty-one
times, with George bagging eighteen. Nothing had been proved, in
other words, other than club soccer in the USA and Canada still
had a long way to go.

Financially, though, the tour achieved its objective, which was to
make money for Newcastle United. Exactly how much has been lost
in the mists of time, if indeed it was ever declared. But, fair to say, it
was a tidy sum. Which, given the players' daily allowance while in
North America had been a paltry $4, didn't exactly endear the suits
in the boardroom to the squad. Not for the last time during George's
stint at Newcastle, player welfare had come second to financial gain
during what was supposed to be the summer recess.

If George took two things from his trip across the Atlantic, they
were the desire to travel and a shuddering realisation as to just how
poorly professional footballers in Britain were paid compared to
leading sporting figures in some other parts of the world. Having
never set foot outside the UK since 1932, touring North America
fired a craving within him to see other parts of the globe. Either
off his own bat or as a footballer, on returning to England George
resolved to, in his words, 'see new places and enjoy the hospitality of
what the world and its people have to offer'. While in New York City,
Newcastle's players had been shocked to discover that some baseball
stars on the Yankees' roster were earning as much as $90,000 per
year in 1949 (approximately £24,400), at a time when the maximum
wage in the Football League stood at £12 per week, falling to £10
during the off season. In other football leagues in other parts of the

world, so George learned, there was no such thing as a maximum wage. Take, for instance, Chile, where players were free to earn whatever they were being offered.

It would take a while to grow, but a seed had definitely been planted.

By the time Newcastle's players arrived in Liverpool on board the *Empress of France* on Friday 1 July they were exhausted. Over the previous forty-three weeks, United had played forty-two league games, one FA Cup tie, three domestic friendlies and ten fixtures across North America, spending countless hours travelling thousands of miles by boat, train and motor coach around England, the Atlantic, Canada and the US. They had met some wonderful people and seen some wonderful sights in the New World. But on the other hand, a few financial truths had hit home. The only real downtime they'd had since August 1948, in an age when football clubs still played league matches on Christmas Day, had been aboard the *Queen Mary* and the *Empress of France*. Even then the players had technically been on duty, exercising every morning of the outward voyage in the ship's gymnasium or on the open deck. And no sooner had the team arrived back on Tyneside than they were straight into pre-season training. When seen through a 21st-century lens, with players now regarded as valuable commodities requiring rest and fine-tuning, it's a scenario which seems nothing short of farcical.

Needless to say, Newcastle's form over the weeks that followed was what you might expect from a group of players running on empty. The opening three games of the 1949–50 league season – against Portsmouth, Everton and Wolverhampton Wanderers – all ended in defeat. On their day United could still be a match for any side, as hefty wins over Everton in the reverse fixture (4–0), Stoke City (4–1) and West Bromwich Albion (5–1) demonstrated. Yet their days were proving few and far between. Word had it that Jackie Milburn, no less, was unsure of his future and wanted away. At one point, a players' meeting was held behind the backs of the manager and the board to discuss poor form, unrest within the squad and discontent on the terraces.

'Soon after I had joined Newcastle we had one of those lean spells which every club suffers,' George recounted in an article written some years later of another meeting convened around the same time to discuss United's poor start to the 1949–50 season.

Three or four matches had been lost in succession, and our manager [George Martin] called a conference one morning and talked the whole problem over, giving what he considered to be the reason for our losses. All, of course, in a very tactful and helpful manner designed not to make anybody a scapegoat, but solely to improve matters for the future. When he had finished he paused a moment and then said 'Anybody like to make any comments?' 'Yes' said a certain well-known player, who must remain nameless. 'How is it I have been played in four different positions in the last five weeks?' The manager pointed out that any player who could fill two or three positions was obviously an asset to any club. One who could fill four so well as the player in question was a great help. 'You are a fine utility player,' he added. Like a flash the player retorted 'Maybe that's alright for you, but not for me. Why, even my shirts are marked "utility" now!' The howl of laughter which went up cleared the atmosphere, which in any case had been quite friendly, like a gust of sea air, and no more was said. The next week we won handsomely.

Although relegation from the First Division was never seriously on the cards, as the 1940s made way for the 1950s, St James' Park was hardly the bed of roses George hoped it would be on arriving from Barnsley. All of which might explain why, in February of 1950, Sheffield Wednesday decided to make what the *Daily Express* called 'a sensational bid' of £25,000 for both George and Ted who, two months previously, had made his first-team debut on the left side of Newcastle's midfield against Aston Villa.

It was, on the face of it, a cunning move. Previous experience told Wednesday they had little or no chance of signing George on his own. It had to be George and Ted. Or to be more precise, George and Ted and Walter and Elsie. George had also been one of Newcastle's more consistent performers, despite their lowly league position, so Wednesday knew they would be landing a player in form.

The bid, which came out of the blue, stunned George, as indeed did Newcastle's decision to accept it. Why, having waited two years to sign him and after moving heaven and earth (or at least Ted, Walter and Elsie) in order to do so, would Newcastle United agree to sell him barely a year later? It made no sense, especially as he'd been playing well and expressed no desire to leave. OK, so the 1949–50 season hadn't panned out as expected, but George was happy on Tyneside, as indeed were the Robledo family. They didn't want to move.

Then, just as surprisingly, two things happened which, combined, put the skids under any talk of a transfer.

First, Jackie Milburn picked up an injury. Second, certain members of Newcastle United's board expressed reservations about the sale of Ted.

That's Ted Robledo, makeweight in George's transfer from Barnsley to Newcastle, the player United hadn't initially wanted, someone who'd sat on his backside for eleven months at St James' Park until opportunity finally knocked. At which point, to everyone's surprise, he'd actually done alright.

On Thursday 16 February, *The Journal* went ahead and published a story which in effect confirmed that negotiations between the two clubs were dead in the water:

Newcastle United FC last night announced two representatives of Sheffield Wednesday have been in Newcastle today with a view to signing George Robledo. No deal was effected. Sheffield Wednesday secretary-manager Mr E. W. Taylor and a director were the visitors. *The Journal* understands that while agreement was reached with the Newcastle officials regarding the transfer of George Robledo, United were unwilling to part with brother Ted when the subject of a dual transfer was broached. Finally the whole deal collapsed when George, after family consultations, decided against a move. It is understood from Sheffield sources that Wednesday were prepared to hand over a cheque for £25,000. Wednesday are known to have been anxious to sign George Robledo for a long time. A year ago, when Newcastle United paid Barnsley £25,000 for the two brothers, Wednesday were also eager to carry through a deal, but United had already come to terms with the South Yorkshire club. A further matter which might have affected the negotiations was the news that centre-forward Jackie Milburn has injured his foot in training and might be out of football for a month.

Darned right Milburn's knock affected the negotiations. Selling one prized asset when you don't have to is nonsensical. Selling that very same prized asset when another of your prized assets is crocked is tantamount to stupidity bordering on recklessness. Between them, George and Jackie constituted Newcastle's overriding goal threat. George, arguably, was also the team's chief creative source. Not even United's oft-criticised board were daft enough to do that.

A line, it seems, had been drawn. George Robledo wasn't going to be sold. Ted Robledo wasn't going to be sold. Jackie Milburn wasn't going to be sold. Nobody was going anywhere. Newcastle would stick rather than continually twisting and see where it got them.

The upturn in results came almost immediately. From the end of February until the beginning of May 1950, United lost just one of their fourteen league fixtures, climbing from the bottom half of the table to finish in fifth place, just three points shy of Portsmouth who had retained their league title.

For George, one match in particular from that sequence would stand out in the mind. On Tuesday 11 April, Newcastle travelled to Yorkshire to face Huddersfield Town. The match drew a sizeable crowd of 37,766, including hundreds of neutral supporters from across the county, there for no other reason than to see the 'Red Shadow'. Newcastle triumphed 2–1 and, appropriately, it was George who scored the winning goal midway through the second half. Headline-grabbing stuff, in other words. And yet, had it not been for a quick-thinking steward, the game might easily have ended in tragedy.

Eight days previously, on Monday 3 April, the entire main West Stand at Huddersfield's Leeds Road ground had been consumed by what the *Yorkshire Post* called 'one of the fiercest fires in the town for many years'. Consequently, Huddersfield's match against Newcastle was switched to Elland Road, home of neighbours Leeds United, which boasted a greater capacity. In fact, the attendance, swelled by those neutrals there to watch George, proved to be Huddersfield's largest for a 'home' game that season.

With around ten minutes of normal time remaining, some wisps of smoke appeared amid seating at the southern end of the main Elland Road stand. Nobody ran, screamed or panicked – in fact, hardly anybody moved at all – but it was enough for several players, George included, to approach the referee and ask if the match should be halted. It wasn't and play continued.

Meanwhile, beneath the stand two firemen, having been alerted by the steward, were doing their level best to extinguish a blaze that had taken hold of a structure made almost entirely of wood. Above them, still hardly anybody moved. 'People were far too interested watching the game to take any notice of the firemen,' one spectator told the *Yorkshire Post*. 'A few people had to leave their seats but the rest stayed where they were.'

Fortunately, their level best was enough to dowse the flames and extinguish the fire. A cursory investigation conducted after the final whistle concluded that a cigarette end dropped between the seats had ignited litter underneath the stand. The actions of the two firemen went almost entirely unnoticed by 'hundreds of people sat unperturbed in the main stand', as the *Yorkshire Post* put it, yet they had almost certainly averted a disaster the likes of which had never been seen before in the UK.

George thought about that evening thirty-five years later when he heard on the BBC World Service that a fire had engulfed the main stand at Valley Parade, home of Bradford City, while a match against Lincoln City was in progress. Over fifty people were feared dead and at least 250 injured. Valley Parade was a ground George knew well, situated just twelve miles from Elland Road as the crow flies. A lit cigarette, it would emerge, had slipped between the floorboards of the largely wooden grandstand and ignited litter beneath that had been allowed to build for years.

'I knew, straight off, that something similar had happened (in Bradford) to what very nearly happened that evening in Leeds,' George told the esteemed Yorkshire based sports writer and editor Benny Hill (no, not that one) many years later.

I don't know what caused that first fire [in Huddersfield], but I do know the one at Elland Road could easily have ended in an inferno from which an awful lot of people would not have escaped. It doesn't even bear thinking about, does it? And how many near misses were there in the meantime that we never got to hear about? Nothing ever changes until someone gets hurt, and as long as nobody got hurt nothing was ever done. All those lives lost, and they really shouldn't have been.

Four days after their last league game of the season, so the curtain finally fell on Newcastle's 1949–50 campaign with a 2–1 friendly win over Ayr United. Having not had any time off since the summer of 1948, United's players could at last look forward to a lengthy period of rest and relaxation. All bar two of them, that is.

For George Robledo and Jackie Milburn, foreign climes beckoned once again. Except this time, they were destined to be adversaries rather than teammates.

6

COME TOGETHER

'The World Cup is a very important way to measure the good players, and the great ones. It is a test of a great player.'
– PELÉ

Robert Guérin had reached a point somewhere beyond frustration. For years, the Union des Sociétés Françaises de Sports Athlétiques (Union of French Athletic Sports Societies or USFSA), along with other similar bodies across Europe, had been waiting for England, ably supported by the other British football associations, to take the lead in establishing an international body that would oversee the sport's governance and growth. It was, after all, the British who had pioneered the game and formulated its rules during the second half of the nineteenth century.

Alas, despite Guérin's best efforts to lead the horse to water, Britannia was showing somewhere between little and zero interest in drinking from football's international waves, let alone ruling them. Throughout 1902 and 1903, Guérin, in his capacity as the USFSA's secretary, had sent copious letters and telegrams to the Football

Association (FA) in London outlining why this was a good thing. The message was simple – lead us and we will follow you.

Still, Britannia shuffled its papers and continued to look the other way.

Eventually, Guérin managed to secure a meeting with his opposite number at the FA, Frederick Wall. 'His head in his hands, Mr Wall listened to my story,' Guérin recalled in his memoirs.

> He said he would report back to his council. I waited a few months. I travelled to London once more and had a meeting with the FA president, Lord Kinnaird. However, that, too, was of no avail. Tired of the struggle and recognising that the Englishmen, true to tradition, wanted to wait and watch, I undertook to invite delegates myself.

And so the inaugural meeting of the Fédération Internationale de Football Association, or FIFA as it's more commonly known today, took place in Paris on 21 May 1904 without any of the British associations being present. The following year, the FA belatedly gave the fledgling organisation its blessing, yet reservations and mistrust continued on both sides. In 1928, this uneasy truce finally broke when the British associations, seeking a stricter distinction between amateurs and professionals, walked out over what they regarded as 'shamateurism' in the form of 'broken time' payments made to amateur footballers who took time off work to play (in Britain, the thorny issue of paying players had been resolved the previous century, whereas in Europe and South America the distinction remained blurred).

Thus, the very first FIFA World Cup took place two years later in Uruguay without the participation of England, Ireland, Scotland or Wales, the four countries that had given the game to the world. Chile were there though, winning two matches and losing one, a tempestuous 3–1 defeat to eventual finalists Argentina, in which both teams indulged in a prolonged full-on brawl that had to be broken up by police (Chile claimed incitement, the uncompromising Argentinean midfielder Luis Monti having kicked their midfielder Arturo Torres as he attempted to head the ball). For better or for worse, at least they had made an impression.

Even so, Chile were no-shows for both the 1934 and 1938 World Cups in Italy and France respectively, played out against the fascist climate of the time (the former) and with Europe in meltdown (the latter). Likewise England, who continued to observe affairs through the window marked 'splendid isolation'. However, by the time the 1950 World Cup appeared on the horizon, the climate had changed. Four years previously, in the spirit of post-war rapprochement, all four British football associations had accepted an invitation from FIFA to rejoin. In a further act of goodwill, FIFA also declared that the 1949–50 British Home International Championships (the annual competition between England, Scotland, Wales and Ireland – later Northern Ireland – which ceased in 1984) could act as a qualifying group for the 1950 World Cup in Brazil, with two nations going through. Long story short, Wales and Ireland fell by the wayside while Scotland, despite finishing second, stubbornly declined to take their place simply because they'd finished second and not first, leaving England as the only British attendee.

In the months leading up to the tournament a whole host of

other countries, for various political, economic, geographic and downright hissy reasons, also decided to give the party a miss. They included Argentina (over a dispute with the Brazilian Football Confederation), Portugal (who refused to take Scotland's place) and Turkey (too far away and expensive to make the journey), all of whom joined the already lengthy list of absentees featuring the likes of Russia, Hungary and Czechoslovakia (now residing behind the Iron Curtain) and Germany (excluded as a result of the war). By the time the draw finally took place in Rio de Janeiro on 22 May 1950, only fifteen countries remained, two of whom (India and France) subsequently withdrew. This left a rump of thirteen teams spread across four hopelessly unbalanced groups (two consisting of four nations, one of three and one of two). Group Two would feature the US and Spain along with, irony of ironies, England and Chile.

Which is how, on Sunday 25 June 1950, inside the brand new Maracanã Stadium in Rio de Janeiro, George Robledo and Jackie Milburn came to be adversaries in what history recalls as England's first ever match at a World Cup.

In the autumn of 1949, while studying in England at the London School of Economics, a Chilean by the name of Aníbal Pinto decided to embark on a spot of matchmaking and bring George Robledo to the attention of football's movers and shakers back in his homeland. A keen sports fan, Pinto had observed George's progress from Second Division Barnsley to First Division Newcastle via the sports columns in the broadsheet newspapers, where he was often referred to as 'Newcastle's Chilean inside-forward' or 'Newcastle's Chilean forward'. The world was a much bigger place in 1949 and Pinto assumed, correctly as it happened, that word of George's exploits probably hadn't filtered through to Santiago. Determined to put that right, Pinto got in touch with Manuel Bianchi, Chile's ambassador to Britain, urging him to make contact with the sport's governing body in Chile, the Federación de Fútbol de Chile. This Bianchi did. Barely able to believe their good fortune, the Federación asked Bianchi to make some follow-up enquiries and, if possible, meet George at the earliest opportunity.

Almost inevitably, meeting George also meant meeting Elsie, Ted and Walter. In the front room of their club house in Fenham, with all four Robledos present, Bianchi went through the process of ascertaining whether this dashing-looking young man, who didn't know a word of Spanish and spoke with a Yorkshire accent, was serious about playing for the country of his birth. 'Yes, certainly,' George was able to assure him. Documentary proof of citizenship was, on request, provided. At some point Elsie, never one to miss an opportunity, told Bianchi that Ted, too, held Chilean citizenship, which the ambassador duly noted.

Formalities in Fenham over, Bianchi then went to meet with Stan Seymour prior to returning to London in order to seek assurances regarding George's availability for international duty during the late spring and summer off season of 1950. With no foreign tour in Newcastle United's diary, Seymour was able to give Bianchi his blessing. All the boxes had been ticked. Thanks to Pinto's initiative and Bianchi's legwork, Chile had got themselves one of English football's leading men.

In 1932, it had taken the *Reina del Pacifico* twenty-four days to wind its way from Iquique to Liverpool by sea. In May 1950, George made the return journey by air from London to Santiago in just two. It was the first time he had ever been on an aeroplane and he rather liked it. The *Reina*, from what he remembered, had sauntered from port to port. Despite stopping to refuel, pick up and set down passengers at various points (including Paris, Lisbon and Dakar), the overriding sensation of flying was one of progress, in every sense of the word. 'The future feels like it has arrived,' he wrote of the experience, even if being up among the clouds had been 'unsettling, at least at first'.

They say Chile is a far-flung place, hidden away from the rest of South America by the barren, towering peaks of the Andes. They say Chile does not lend itself easily to maps, measuring as it does some 2,600 miles in length and no more than 200 in width. They say, 'Such a country should be called an island,' as the writer Benjamín Subercaseaux put it while describing the 'crazy geography' of his homeland. Old perceptions, perhaps, yet ones which continue to apply as much today as they did in 1950, the year word reached Chile that some kind of superman was on his way from England to lead the country's relatively young, inexperienced football team into the forthcoming World Cup finals. It was almost, some of an older disposition couldn't help but think, as if history was repeating itself.

First came the Spanish. Then, in the nineteenth century, came the British, many of whom set themselves up as bankers and merchants, the kind of professions that enabled Chile's economy to grow and prosper. They brought with them traditional British family names such as Cox, Edwards and Grove, which became well known throughout the country. In the latter part of the century, the Brits also imported football, initially played by immigrants and sailors in the parks and on the quaysides of Valparaíso, second home (behind Liverpool) to the *Reina del Pacifico*. In time, having been adopted by local people, the game spread to the hinterlands, giving rise to amateur teams and eventually professional outfits such as Colo-Colo, widely regarded as the largest and most popular football club in Chile.

Now, an emigrant was returning from Britain to play football for the country he had last set foot in some eighteen years previously. George's arrival fostered a sense of anticipation, if not expectation, among Chileans. Few seriously expected their country to win the World Cup. Even so, with a top-class creator and getter of goals in the side, things might at least get interesting.

That sense of anticipation duly went up a notch when the draw for the World Cup was made in Rio de Janeiro, pitching Chile into the same group not only as England but also Spain. It seemed to be 'written in the stars', as George later remarked of the sub-plot involving his adopted homeland.

Prior to facing England at the Maracanã Stadium in Rio, George had the best part of three weeks to get to know his teammates and, if possible, see a bit of Santiago and its surroundings. His almost total lack of Spanish could, in theory, have been a problem. George, though, had been here before. On first moving to Yorkshire, he'd barely been able to understand what many people were saying, such was the strength of the local accent. On moving to Newcastle he had struggled again, such was the tricky nature of the Geordie dialect (United even went as far as assigning two of the dressing room's broader Geordies to help George who, by his own account, 'just couldn't get the hang of the accent at all'). This, sensed George, was something similar, another linguistic challenge there to be tackled and ultimately enjoyed.

Time, however, was of the essence. And so, during his first few days on Chilean soil, 'Jorge', as he was immediately christened by his teammates, set about learning the Spanish words for some universal football terms, including:

- Pass (as in 'pass me the ball'): *Pasa*
- Shoot! (as in 'have a shot'): *Chuta!*
- Go left: *Izquierda*
- Go right: *Derecha*
- My ball!: *Mia!*
- Cross: *Centra*
- Leave! (as in 'leave the ball to me'): *Deja!*
- The back post (George's favourite attacking position for headers): *Al palo largo*

In addition, George's teammates taught him a few words which, it turned out, had absolutely nothing to do with football. As in rude ones. The tradition of playing practical jokes on your amigos in the dressing room was, he soon realised, as alive and well in Santiago as it was at St James' Park.

It was difficult, but in those first few training sessions, 'Jorge' tried communicating only in Spanish with his teammates who, on a personal level, he found hugely welcoming and encouraging. From a footballing perspective, whatever the team lacked in skill they more than made up for in heart. 'The enthusiasm of the public for soccer out there is amazing, and so is that of the players themselves,' wrote

George in an annual called *Soccer Fanfare*, the latest publication to utilise his literary skills.

> Although most of them are amateurs, they were all as keen as mustard to better themselves. Both the amateurs and professionals work during the week and are allowed time off for training, the amateurs getting just their expenses. One of the latter with whom I played [Andrés Prieto, a forward], however, came from a very wealthy family and never even bothered to claim his expenses. He was a university student and an international although only just 20 years of age, and a really first class player.

There was, of course, also the elephant in the room surrounding George's return to Chile – namely, the spectre of his father, Arístides Robledo. At some point during his pre-World Cup stay in Santiago, George became the only one of the Robledo brothers to, as an adult, meet their dad. Today, nobody knows where exactly that meeting took place or who reached out to who or what they discussed. Where do you possibly start when so much water has gone under the bridge?

George, a man of few words, barely spoke about their meeting to other members of his own family, let alone friends and acquaintances. 'Ted and I never saw him again, but George did,' confirmed Walter Robledo in a 2019 interview with journalist Chris Waugh of *The Athletic*. 'He didn't talk about him much, though. We'd been away from him for so long.' As Richard Williams, grandson of their former Brampton Ellis Senior School headmaster Harold Steer – who also interviewed Walter for *The Independent* in 1999 – says, 'I don't think Arístides was ever really much more than an old wedding photograph to Ted and Walter.'

Within a year, Arístides would be dead of natural causes, aged just fifty-seven. How things were left between the two men is anyone's guess. George's almost complete silence on the matter, even for a man of his reserved nature, is perhaps telling. Then again, they could have been open to further dialogue and simply been defeated by time.

Either way, George certainly didn't let the experience or Arístides's almost complete absence from his formative years interfere with his own responsibilities as a father later in life. 'I was a spoiled girl, but a very down-to-earth spoiled girl,' says Elizabeth Robledo.

I had all the latest Barbie dolls, but he was also the kind of dad who spent time with me and talked to me. He and my mum used to say, 'There will be stages in life when we can give you everything, but maybe one day that won't always be the case.' I've never forgotten that, because football was so different then to how it is now. They were paid well but they didn't receive anything like as much as footballers do today, so there could be tough times as well as good times, especially when they finished playing. The main thing was that I always felt loved by him. He was adorable, he really was, a very loving dad who will always be very special to me.

He trained. He learned a bit of Spanish. For whatever it was worth, he met his father. He went out for dinner with his teammates. He took afternoon tea, which, to his amusement, seemed as much of a ritual in Chile as it was in England. He watched as Santiaguinos sipped coffee and ate empanadas (pastries filled with meat and olives) during their work breaks at the little refreshment bars and stands dotted around the city centre. He marvelled at the purple shadows that, come dusk, marched from the foothills to the peaks of the nearby Andes. That desire to 'see new places and enjoy the hospitality of what the world and its people have to offer', born out of the previous summer's trip to North America, was being satisfied. And all 'at somebody else's expense', as he would quip on his return to England.

• • •

Considering the relative youth, inexperience and amateur status of some of their players, Chile trained hard and prepared well before heading to Brazil for the World Cup, with George on hand to provide some inside information about what to expect from their opening opponents.

As for England, all that was standing between them and an early exit from the tournament was, in hindsight, time.

Without any question, England had the players to win the 1950 World Cup. But then, as we've already seen, the sharpest minds weren't always found at the Football Association who, for reasons best known to themselves, had organised a goodwill tour of Canada at exactly the same time as things were scheduled to get underway in Brazil. Consequently, England's most famous player, Stanley Matthews, found himself bound initially for North America until common sense prevailed and he was diverted to Rio.

To make matters worse, team manager Walter Winterbottom,

battling the club versus country squabbles prevalent at the time, also had to factor in Manchester United's request that none of their players be considered as they would be touring the US. On arriving in Rio, he discovered the food being served in the team hotel was too spicy for the players to eat. Not one to be undone, Winterbottom decided the best way around the problem was to lock away the garlic, don an apron and do the cooking himself.

'When I think back now to the World Cup, we had a three or four day get-together in London after a hard season,' recalled Tom Finney.

> We went off and stopped in Rio right on the Copacabana Beach, in a hotel where you were very fortunate to get any sleep with the noise that was going on. It was early hours and there were car horns blazing away, and of course you went from a temperature here of some sixty degrees into something like ninety degrees, and bone hard grounds.

'There was no preparation as there is today,' added Stanley Matthews later in life, speaking about the make-do-and-mend nature of the trip. 'Tommy Finney and Wilf Mannion and I shared our rooms and we were eating bananas mostly.' As for Mannion's own memories of this baptism of Brazilian fire? 'You got out there into a [hot] climate where you needed to [acclimatise for] a few weeks, after having a hard season,' recounted the Middlesbrough inside-forward. 'Just walking about [was tiring] but he [Winterbottom] had you training in the heat and things like that. It was all against us.'

In that respect, England weren't alone. 'There is no doubt that the arrangement of the tournament greatly and grossly favoured Brazil, who played every one of their six matches but the second in Rio, while the other teams were obliged to traipse exhaustingly around the whole of this huge country,' wrote Brian Glanville, who reported from no fewer than ten World Cups, in his 2001 book on the history of the finals. 'The idea seems to have escaped everybody that if there were groups, these should logically be centred on one place. Moreover, the muggy, humid, debilitating climate of Rio was certainly a handicap to visiting teams.'

The paint had barely dried on the brand new Maracanã Stadium when, on Saturday 24 June 1950, Brazil and Mexico went head to head in the opening game of the tournament, the hosts barely getting out of third gear on their way to a comfortable 4–0 victory. Twenty-four hours later, it was Chile and England's turn to take the stage. 'Their welcome was tremendous, cheers and whistles mingling with the explosion of hundreds of firecrackers which sounded like a battery of machine guns,' wrote the former Sunderland and Arsenal centre-forward-turned-journalist Charlie Buchan in his memoirs.

> Before the kick-off, something like 5,000 pigeons were released and circled the ground. But, just as the [Brazilian] president was delivering a welcome address and a gun salute was being fired, the game started. You see, three o'clock was the time scheduled for the kick-off and the referee had been instructed to start the game on time. He did so amid an indescribable din.

On referee Karel van der Meer's whistle, George Robledo became the very first Football League player from outside the British Isles to face England in an official international. 'Play the game, not the occasion,' he remembered thinking to himself walking onto the pitch beforehand. And, right from the word go, that's what George did, encouraging and cajoling his teammates while also dictating Chile's forward play. Prior to kick-off, he had managed to convey to the rest of the dressing room the news that England, for reasons best known to themselves, were going without two key players for this fixture, namely Stanley Matthews and Jackie Milburn. With some members of the Chilean team under the impression they were facing England's 'B' team, 'La Roja' ('the red one', as Chile's nickname goes) gave as good as they got during the opening stages, creating yet wasting several good opportunities to take the lead. Nevertheless, it was England who drew first blood in the thirty-eighth minute, with Stan Mortensen climbing high to send a looping header beyond Chile's goalkeeper, Sergio Livingstone.

At half-time George fired up his customary cigarette, while in the dressing room next door, England's players took turns wearing oxygen masks as a way of dealing with the conditions. After the restart, both teams continued to press. Twice England hit the frame of the goal, as indeed had Chile in the first half through midfielder Hernán Carvallo and centre-forward Manuel Muñoz. As the opportunities continued to come and go, so George sensed the need for him to take control rather than play the role of creator and mentor. When England conceded a free kick some thirty yards from their goal, it was he who immediately grabbed the ball and sized up the situation.

Was it within his shooting range?

Yes.

Would he be better off trying some kind of set-piece move?

No. The free kick was head-on to England's goal, and Chile were unlikely to get a better opportunity to score from a dead-ball position all game.

Then there was the weather to factor in. Sure, it was Rio de Janeiro. Sure, it was muggy. And yet, remarkably for Brazil's sunshine coast, it was also raining. Goalkeepers hate rain as it makes the ball slippery. Through a series of hand signals, George instructed both Carvallo and Muñoz to close in on goalkeeper Bert Williams in search of rebounds, should England's last line of defence spill the shot that was about to come his way.

From the moment the ball left his right boot, George had rarely, if ever, been more certain that he'd scored a goal. Off it flew through the clammy Rio air, as sweet as a well-struck golf shot. England's defensive wall couldn't stop it and neither could Williams, whose dive was in vain. But then, right at the last nanosecond, the ball deviated fractionally from its arrow-like trajectory, cannoning back into play off an upright before being cleared to safety by a defender. For the third time that afternoon, Chile had been denied by the woodwork. Besides the likes of Mannion, Mortensen and Finney, England also appeared to have a certain Lady Luck on their side.

Maybe it's true, or maybe it's apocryphal. Either way, there's an old story that goes something like this. With the frame of the goal still shaking from that thunderous free kick, so one of England's defenders is supposed to have turned to Chile's number nine and drolly delivered the following words: 'Steady, George, you're not playing for Newcastle now, you know.'

'As if you had weights on you,' was how Mannion described the experience of playing in Rio that day. Yet it was his second-half goal, a low drive despatched into the corner of Livingstone's net, which ultimately killed the game off in England's favour. Afterwards, Winterbottom declared himself thoroughly unimpressed with the standard of officiating, highlighting the 'culture clash' that existed between South America and the UK in terms of competing for the ball, something he elaborated on following his resignation as England's manager in 1962:

> They had different attitudes in South America to the way players could handle you and push you off the ball with impunity. If you brought them down by tackling their feet they used to get furious. I used to think this was really difficult. Our game was based on fierce tackling for the ball, and that used to get all the spectators up in arms in South America. So there was a contrast between the two.

Four days after their 2–0 defeat to England, Chile returned to the Maracanã Stadium and lost by the same scoreline to the highly fancied, combative Spanish side. Once again George and his inexperienced teammates competed well but failed to make the most of the chances that came their way, with first-half goals by Estanislau Basora and Telmo Zarra putting the game to bed in Spain's favour. So far Chile had acquitted themselves admirably against tough opponents, which in itself amounted to some kind of success. However, the abiding memory of that day for George, and indeed the vast majority of people who followed world football in 1950, had absolutely nothing to do with events at the Maracanã.

Having beaten Chile in Rio, England then made their way north to face the US, the fourth team in Group Two, in Belo Horizonte. It was a game England were expected to win comfortably. As George himself had witnessed the previous summer during Newcastle United's tour of North America, football, or 'soccer', had little or no identity in the US, where baseball, basketball and American gridiron football dominated the sporting landscape. True, they had some talented young players, but none who were on a par with Matthews, Milburn or Finney. But even so, there were some who sensed trouble ahead.

'I had a vague feeling of discomfort about the future,' wrote Charles Buchan after England's performance against Chile.

I thought the England team had put too much emphasis on copybook football to the sacrifice of punch and finish in front of goal. Their midfield movements were perfectly carried out, but they were mainly across field, not direct enough to get the Chilean defenders in a panic. My doubts were not dispelled even by Mortensen's great first goal, nor by the superb shot with which Mannion increased the lead. It was exhibition soccer, not World Cup winning stuff.

'I remember their [the US's] coach was born in Scotland, a fella called Bill Jeffrey,' recalled journalist Frank Butler, who covered the 1950 World Cup for the *News of the World*.

I flew up [from Rio to Belo Horizonte] with him and he said to me, 'I don't want to pump you too much, I'm not trying to get information, but is it true they're not playing Stanley Matthews against us? The greatest footballer in the world. Surely they've got a trick, they're going to bring him on?' And I said 'No', and Stanley sat next to me in the tiny little ground at Belo Horizonte and we played like chumps, not champs.

Despite having his hands tied when it came to team selection matters, Walter Winterbottom had pushed the case for including Matthews, if not Milburn, in England's side to face the US. The chairman of selectors, a Grimsby fish merchant by the name of Arthur Drewry who doubled as the president of the Football League, was not for turning. 'My policy is to never change a winning team,' he declared from the team's base in the mountain village of Morro Velho, home to a British-owned gold mining company employing some 2,000 UK workers. For the second game running, Matthews, as well as Milburn, would be no more than a spectator, the concept of substitutes still being some years off in international competition.

The following day, England lost 1–0 to a US side whose captain, a Scot called Ed McIlvenny, had emigrated eighteen months previously, having been given a free transfer by Wrexham of the Football League's third tier. On the final whistle, hundreds of people broke through what little security there was and chaired the victorious US players shoulder-high from the field. It was, and indeed remains, one the greatest upsets ever witnessed at a World Cup.

'It was the biggest freak result I ever experienced throughout my playing career,' England captain Billy Wright later admitted in a television interview.

> I promise you that ninety-nine times out of 100 we would have won the match. It was played on a cramped, narrow pitch that meant we were unable to make full use of our strength down the wings. I recall that the dressing rooms were so dingy and rat-infested that Walter [Winterbottom] ordered us on to the coach, and we changed in a sports club a ten-minute drive away. During the most frustrating game in which I ever played, we must have had twenty shots to their one, when the ball deflected off the head of [Joe] Gaetjens [the US's Haitian-born centre-forward] and into the net. I had never felt worse on a football pitch than at the final whistle.

'One of the papers put a black border around the front page and said, "The Impossible Result, United States 1 England 0,"' added Frank Butler.

> It was incredible. That day Walter Winterbottom got the blame for it but he didn't pick the team in those days. He was just the manager and he carried the can. We had about 23 selectors capable of going into a geriatric ward and they used to pick teams, but on that occasion it was left to one man, Arthur Drewry, who was president of the Football League, and he chose the team.

Back in Rio, George had just returned to Chile's team hotel from the Maracanã Stadium when word of England's demise came through from Belo Horizonte. Any assumptions he'd harboured regarding the supposed weakness of the US team had already gone out of the window when, in the first round of matches, they'd led Spain for over an hour in Curitiba, a city south-west of São Paulo, before fading during the dying minutes to lose 3–1. Even so, he hadn't seen this scoreline coming within a month of Sundays.

'I refused to believe it when I was told, and still could not credit it when somebody showed me a paper giving the result,' George wrote in his piece for the *Soccer Fanfare* annual.

I said 'Oh, it must be a misprint.' Unfortunately, it was nothing of the kind, but only too true. At that period we had not played the US, and it made me wonder what sort of a side they had. In their game with Spain they had been leading 1–0 with only eight minutes to go, and then the Spaniards turned on the heat and got three goals. Our last game of the series was against the States. 'This is going to be tough' I thought. 'If they can beat England, we have had it'.

All the sides in Group Two had only three days between the second and final round of games to recover, and in that time, Chile had to travel the furthest of the four teams. Recife, situated on Brazil's north-eastern coast four hours by air from Rio, hosted just one match during the 1950 World Cup and that was Chile versus the much-talked-about US on 2 July. Only one team in Group Two was still without a win. Only one team in Group Two was still without a goal to their name. Regardless of what the US had done to England, George was determined that it wasn't going to finish that way against Chile.

Like an English lower-league football ground with palm trees. That was George's first impression of Recife's Estádio Ilha do Retiro. About as far removed, in other words, as it was possible to get from the Maracanã Stadium, with its multiple tiers stretching away into the gods. For the third and final time that summer, goalkeeper and captain Sergio Livingstone, the oldest member of Chile's squad at age thirty, gathered the team together before kick-off for a pep talk, none of which George could understand. Not that it really mattered. Having seen other players fail to convert chances he'd normally bury in his sleep in the previous two games, George had already decided to play further upfield, dovetailing his usual inside-forward position with that of centre-forward. It would be exhausting work in the mid-afternoon sun, with kick-off scheduled for 3 p.m. Brazilian time in the closest host city to the equator, but he could see no alternative if Chile were to avoid a Group Two whitewash.

In the sixteenth minute, having attacked from the outset, Chile moved the ball to the right flank, where Andrés Prieto gained possession level with the US's penalty area. Instinctively yet somewhat naively, four American players moved towards the near post attempting to shut down the danger, leaving an area as wide as Iowa at the back post for George to attack. Prieto's cross was a pinpoint one and, unmarked, 'Jorge' sent a bullet of a header beyond US goalkeeper Frank Borghi to give Chile a deserved lead.

'One peculiar aspect of our game against the Americans was that their centre-half [Charlie Colombo] wore a pair of leather mittens throughout the match, which was something I had never seen before – or since – apart of course from goalkeepers,' wrote George in a magazine article on his return from the World Cup.

The Americans' coach told me afterwards that it was just due to a superstition. This centre-half used his weight on every opportunity. After a bit I got tired of his tactics, so used my own shoulders to good purpose. He wasn't pleased at this retaliation, and kept up a steady flow of adjectives – needless to say they were not complimentary – through the rest of the play until at last, having had enough of this too, I told him what I thought of him in no uncertain manner. He seemed so dumbfounded that he just stood and stared.

Whatever colourful language or tactics they employed, Colombo and his teammates were no match for George and his compadres on a day when, at last, Chile's impressive approach play had an end product. In the thirty-second minute, Atilio Cremaschi added a second with a left-foot drive from just outside the penalty area. Although the Americans managed to square the game at 2–2 early in the second half, through goals from Frank Wallace and Joe Maca, Chile then proceeded to run riot with further strikes by Prieto, Cremaschi and Fernando Riera. As George reflected afterwards of their 5–2 victory, 'Although the Americans were forceful and robust, we had little difficulty beating them, which made their victory over England all the more surprising to me. I just couldn't understand it.'

George certainly wasn't alone in that department. Stung by the criticism that had come their way in the wake of losing to the US, England – or rather the Football Association committee members present in Brazil, including Arthur Drewry – chose to shut the stable door after the horse had bolted by restoring Stanley Matthews and Jackie Milburn to the team for their final Group Two game against

Spain at the Maracanã Stadium. It proved too little, too late. The Spanish pushed, pulled, fouled, obstructed and time-wasted flagrantly on their way to a 1–0 win, a result that sent them through to the complex and somewhat controversial round-robin final group stage implemented by the Brazilian organisers (ensuring more matches and extra ticket revenue to help offset the substantial costs of staging the tournament), as opposed to the customary straight knockout format.

For England, Chile and the US – who finished second, third and fourth in Group Two respectively with two points each – all that remained was the plane journey home. Even then, on arriving at Galeão Airport in Rio, the England team, as if caught in some never-ending farce, discovered their flight had been delayed for twenty-four hours. As Charles Buchan diplomatically phrased it in one of his newspaper dispatches, 'The players were in no mood to enjoy the extra freedom.'

George, however, had loved the whole World Cup experience. Of the 286 players competing in Brazil that summer from across thirteen nations, he'd been the only one signed to a professional club based outside his own country. Not that anyone, somewhat surprisingly perhaps, made a big deal of it at the time. He had made new friends within the Chilean team and together they'd competed on football's greatest stage. In George's words, 'Nobody expected much from them, yet I was agreeably surprised at the quality of their play, and actually they gave a very good account of themselves.'

What's more, George also loved being in Brazil where football, he couldn't help but notice, seemed to have become a new form of church. Given the opportunity, he would have stayed for the last match, which fortunately for the organisers (who, incredibly, had failed to incorporate a final into their flawed round-robin format), ended up being between the top two teams in the final group stage, namely Brazil and Uruguay. Alas, he had been away for almost two months and duty called back in Newcastle upon Tyne.

'If the defeat of England by the USA was a bitter pill to English folk, their disappointment was nothing to that felt by Brazilians when their country was beaten in the final,' reflected George in his *Soccer Fanfare* article.

So seriously do they take their football over there that it was regarded almost as a national catastrophe. Unfortunately I was on my way home when the match took place in the magnificent Estadio Municipal in Rio de Janeiro [the Maracanã Stadium] before a crowd of 200,000 people, who paid the almost fantastic sum of £125,000 to see the match. Uruguay, as you know, won 2–1, and it almost broke the hearts of thousands of loyal Brazilians. They had never visualised such a dire possibility. A friend of mine who was at the match wrote me afterwards and said that when the final whistle went scores of folk near him wept unashamedly. I'm rather glad we don't take football quite so seriously in this country. Generally speaking, we are excellent losers, and although naturally every player likes to be on the winning side, British footballers can take a reverse philosophically and sportingly.

History has shown that England, and by association Britain, failed to learn from the mistakes of 1950. At the Football Association, the selection of the international side by committee continued.

In November 1953, Hungary, sporting V-neck collars and low-cut boots, demolished an England XI wearing heavy cotton shirts and long baggy shorts 6–3 at Wembley in a blur of visionary tactics and one-touch passing (which they duly repeated on the banks of the River Danube the following May, winning 7–1 in Budapest). In 1958, England arrived in Sweden just two days before the start of the World Cup without having sourced anywhere to train. Four years later, when the World Cup came, ironically, to Chile, England's players found themselves based 8,000 feet above sea level in a village with no road access. The times, as Bob Dylan would soon point out in song, were a-changin'. It's just that England, and Britain at large, seemed reluctant to move with the times when it came to football.

Fair play to George though, who at least tried dragging his adopted homeland kicking and screaming into the 1950s. Before leaving Rio for England, entirely off his own bat he went out and bought eleven pairs of low-cut, lightweight rubber-studded boots, similar to the ones Chile had worn at the World Cup. Goodbye ankle-length, bulging, toe-capped Luddite British clogs – the revolution was coming to St James' Park!

Could he persuade any of his Newcastle United teammates to wear them? Could he heck.

7

NOBODY TOLD ME (THERE'D BE DAYS LIKE THESE)

'It's not who you know. It's who knows you.'
– HOLLYWOOD MAXIM

There's a wonderful picture, taken in black and white by a photographer whose identity has long since been lost to time, which shows George Robledo waving goodbye to his Chilean teammates at Rio's Galeão Airport before boarding the aircraft that will take him on the first leg of his journey from Brazil to London. George is facing the camera, his right hand raised in salute while holding what appears to be a Panama hat. His teammates stand facing him with their backs to the photographer, waving to 'Jorge' in return. The picture looks staged, though by all accounts it wasn't. The photographer was merely in the right place at the right time. Published in a Spanish-language magazine, the caption accompanying the image quotes George as saying, '*Hasta luego, muchachos. Ya estaré en Chile con ustedes.*'

'See you later, boys. I will be back in Chile with you.'

If those really were his words, then George's rapid grasp of the Spanish language was impressive, to say the least. Quite possibly they're the work of a sub-editor sprinkling a little fairy dust over the moment. Either way, it's a picture which encapsulates the warmth and mutual affection that existed between George and his Chilean teammates, fostered during the summer of 1950. Friendships and bonds had, unquestionably, been forged.

Be that as it may, exactly how or indeed when George would get back to Chile was anyone's guess. His closest family were in England. His employers were in England. Travelling by air wasn't anything like as smooth, quick or comfortable as it is in the twenty-first century. It's hard enough now, even with the relatively recent concept of international breaks in the football calendar, to represent both a club and a country at opposite ends of the globe. In 1950, it was nigh on impossible. In the event, another three years would pass before George played again for Chile, by which time his life had been turned completely on its head.

Isolated. Set apart. Distant. Bloody awkward to get to. Chile is all of these things and more. But then so is north-east England. Throughout the lion's share of their existence, the region's three largest professional football clubs – Middlesbrough, Sunderland and Newcastle United – have all struggled, to a greater or lesser extent, to attract the best talent from further afield. The very thing that gave England's top-right-hand corner its unique cultural identity – that feeling of being detached, different, special – was also what worked against it in terms of recruiting football players. 'They used to say that if you had any aspiration to play for your country, then you didn't go to Sunderland, Middlesbrough or Newcastle,' Dave

Hollins, United's goalkeeper during the early 1960s, once remarked. 'The north-east was out of sight, out of mind, and you didn't further your progress in football by going there. That was the feeling within the game.' Hollins, it should be said, also kept goal for Wales. If that was the consensus in post-war Cardiff, then what possible hope did north-east England have of raising pulse rates in, say, Caracas?

And yet, in the wake of the 1950 World Cup, many of a South American disposition began casting envious eyes in the direction of Newcastle – not through any desire to move there or wear United's famous black and white shirt, but because of a certain football player, namely George Robledo. Word had it in South America that 'Jorge' scored and created goals by the hatful. Word had it in South America that Newcastle United were more obsessed with bank balances than winning silverware and would, in all likelihood, be prepared to sell at the right price. Word had it in South America that he spoke Spanish fluently (well, they couldn't possibly be right about everything). In short, word had it that George was the complete footballer, a Chilean Englander who combined the very best elements of the British and South American games – strong, skilful, creative, combative, devastating on the ground and in the air on muddy, heavy pitches but also devastating on the ground and in the air on dusty, bumpy pitches.

In the months that followed, several clubs from Latin America got in touch with Newcastle United about taking George south of the equator. Colo-Colo, traditionally regarded as Chile's largest and most successful club, made enquiries as, reportedly, did Argentinean giants River Plate. Club Deportivo Universidad Católica of Santiago went one better by making an offer. Not just any offer, but one which amounted to an eye-watering (for the time) transfer fee of £30,000. At one stage, Ambassador Bianchi returned to the Robledo's front room in Fenham on behalf of the Federación de Fútbol de Chile to try and persuade George that his future at club level lay not on the banks of the Tyne but beyond the Andes.

To their credit, Newcastle United turned away from temptation, declining all advances regarding George over the course of 1950, 1951 and 1952, staying true to their decision (made following Sheffield Wednesday's bid of February 1950) to stick rather than continually twisting in terms of key team personnel, just to see where it got them. As for George, despite his growing sense of wanderlust, he was happy, for the time being at least, to stay on board and see where the Newcastle ride took him.

Like disciples, George's Chilean teammates – not to mention those opponents, journalists and spectators who'd witnessed his performances at the World Cup – had gone their separate ways after Brazil, singing 'Jorge's' praises and fuelling the interest in him. However, none of that would have counted for anything had he not continued to deliver on the field at club level for Newcastle United. Having climbed to the top of the First Division table in mid-September of 1950 with a 3–1 home win over Chelsea, the Magpies continued to impress throughout the autumn, losing only one of their opening sixteen league games of the 1950–51 season. It took something back then to steal the headlines from Stanley Matthews, but that's exactly what George did by scoring a hat-trick against Blackpool at St James' Park on 28 October. The following Saturday he did it again, bagging another triple in a 4–2 win over Liverpool at Anfield. 'Robledo's three goals in six minutes conjured a hat-trick out of the blue for the second time in eight days,' wrote the correspondent from *The Journal*. 'It was his conversion of the improbable which won the day. Twice he moved quicker than the defenders to balls which looked covered. Simple, but effective.' Of his performance against Blackpool, the same newspaper commented that George had 'kept the ball running as if in prepared grooves', adding that his movement in attack 'tore them [Blackpool] up repeatedly'.

As the plaudits poured in, so George's army of admirers continued to build. 'My father used to take me to St James' Park when there was sixty or seventy thousand people there, the vast majority of them standing on the terraces,' says Barry Murphy, who grew up in nearby Consett and in later life played 569 times for Barnsley, a club appearance record that stands to this day.

That was when, if you were stuck at the back, they used to shuffle us kids down to the front over everyone's heads. Joe Harvey was the captain and we had players like Bobby Mitchell, who created loads of opportunities for everyone else, along with Jimmy Scoular and Ronnie Simpson, who took over in goal from Jack Fairbrother. Then there was George and his brother Ted. Everyone raved about them both, but George was something else. Watching him, you got the feeling that people had never seen anything like him before. He had so much ability on the ball and seemed to go through players like they weren't there. As soon as he got possession, you could sense the expectation levels rising among the crowd. You knew something special was going to happen. He was a fantastic player.

'I just thought he came from another planet, another world,' Bobby Robson, another boyhood fan of George, once enthused.

> Thick-set, swarthy, he had a Chilean countenance, half sunburnt. Good looking chap actually. Compact, solid player, a goalscorer. He got in with the centre-forward, he saw the crosses, he got in the box. He worked very hard, he could turn on the ball, he could play a good pass. He was a bit like Alan Shearer really, a good solid body, good legs, strong thighs. He got up and down and he played in that attacking half. He could turn on the ball and he was adept in the air. Most of my heroes were Newcastle United players, and they do not come any bigger or better than George Robledo in my eyes.

George's handsome features are something that Professor Stacey Pope of the Department of Sport and Exercise Sciences at Durham University has come across in her extensive research into female sports fans. While conducting interviews between 2017 and 2022 with women who followed Newcastle United as far back as the 1950s, Pope noticed the names George and Ted Robledo cropping up with some regularity. One fan by the name of Joan recalled how, together with a friend, she would doorstep the Robledo house and 'watch for him [George] coming out and we'd follow him to see where he was going. Ey, God, honestly! The very idea! Our Deirdre and me, "Ohhh George!" we used to go.' Another interviewee called Simon remembered his aunt, a big admirer of the Robledo brothers, knitting scarves for them as presents. 'I guess that was 1950s flirting at its best!' he told Pope.

'Maggie and I found out where they lived up Barrack Road [leading towards Fenham], so we decided we'd try and find the house,' one supporter called Mary recounted.

We did find it but they were away. His mam was in the garden. I knew it was his mam because I'd seen a photograph of her and the two boys. She couldn't really speak to us and just said 'Newcastle supporters' and we gave her a wave. We thought 'Eh, that's great!' But they were away at the football. Oh, George Robledo was fantastic, he really was, a brilliant player.

'I found that what people like Joan and Mary had to say really illustrates the appeal and star quality back then of players like George, even when those players lived in the very same streets and communities as the supporters who idolised them,' says Professor Pope. 'Women football fans have been largely hidden from history, but this shines a light on how they, as well as men, followed the game as well as particular players at that time.'

For all George's brilliance, it was perhaps too much to expect Newcastle United to continue to challenge for the 1950–51 Football League title. Tucked into fifth place at the turn of the year, five points behind leaders Tottenham Hotspur with a game in hand, they eventually finished the campaign in a highly respectable fourth position despite winning only three of their last thirteen league fixtures. Why the sudden dip in form towards the end? Because United had reached the FA Cup final, where they would take on Blackpool and Stanley Matthews et al. As any professional who played the game prior to the advent of the Premier League will tell you, the prospect of appearing in an FA Cup final at the old Wembley Stadium had a habit of commandeering the mind to the exclusion of all else.

It's hard, now that football is dominated to such an extent by the Champions League and the Premier League, to impress upon anyone born prior to, say, 1980 just how big a deal the FA Cup used to be. For many fans, FA Cup final day rivalled, if not exceeded, the excitement of Christmas Day or a birthday, regardless of whether your favourite team had even made it to Wembley. In 1951, the League Cup had yet to be conceived, let alone the end of season play-offs. The only way a professional football player from these shores got to play at Wembley was by representing England (a slim chance), one of the other home nations (slightly better odds) or appearing in the FA Cup final (next to no chance for the vast majority due to the highly competitive nature of a tournament that played second fiddle to no other). The actor Alan Alda tells a story of being out in his car on the evening when the final episode of the television series *M*A*S*H*, in which he starred, was aired in the US and being amazed that the roads were devoid of traffic. In the UK, that used to happen every year when the FA Cup final was on. If you wanted to avoid the Saturday queues in Sainsbury's, that's when you did your shopping.

Unsurprisingly perhaps, the pressure of appearing – or potentially appearing – in an FA Cup final could get to even the most experienced of players, causing teams to buckle under the strain. Ever wondered why so few clubs pulled off the much-coveted league and cup double during the second half of the twentieth century? Well, now you have your answer. Likewise, middle-of-the-road teams with zero chance of winning the top-flight title (or indeed second-tier clubs chasing promotion) could easily become distracted by the prospect of walking out at Wembley. Take, for instance, Brighton & Hove Albion, who reached the FA Cup final in 1983, defeating Newcastle United along the way, only to get relegated the same season. As one of Albion's players once told this author, 'With every round that we won, the FA Cup just took over, and our league form fell apart. Before we knew it, it was too late for us to save ourselves.'

The early rounds of Newcastle's run to the 1951 final were not only eventful but also laced with tragedy. Having overcome Second Division Bury 4–1 on a waterlogged pitch at St James' Park, with George and Jackie Milburn among the goalscorers, United came up against far tougher opponents in the form of Bolton Wanderers at home. Once again, there were way too many people in the ground for it to be safe. The electric apparatus installed by the club to limit entry through the turnstiles broke down, leading to supporters being admitted without anyone keeping a headcount on the attendance.

In his seminal book *Fever Pitch*, Nick Hornby recalls attending an Arsenal versus Southampton game in August 1980 when severe crowd congestion outside Highbury caused him and others to sit down on steps once inside the ground to get their breath back. 'I trusted the system,' admitted Hornby, writing after the Hillsborough disaster of April 1989, when a crush at the Liverpool versus Nottingham Forest FA Cup semi-final led to ninety-seven fatalities and over 750 injuries. 'I knew that I could not be squashed to death, because that never happened at football matches.' Except it did, and had been for years. Two people died that January 1951 day at St James' Park, with many more requiring medical attention. Again, there was no degree of soul-searching afterwards by the authorities. Many more would die over the years to come, on the long and somewhat inevitable road to Hillsborough, sixty-six of them in one afternoon in January 1971 as supporters funnelled out of Ibrox, Glasgow, following a Rangers versus Celtic game.

'How could anyone have hoped to get away with it?' added Hornby of the decades when colossal numbers of people, often dispersed unevenly, stood shoulder to shoulder on the terraces at football grounds. 'With sixty-thousand-plus crowds, all you can do is shut the gates, tell everyone to squash up, and then pray, very hard.'

Despite the calamitous scenes witnessed at the Bolton Wanderers match (won, for what it was worth, 3–2 by Newcastle), there was never any question of the Magpies withdrawing from the FA Cup either out of respect or as some form of penance. In the fifth round, not far short of 50,000 people (including approximately 12,000 away supporters) squashed up and prayed very hard at the Victoria Ground as Newcastle overcame Stoke City 4–2, with George scoring twice.

At the quarter-final stage, Bristol Rovers were overcome 3–1 in a replay, the first game having finished 0–0 on Tyneside, setting up a semi-final clash against Wolverhampton Wanderers at, ironically, Hillsborough. The match proved to be a belter, with both sides having early goals disallowed, yet ultimately finished scoreless thanks largely to the heroics of Wolverhampton goalkeeper Bert Williams. Not to be disheartened, two goals within the space of a minute by Milburn and Bobby Mitchell saw Newcastle prevail 2–1 in the replay at a sodden Leeds Road, Huddersfield. For the eighth time in their history, United were through to the FA Cup final.

At which point, cup fever kicked in to the detriment of Newcastle's league form. Between defeating Wolverhampton in the replay and facing Blackpool at Wembley on 28 April, the Magpies played eleven First Division fixtures, winning just one and conspiring to lose five. Try as they might to focus on bread-and-butter matters in the league, minds were inexorably turning towards the big day. 'If you ask 100 footballers what was their main ambition, I think at least ninety would say to be on the winning side in a cup final at Wembley,' said George in one interview. Being United's first appearance in a cup final since 1932, nerves were, so he believed, 'inevitable'.

Newcastle, mind, weren't alone in that department. 'Between the semi-final and the final, there were about eight league matches,' Jackie Mudie, Blackpool's long-serving centre-forward, said long after the event.

We won the majority of ours and Newcastle, our opponents at Wembley, lost five or six. We were the unquestionable favourites, though we weren't over confident. We didn't go away for special training before the final but stayed at home, going down to St Annes to practice on some lush grass in anticipation of Wembley and having salt water baths at Lytham. Stan [Matthews] revels in the big event, but I think on this occasion he was more nervous beforehand than anyone else in the team.

'The FA Cup is like no other football game in the world,' wrote Ken Sheppard in *The Journal* of those whose nerves threatened to get the better of them beneath Wembley's old twin towers. 'The soft springiness of the almost virgin turf affects the players as much as the cup fever affects the spectators. I have been told of famous stars unable to lace their own boots because their hands were shaking too much.'

Unlike Blackpool, Newcastle did go away before the final. Not to Tenerife or the Algarve, or to any of the other sun-kissed retreats favoured by clubs today during pre-season or before big occasions, but to Buxton. As in the English Peak District. Where, by all accounts, most of the talk among United's players focused on how they would counter the combined threat of Blackpool's two Stans, Messrs Matthews and Mortensen.

'The plan was that Matthews would be left to the nearest man,' recalled Newcastle defender Bobby Cowell. 'Bobby Corbett and Charlie Crowe, our full-back and wing-half, would try and handle him between them.' By shutting down Matthews, the supply line to Mortensen (already closely marked by Frank Brennan, United's colossus of a centre-half) would, in theory, be cut. With that, United made for their team hotel in Weybridge, Surrey, a relatively short drive from Wembley.

At 9.25 p.m. on the evening before the game, the first of seventeen charter trains departed Newcastle Central Station, conveying thousands of United supporters down the main east coast railway line to London. They left at twenty-minute intervals in what was dubbed 'Operation Magpie', bound alternately for King's Cross and Wembley Park Stations to avoid bottlenecks building up on the approaches to the capital. In something resembling a scene from a *Wacky Races* cartoon, thirty-two supporters chose instead to hire a Dakota aircraft to take them from what is now Newcastle

International Airport to Elstree, the nearest available airfield to Wembley. By breakfast time, Trafalgar Square was full of ebullient yet good-natured Geordies enjoying a spot of sightseeing. As one supporter, mindful of the all-too-recent war years, told the *Daily Express*, 'It's nice to see the place is still standing.'

Unlike hundreds of others, Elsie Robledo didn't climb on the lions in Trafalgar Square that morning. Neither did Walter Robledo, now nineteen years old, who went to London with his mother to support not only George but also Ted, overlooked by Newcastle for the final but who travelled to Wembley with United's official party. It would, of course, have been poetic if Arístides had been there too. His oldest son was, after all, about to become the first Chilean, and indeed the first South American, to play in an FA Cup final. But not all stories have Hollywood endings. In the same week as George scored a brace away to Stoke City in the fifth round of the cup, Arístides had died on the other side of the world in the country he'd felt unable to steam away from on the MV *Reina del Pacifico* that fateful morning in March 1932. The Robledo family annals bear no mention of when, where or how his sons learned of their father's death. Likewise, there's no record of their reactions on being told. To quote Hamlet's last words, the rest is silence. And not, in the case of the Robledos, necessarily in a way that brought peace or a sense of ease to either the living or the dead.

The headlines that beautiful spring weekend belonged to Milburn. But once again, it was George who did much of the legwork at Wembley, building a platform on which 'wor Jackie' ('our Jackie') could shine. The first half finished goalless but provided clues as to what would follow after the break. George, for one, had noticed during the early exchanges that Blackpool appeared to be playing a risky offside trap, pushing high up the pitch in an attempt to catch out Newcastle's pacey attackers. What's more, this trap was frequently malfunctioning. Sooner or later, so George reckoned, one through pass in Milburn's direction would split Blackpool wide open.

Shortly after the restart, Stanley Matthews made ground down Blackpool's right flank, cutting inside Newcastle's penalty area before pulling the ball back to where he believed the other Stan would be. Except Mortensen wasn't there. Gaining possession, George looked up and played a left-footed pass to Milburn, standing near the centre circle. Despite being tackled, Milburn managed to touch the ball back towards George, who was arriving at speed in support. He in turn played a defence-splitting through pass for Milburn to canter onto. Blackpool's rearguard had been undone. The rest was down to wor Jackie.

'I found a wide open space between me and goalkeeper George Farm, who looked so far away I assumed he might well be on his own front garden in Blackpool,' wrote Milburn in his autobiography.

Then followed the longest run I've ever experienced with a football at my feet. It seemed to take hours for me to reach the eighteen yards, and all the time I felt as though the world was on my heels. I was wearing my heavy boots, with a thick sole, so that I could really put some punch into my shots, but as I approached Farm, who was now bobbing up and down like a jack-in-the-box, for a second I forgot all about the crowd, the defenders on my heels, and the King watching in the royal box. Two questions had to be answered quickly. Should I have a crack at goal and hope for the best? Or should I try to place the ball past goalkeeper Farm? I did not have to make my own decision. On the eighteen yards line I noticed Farm had left a little more space on his right hand. It wasn't much, but it was enough for a forward to decide which was the bigger target. So, taking a big chance, for George Farm's an agile fellow with tremendous reaction, I made up my mind to glide the ball past him. As the ball left my foot for one dreadful moment I feared I hadn't hit it hard enough, but the roar of the crowd told me I was wrong.

'The first half was a pretty even affair,' countered Matthews in his own autobiography.

To my mind, we had the better of the chances but never made one tell. Our ploy was for our defence to push up quickly to try and catch the Newcastle forwards offside. This worked well in the first half, but it proved our undoing after half-time. Five minutes into the second half, Chilean George Robledo played a wonderful defence-splitting ball. With our defenders pushing on, Jackie Milburn timed his run to perfection and raced away enjoying more space than Captain Kirk as George Farm came off his line in an attempt to narrow the angle. At one point Jackie glanced over his shoulder to check that he was onside. He was, and faced with a one-to-one with George Farm, Jackie didn't miss such gilt-edged chances. He coolly side-footed the ball wide of George into the net and we were chasing the game.

Five minutes after taking the lead, Newcastle doubled their advantage when Newcastle inside-forward Ernie Taylor, who would sign for Blackpool later that year, back-heeled the ball into Milburn's path some twenty-five yards from goal. Without breaking stride, Newcastle's centre-forward let rip with a searing shot, which screamed into the Blackpool net. 'When Geordie soccer fans who were at Wembley grow old, and take a sentimental soccer journey back over the years, they will tell their wide-eyed grandchildren of the greatest goal they ever saw,' wrote Henry Rose of the *Daily Express*. Stanley Matthews was equally fulsome in his praise of Milburn's wonder strike. 'It was a goal fit to win any cup final, an absolute cracker, and though we battled back and seized the initiative, Newcastle remained steadfast and survived our onslaught,' he added. 'I played my heart out in that game, at times cutting inside to have a pop at goal myself. I gave it my all, even during the latter stages, but on the day it simply wasn't enough.'

As the game drifted towards its conclusion, George produced another slide rule of a pass to send Milburn away towards Blackpool's goal. With a Wembley hat-trick beckoning, Milburn uncharacteristically prevaricated, allowing defender Eric Hayward to make a last-ditch tackle. At the final whistle, George stood inside Newcastle's half of the field, arms wrapped around the back of his head, staring out into the middle distance, caught somewhere between disbelief and exhaustion. His Wembley 'baptism', as he would later call it, had resulted in victory, a cup winner's medal and an assist – not that such terminology existed at the time.

Matthews, gracious as ever, came to shake George's hand, as did Blackpool's captain Harry Johnston, who prior to kick-off had momentarily thrown George's pre-match concentration. On emerging from Blackpool's dressing room, Johnston had spotted Newcastle's inside-forward and come across for a chat, during which he reminded George of their first ever meeting at Oakwell back in January 1949. 'I think you and I are going to be seeing a fair bit of each other soon,' had been Johnson's words to George following Blackpool's 1–0 win over Barnsley in the FA Cup. George didn't need any reminding, but the mere mention of what had been a special moment caught him off guard. 'Yes, I suppose I have come a long way,' he found himself thinking. Not, however, for long. By the time both teams emerged side by side from the Wembley tunnel, George's blinkers were firmly back on.

In the north-east of England, the majority of those who hadn't been fortunate enough to secure a ticket or who simply couldn't afford one listened to the match on the radio – or the wireless, as such things were then known. If someone in any given street was fortunate enough to have a television, then the rest of the street would in all likelihood gravitate towards that particular house. 'The idea of travelling down to Wembley was unthinkable for a family like ours,' says Barry Murphy, who was eleven at the time of the 1951 FA Cup final.

We didn't have that much money. I'm the youngest of three brothers and they all worked in pits or steelworks. My father was a miner for fifty years. He would come home black to the eyeballs with coal dust, which put me off going underground straightaway. I'll be a professional footballer, thank you very much! We weren't the kind of house that had a television, so we'd go to another house at the bottom of our street in Consett where the Kyle family lived. They had a television. All the street would be sat in their lounge, watching the final. To see George and the rest of the lads passing the ball around at Wembley on that black and white screen was marvellous. It was a real occasion, like watching the coronation.

It is often said that football players struggle to remember anything about the big occasions in their careers, such as semi-finals or finals. They're too in the moment, too focused, to take it all in. As a consequence, such occasions pass them by in the blink of an eye. For George, the 1951 FA Cup final wasn't like that. He remembered everything – walking out onto the field beforehand, shaking hands with King George VI prior to kick-off, cracking Blackpool's high-risk offside code early on, the sight of Jackie Milburn galloping in on goal to give Newcastle the lead, climbing the thirty-nine steps to Wembley's royal box after the final whistle and making eye contact with Princess Margaret, shaking hands for a second time with King George VI, being presented with his winner's medal by Queen Elizabeth, the future Queen Mother. It was all there, crystal clear, and would remain so for the rest of his days.

Making eye contact with a princess and shaking hands with a king. Twice. Not bad for a lad from the moon-like wastes of the Atacama Desert via a Yorkshire pit village.

And within a very short space of time, it would get even better.

8

I FEEL FINE

'There's a trick to it, you see. When you arrive on set, you have to have
total confidence in yourself. In my tiny kingdom, I have to be king.'
– ANTHONY HOPKINS

There was a time when the FA Cup final constituted the full-
stop to the domestic Football League season in England and
Wales. Everything built to the big day, after which, hard as it might
be to believe in this era of 24-hour rolling sports news, football re-
ceded into the shadows for three months, barely to be discussed
outside of working men's clubs or school playgrounds.

For Newcastle United, though, the 1950–51 season proved an
exception to the rule. A fixture backlog caused by winter post-
ponements and progression in the FA Cup meant the Magpies
still had games left to play after winning the final at Wembley. For
George and his teammates, there would be no victory procession
through the streets of Newcastle on the Sunday or Monday. Instead,
they'd have to wait until Thursday 3 May to accept the adulation
of the Geordie public, shoehorning the celebrations into a 48-hour

window of opportunity that fell between fixtures against Wolverhampton Wanderers (away, on 2 May) and Middlesbrough (home, on 5 May). Accordingly, United's team remained in the south of England for much of the week that followed, enjoying a reception at the Savoy on the Saturday night and three days on the coast at Brighton before travelling to Wolverhampton on the Wednesday. Where, with the weight of Wembley finally off their shoulders, they prevailed 1–0 thanks to a 77th-minute winner scored by George, the FA Cup having been paraded around the Molineux ground at half-time for all to see.

The following morning, Newcastle's players boarded the train that would take them back to north-east England ahead of the victory procession later in the day. At York Station, with hundreds of people lining the platforms to catch a glimpse of the Wembley heroes, a specially created headboard was attached to the front of the steam locomotive bearing the words 'It's wors agen' (It's ours again) accompanied by '1910, 1924, 1932, 1951', United's four victorious FA Cup campaigns. More stops followed at Hartlepool and Sunderland as the train took the more circuitous coastal route north, seemingly intent on pulling as many people as possible in on the celebrations.

'And then the thunderous voice of the happy thousands at the [Newcastle] Central station,' wrote one of the many correspondents from The Journal assigned to the homecoming. Local police had reckoned on 100,000 people thronging the streets. In the event, double that number turned out as three open-topped motor coaches chaired the players and club officials from the station to St James' Park, where a reserve team fixture, attracting a further 30,000 spectators, took on the form of one big party, prior to a celebration bash being held that evening at the Oxford Galleries dance hall on New Bridge Street. In the words of team captain Joe Harvey, 'We knew we'd get a terrific reception, but I never imagined it would be like this. It was wonderful.'

Wonderful it may have been, yet Newcastle United, as history has shown, are rarely Newcastle United without some form of discord in the ranks. Five months prior to beating Blackpool at Wembley, manager George Martin had left the club to take over the reins at Aston Villa, with Stan Seymour's strong influence when it came to team affairs reportedly easing his departure from St James' Park. To the naked eye, with United closing in on Wembley, Martin appeared not to be missed. Behind the scenes, however, the buffer-like role that he'd occupied between the players and Seymour, along with the suits in the boardroom, had been removed.

As FA Cup final day drew closer, so a number of gripes came to the surface, which may just have been nipped in the bud had Martin still been in position. There were arguments over bonuses, with players resorting to selling their own Wembley-related promotional items to make a bit of cash on the side. Instead of being allocated seats for the final, the players' wives were initially given standing tickets on the terraces (space was eventually found to accommodate them two rows behind the Royal Box). Even after the final had been won, the chagrin continued. Jack Fairbrother kept a clean sheet at Wembley, but that didn't prevent one loose-tongued director from publicly declaring he was 'on his way out', much to the goalkeeper's annoyance. Handbags which were, allegedly, to be stuffed with money and given to players' wives at the Oxford Galleries gathering duly materialised, only with old newspapers inside instead of the anticipated cash (illegal payments were rife within English football at the time, not that Newcastle's players benefitted to any real degree).

At that point in time, George didn't have a wife or even a girl-friend. But he did have a mum and she meant an awful lot to him. Prior to arriving back in Newcastle after the FA Cup final, George asked Seymour if Elsie could accompany him to St James' Park to see the players parade the trophy in front of the 30,000 fans attend-ing the sideshow that was United's reserve team fixture. Seymour had been noncommittal and George received no answer. When the day came, George found himself at St James' Park without his mother, being asked by Seymour to fulfil club duties, such as meet-ing local dignitaries, which he was in absolutely no mood to do. At first, he flatly refused. 'Why is it at the reception the room is full of strangers?' George's teammate Charlie Crowe recalled him asking Seymour. 'Why is that, when you have refused to let my mother be present, eh?' George wasn't prone to temper tantrums, but like many a man, he had his limits. It didn't matter that Seymour was, in theory, his boss. On that occasion, George let him have both barrels. As Newcastle's manager, and indeed anyone within earshot discov-ered, if you crossed one Robledo – be it mother, brother, brother or brother – then you crossed them all.

Not that Seymour appeared to take it personally. That summer, for the first time in three years, George actually got a holiday. As in a break from playing the game, rather than two weeks relaxing on the beach. The following season George went straight back into the team, with Seymour fielding him less as an inside-forward and more as a second centre-forward alongside Milburn. The effect was instantaneous. On the opening day of the campaign, Newcastle battered Stoke City 6–0 at St James' Park with Milburn grappling a hat-trick and Bobby Mitchell, Crowe and George notching one apiece. A fortnight later, Tottenham Hotspur, the reigning Football League champions, came to Tyneside and were smashed 7–2, with George scoring a hat-trick. In the next home game, Burnley were dismissed 7–1, four of United's goals coming from George. 'Robledo, the goal-getter, was dynamite,' proclaimed *The Journal* in its match report. Few who witnessed his performances throughout the majority of the 1951–52 season would argue with that assessment.

'We were lucky at that time because we had Jackie Milburn and George who, together, formed such a prolific partnership,' says Peter Donaghy, a Newcastle United supporter and, until relatively recently, season-ticket holder since 1947.

Jackie was like a jet engine – put the ball a few yards in front of him and off he'd go, sprinting from the halfway line towards the goal. George, however, had the physical strength which Jackie didn't have. He was never afraid to get involved. Not in anything dirty, but in the way he'd slide in with perfect timing to win a tackle or convert a chance. A lot of his goals were from close range, managing to be in the right place at the right time through a combination of clever positioning, strength and sheer bravery. When George was in or around that six-yard box, he ruled. Given half a chance, he would not hesitate. It helped as well that he had the right temperament. There was none of that agro that you sometimes get with South American players, who can get pretty excitable. George wasn't like that at all. He always came across as very balanced, although you probably wouldn't want to argue with him. He might not have been that tall, but he certainly had a presence.

Presence, yes. Access to a telephone? That would be a no. Which is where the Donaghy family were able to help out. 'Our house was about 200 yards from where the Robledos lived in Fenham,' adds Donaghy.

My parents were very keen on football and my mother became very friendly with Mrs Robledo. The house they lived in belonged to the club but, believe it or not, it didn't have a phone, which made it difficult if anyone at the club wanted to contact George. Frank Brennan, who played centre-half for Newcastle for years, also knew my family, so he'd ring my mother and say, 'Look, would you mind nipping down the road and telling George that he needs to be at the ground for two o'clock,' or whenever. My mother would then go and pass the message on to George or his mother. A couple of hours later he'd be out on the park, doing his thing. It's amazing to think that's how it was then, almost like something from another world. Which I suppose it is now.

Despite a smoking habit that would've put many a Tyneside chimney stack to shame, not to mention his exhaustive summer expeditions to North and South America during 1949 and 1950 respectively, George noticed no discernible dip in his performances or fitness levels while playing for Newcastle during the 1949–50 or 1950–51 seasons. Yet, by his own admission, August 1951 saw him feeling sharper, healthier, more focused and 'like there was more fuel in my tank'. Amazing what a proper rest can achieve. Not, it should be said, that George sat at home with his feet up during the summer of 1951. Contrary to popular belief and regional stereotypes of the time, George discovered there was far more to the north-east of England than coal mines, shipyards and whippets. Like, for instance, the rolling hills and sand dunes of Northumberland, Bamburgh with its spectacular castle and Whitley Bay's Spanish City concert hall and restaurant (immortalised thirty years later in the Dire Straits song 'Tunnel of Love'), the latter becoming a favourite hang-out for the entire Robledo family.

He also, briefly, took to river fishing. 'We had a group in Fenham who used to go out, people I knew from the area,' George recalled.

I never really caught anything but I loved the company and venturing out into the wonderful countryside. Northumberland is so beautiful with so many places to explore. And the people you meet are always so hospitable. I became very attached to the Geordies. There was a time when I used to sign all my letters 'Geordie Robledo'. Then one day a friend of mine reminded me that there were no Geordies born south of the [River] Tees!

Mentally as well as physically rejuvenated, and high on Northumberland air, George took his early season form and ran with it. Sandwiched between his hat-trick versus Tottenham and four-goal salvo at the expense of Burnley came a brace in the 3–3 draw with West Bromwich Albion and another pair in a 2–1 win over Preston North End. Eleven strikes in four games – not a bad return for someone who wasn't actually a centre-forward. While playing for Barnsley, George's ability to operate almost in plain sight, causing maximum damage to the opposition with the minimum of fuss, had frequently left observers as well as opponents confounded. And so it proved to be the case with Newcastle. 'Robledo can look very obvious and this season very one-sided but again on Saturday, besides making orthodox leadership very insistent, he was often quick to move free of his policeman,' wrote the erudite correspondent covering the Preston North End match for *The Journal*. Or, as the reporter from the *Daily Express* attending the same fixture succinctly put it, 'With Robledo, you almost always know what he is about to do. Stopping him from doing it is something else entirely.'

Less obvious, certainly in terms of how most forwards were (and continue to be) wired, was George's willingness to put his neck on the line at the other end of the field, dropping back when necessary to help out his defenders. Rarely was this more evident than at Old Trafford on the afternoon of Saturday 25 August 1951. Early in the second half, with the match finely balanced at 1–1, Newcastle goal-keeper Jack Fairbrother suffered a suspected fractured collarbone in a collision with an opponent and had to leave the field. Substitutes didn't exist in 1951, meaning Newcastle were down to ten men and facing the prospect of an outfield player having to go in goal.

But who would that player be?

George didn't even wait to be asked, falling back at the drop of a hat to assume the position of last man. He played well, making two fine saves to deny Manchester United's prolific striker Jack Rowley, but couldn't prevent the home side from ultimately triumphing 2–1. George, it should be said, had earlier put Newcastle ahead with one of his trademark cannonball blasts from close range. 'Several days later I received a letter enclosing a stamped addressed envelope from a Manchester schoolboy,' George would tell David Watson, the Yorkshire-based author, many years afterwards. 'The letter requested I send the writer my autograph as I was the best goalkeeper he had ever seen!'

By the end of the 1951–52 campaign, George had a grand total of thirty-three league goals to his name, more than any other player in English football's top flight that season. Had the Golden Boot existed at the time, he would have won it. No overseas registered, foreign-born player had ever reached that number before (and, at the time of writing, only Erling Haaland has 'officially' passed it since, the caveat being that he wasn't born in Norway, the country he represents at international level, but in Leeds, Yorkshire, where he lived until the age of three). Then again, England wasn't exactly teeming with overseas registered, foreign-born players in 1952, which helps explain why the media barely mentioned George's feat. In football, records don't tend to be championed when they're created, only when they are broken. Even so, thirty-three goals was, and indeed remains, a formidable achievement and George had every right to be proud.

There was, however, something else about the 1951–52 season that made him even prouder. Since arriving on Tyneside from Barnsley as part of the deal to secure George's signature, Ted Robledo had barely figured in Newcastle United's plans. There was, initially, no guarantee that would ever change, bar the odd fleeting appearance as a stopgap for someone further up the pecking order in the squad. Newcastle had, after all, wanted George, not his brother.

But then something strange happened. A few weeks into the 1951–52 season, Ted broke into United's first team, playing on the left side of midfield. One appearance turned into two, which turned into three, until he became a regular starter. Ted's hard work in training, based around his desire to become a better player, had at long last paid off. Having his brother alongside him as the goals flowed in the league and FA Cup, with Newcastle reaching the final for the second year running, made 1951–52 easily the most enjoyable season of George's entire career.

'It had always been George up until then, but from that point on it became George and Ted,' says Barry Murphy.

> Everyone raved about George because he scored the goals and did things no other player seemed to do, but Ted was a good player too. George grabbed the headlines, whereas Ted was the steady one. In many ways they were like a double act. Here were these two Chileans who'd come through Barnsley to get to us in Newcastle. They obviously stuck together in life and people liked that about them.

'There was a lot of fascination because there were two Chileans playing for Newcastle and there weren't any foreign players then,' Sir John Hall, the one-time fan who went on to become United's owner, said in a 2019 interview with *The Athletic* while reflecting on the idols of his youth. 'George was a strong forward and a goalscorer, while Ted was workmanlike. George and Jackie [Milburn] were absolute heroes together. What a team that was. They were very exciting times.'

You can say that again. Newcastle finished eighth in the First Division table that season. For entertainment value, however, they came second to none, scoring ninety-eight goals in forty-two league games. Throw in the added drama of United's defence of the FA Cup (which very nearly came a cropper at the first hurdle) and you can see why 1952, even after all this time, remains one of the standout years in the club's entire history.

'The road to Wembley is a hard one,' wrote George in one of his magazine commissions.

In addition to the necessary skill, determination and team spirit, the club that wins the cup must also have the run of the ball and a certain amount of luck. Without wishing to boast in any way, I think it true to say that the Newcastle United teams of 1951 and 1952 had the requisite qualities for success. Yet, at the start of the 1952 cup ties, it hardly seemed possible that we should reach Wembley again. Usually the cup holders make their exit fairly early the year after their success. That, indeed, seemed likely to be our fate in the third round tie against Aston Villa at Newcastle. Villa were two up in twenty minutes, and although we reduced the arrears before the interval, Villa were still a goal in front with ten minutes to go and it looked all up with us. Then Bobby Mitchell hit a screamer to level the scores, got another on the volley to put us in front, and with three minutes still to go Villa were two goals behind [George having weighed in with Newcastle's fourth]. That was a real grandstand finish, and a tribute to a side that refused to give up when things looked black.

The draw did not favour us after that. We had to meet Tottenham

Hotspur, Portsmouth and Swansea, all away. When the lads knew what they were up against, all that was said was 'We'll do our best.' And how well they did, everybody knows.

The general consensus among the majority of English football statisticians is that Newcastle United's Wembley odyssey of 1952 involved more mileage than any other club in the history of the competition, taking in as it did trips to north London, south-west Wales, the south coast of England, Sheffield (for the semi-final), Leeds (for the semi-final replay) and, finally, north-west London.

Back then, there were no motorways. Few people owned cars or had the means to fly. The trains did their best, but it still took much longer to get anywhere than it tends to today. That didn't prevent around 15,000 Newcastle supporters from travelling to White Hart Lane to watch the Magpies take on Tottenham in the fourth round, their loyalty being rewarded by a performance which Paul Joannou, United's long-standing official historian, once referred to as 'one of the finest team efforts in the club's history'. It was George, though, who put the Londoners to the sword, dancing his way through the heart of Tottenham's defence on a mud bath of a pitch to score with his right foot in the first half and his left in the second, both goals coming either side of a twenty-yard thunderbolt from Mitchell just before the break.

'The team that wins this one will win the cup,' Stan Seymour had declared prior to kick-off at White Hart Lane. Few who witnessed Newcastle's commanding 3–0 win were prepared to argue with him, even after the Mapgies had made heavy weather of Second Division strugglers Swansea Town (as Swansea City were then known) in the

The MV *Reina del Pacifico*, the ship on which the Robledo family sailed from Chile to the UK, berthed in Liverpool towards the end of its working life.

Source: Liverpool Maritime Museum

BRAMPTON ELLIS SENIOR SCHOOL 1938-39

ABOVE The all-conquering 1938–39 Brampton Ellis Senior School football team, with George sitting front and centre.

Source: Chris Brook

LEFT 'Swooping down upon the foe, the fearless shadow streaks.' George smiles for the camera before making one of his 114 appearances for Barnsley.

Source: David Wood

'Watching him, you got the feeling that people
had never seen anything like him before.'
George goes through his warm-up routine
ahead of a Newcastle United match.

Source: Robledo family collection

George (*far left*) lines up alongside his Newcastle
United teammates at St James' Park, including Jackie
Milburn (*second from the left*) and Ted Robledo
(*fifth from the left*).

Source: Chris Brook

Ted (*left*) and George touch down in South Africa
during Newcastle United's summer tour of 1952.

Source: Robledo family collection

The image that inspired the young John Lennon to reach for his paintbrushes – George scores the winning goal for Newcastle United in the 1952 FA Cup final.

© *Newcastle Chronicle*

LEFT George, Walter, Elsie and Ted Robledo (*left to right*) sift through a typical day's fan mail. George was very close to his family and refused to move clubs throughout his career unless they all wanted to come with him.

Source: Robledo family collection

BELOW St James' Park, Newcastle, as it was in the early 1950s. The stadium is located right at the centre of Newcastle upon Tyne, visible from every approach. Here, George is seen scoring in the snow against Preston North End.

Source: Robledo family collection

George leads Newcastle's reserve
team out ahead of his last appearance
in a United shirt, 2 May 1953.

Source: Robledo family collection

George is mobbed by the crowds at Los Cerrillos Airport,
Santiago, having signed for Colo-Colo from Newcastle United.
More than 2,000 people turned up at the airport to witness
George and Ted's arrival.

Source: Robledo family collection

George (*centre*) in the white
shirt of Colo-Colo, surrounded
by teammates and admirers.
George was astonished to learn
that his and Ted's transfer to
Colo-Colo from Newcastle
United had in part been
funded by an increase in the
club membership fees paid
every month by supporters.

Source: Robledo family collection

Brothers in arms. George (*left*) and Ted join forces for the Chilean national side.

Source: Robledo family collection

'A gentleman on the field, a gentleman off the field.' George relaxes at home with his mother, Elsie, for company.

Source: Robledo family collection

The only known photograph of Arístides Robledo, George's father, who disembarked the ship that took the rest of his family to the UK at the very last minute, without telling any of them.

Source: Robledo family collection

George with his baby daughter Elizabeth, born in April 1961. Perhaps conscious that his father had missed out on the majority of his childhood, George resolved to be there for Elizabeth no matter what.

Source: Robledo family collection

ABOVE Family man. At home in Rancagua with wife Gladys and daughter Elizabeth.

Source: Robledo family collection

LEFT George with England manager Walter Winterbottom (*left*) preparing for the 1962 World Cup in Chile. The England team stayed in Rancagua and George was their liaison officer, attaché, interpreter and all-round fixer.

Source: Robledo family collection

'I am quite overwhelmed but so happy to be back among old friends.' George returns to St James' Park and to England for the last time in April 1981.

Source: Robledo family collection

5 Ridgeway, Fenham, Newcastle upon Tyne, a 'club house' owned by Newcastle United, which served as the Robledo family home from 1949 to 1953.

Author's collection

The blue plaque on the wall of 97 Barnsley Road, West Melton, Yorkshire, home to the Robledos from 1932 to 1949.

Author's collection

George's funeral service at the Iglesia Las Carmelitas, Viña del Mar, April 1989. George's body was driven through streets lined with people before being laid to rest in the Mausoleo de Colo-Colo, the club's own dedicated mausoleum.

Source: Robledo family collection

ABOVE 'People are right when they say it looks like the Moon or Mars.' Elizabeth Robledo returns to George's birthplace of Oficina Alianza, September 2023.

Source: Robledo family collection

LEFT Lifelong Barnsley supporter Don Wearmouth with his one remaining signed photograph of George.

Author's collection

fifth round, with Mitchell scoring the only goal in a keenly contest-
ed game at a jam-packed Vetch Field. In the quarter-finals, it was
Milburn's turn to shine as highly fancied Portsmouth were beaten
4–2 at Fratton Park, Newcastle's number nine scoring his side's first,
second and third goals prior to George wrapping things up with a
late fourth.

And so to Hillsborough for the semi-final against Blackburn
Rovers, watched by 20,000 fans from Lancashire, 20,000 fans from
the north-east of England and what appeared to be 25,000 George
and Ted devotees from their old Yorkshire stomping ground, the
trains out of Barnsley and the Dearne Valley being 'full to the brim
all morning' according to the *Barnsley Chronicle*.

Without wishing to labour the point, you know the thing about
there being too many people inside football grounds during the
post-war years for it to be safe?

Well, it happened again. At Hillsborough, of all places.

In the years since the Hillsborough disaster of April 1989, much
has been made of the warnings that went unheeded in the decade
leading up to that fateful day. Many of those who attended FA
Cup semi-finals between Tottenham Hotspur and Wolverhampton Wanderers (1981), Coventry City and Leeds United (1987) and
Liverpool versus Nottingham Forest (1988) returned from Hillsborough with horror stories of overcrowding at the Leppings Lane end
of the ground, leading to broken arms, legs and ribs. Over time, the
geography of this particular part of the stadium had changed – for
example, in 1981 when the terrace behind the goal was split into
pens to restrict sideways movement by supporters. Nevertheless,
the story remained the same – whenever Hillsborough was chosen

as a neutral venue to stage big games, there always seemed to be too many people in the Leppings Lane end for it to be anything like safe.

On Saturday 29 March 1952, the standing areas at Hillsborough were already full sixty minutes before the scheduled 3 p.m. kick-off. Yet more people gained access through the turnstiles and, inevitably, crushes developed, the worst of them being at the Leppings Lane end. With nowhere else to go, sizeable numbers trapped towards the front began climbing over the low brick wall surrounding the pitch, seeking refuge on the grass behind the goal. Many subsequently required first aid. Efforts by the few police officers on duty to keep the crowds back came to nothing as the crowd chose instead to marshal itself, passing those in most distress over the wall to others who'd made it to safety, almost certainly saving lives in the process. Needless to say, there was no delay to the kick-off time, with Blackburn getting proceedings underway as people lay on the side of the field recovering or receiving attention.

Shut the gates. Tell everyone to squash up. Pray, very hard.

Except praying makes it sound as if those in charge actually cared. Which, given these things kept happening for years on end, is debatable.

For what it was worth, the match that unfolded singularly failed to live up to expectations as Newcastle underwhelmed against their Second Division opponents. Both sides wasted glorious chances to seal it in the dying minutes, with Blackburn's Albert Nightingale being denied from close range by United goalkeeper Ronnie Simpson, while George somewhat uncharacteristically fired wide at the other end with the goal at his mercy. A 0–0 draw wasn't what anyone wanted or indeed expected, given Newcastle's free-scoring form in both the league and cup, but at least everyone made it home alive that evening.

Barry Murphy wasn't at Hillsborough that day. Money, or rather the lack of, prevented him travelling from his home in Consett. But he was there on 15 April 1989. He'd supported Newcastle United, played for Barnsley, coached at Barnsley, coached at Leeds United and by the late 1980s was scouting for Nottingham Forest, Liverpool's opponents at Hillsborough in the FA Cup semi-finals for the second year running. He went with his wife, Josie, and no sooner had the pair taken their seats in the directors' box than she realised something was seriously amiss at the Leppings Lane end of the ground.

Sitting in the conservatory of their home in Barnsley thirty-five years later, Josie Murphy recalls what happened next.

I could see the people coming in behind that goal and I said to Barry, 'Oh, it's getting crowded in there.' Nobody seemed to be doing anything about it. It just got fuller and fuller, and still nobody did anything. Barry was saying 'Don't worry, sit down and watch the match' because I don't think he thought anything was wrong. But I could tell there was. One thing I'll always re-member is this lad we'd come across when we went to pick our tickets up. He was a Liverpool supporter, but his ticket was among the Nottingham Forest supporters, and he was begging this chap to swap tickets so he could be with his pals at the Leppings Lane end. I often wonder about him and if he did go to that end or whether fate spared him.

'They used to shuffle you down, all the way down to the front, and not once did I ever think I was in any danger,' adds Barry Murphy, remembering the St James' Park crowds of his childhood. 'All those times we went to watch George and Ted and all those fantastic players, and it never crossed my mind. You look back now at those huge crowds and you think "Really?" But we didn't know any better. It [Hillsborough] was awful. It was frightening.'

Four days after failing to deliver a knockout punch, Newcastle and Blackburn went head to head again in the replay at Elland Road, Leeds – no less of a safety risk in hindsight, with its combustible wooden stands. This time, George was in no mood to pass up any gilt-edged opportunities that might come his way. It was his header midway through the second half which put United ahead, and after Blackburn had equalised, it was another of his headers that was handled on the line by a defender, giving the Magpies the chance to win it in the closing minutes from the penalty spot. With several of his teammates unable to watch, up stepped Mitchell to score. 'I just looked at a spot in the net and hit the ball as hard as I could,' he told one journalist afterwards.

And with that, Newcastle were back at Wembley.

'The run of the ball and a certain amount of luck.' A team needs both, so George once wrote, in order to successfully negotiate the road to Wembley. In reality, luck played little to no part in Newcastle reaching the 1952 FA Cup final. Aston Villa, Tottenham and Portsmouth were all among the fancied teams that year, each one destined to finish inside the top six of the Football League, and yet United blew two of them away in their own back yards. The victories against Aston Villa, Swansea and Blackburn owed more to a combination of dogged determination and astute game management than any slices of good fortune. In the final the Magpies would face Arsenal, winners of the trophy in 1950 and the third-best team in the country going by the 1951–52 First Division table. If ever a side deserved to be at Wembley on merit, then it was Newcastle United's class of '52.

Even then, right in the eye of the hurricane, George got the feeling that perhaps this was his high-cotton moment. Those thirty-three goals in the league had made him the top First Division marksman in the country. He'd made it to Wembley, playing in every round of Newcastle's FA Cup campaign and scoring another five goals along the way. What's more, his brother had played in every round too. He was happy on and off the field. Short of getting a date with Ava Gardner, things couldn't really get much better. Or could they?

In the twenty-first century, the majority of professional sportsmen and women in Britain tend to get where they're going as a result of 'pathways'. Put simply, pathways identify those who excel in sport at a young age, sending them off on a journey towards realising their potential, at whatever level that may be. From jumpers for goalposts to international recognition through a series of performance hoops and programmes overseen by governing bodies, professional clubs, universities... you get the picture.

In 1952, things were slightly different. Take George, for instance. Prior to becoming a professional footballer, he'd emigrated from one end of the world to the other in the middle of a global depression, become estranged from his father, seen his adopted homeland become embroiled in a six-year war against fascism, been sent to work in a mine as a consequence of that war and watched his well-meaning mother chase Wolverhampton Wanderers from the door in the name of education. No magic carpet ride of a plan was ever going to work for George and his kind.

But that's not to say the generation of footballers born between the wars didn't have dreams or weren't determined to make the most of whatever opportunities came their way.

So, how could things get even better for George?

Well, with no sign of Ava Gardner on the horizon, winning the FA Cup for a second time would be champion, as they say on Tyneside. Even better, in all likelihood, than the year beforehand, as his brother would be there alongside him (providing, of course, both were fit and selected for the final).

Then there was the small matter of scoring the winner at Wembley. Because, let's face it, who hasn't dreamed of scoring the winning goal in a cup final?

9

A DAY IN THE LIFE

'Perhaps what one wants to say is formed in childhood,
and the rest of one's life is spent trying to say it.'
– BARBARA HEPWORTH

'**C**ome on, come on.'

Jackie Milburn said the words under his breath but, even with 100,000 noisy spectators for company, George Robledo still heard him loud and clear. Like salt and pepper pots set out on a banquet table, so the two men stood alone at the centre of Wembley's colossal playing field, ready to get the 1952 FA Cup final underway. One blast on the whistle from referee Arthur Ellis and they'd be off. Except that it wasn't three o'clock yet, hence the wait.

Which, Milburn couldn't help but think, was going on rather a long time. But no way was Ellis, a Yorkshireman who prided himself on punctuality, going to start the match a second before or after 3 p.m.

And so the waiting continued, with George rubbing his hands together for something to do as Milburn danced from foot to foot in a bid to maintain concentration.

'Come on, come on.'

When, at last, the whistle sounded, that all-important focus was lost. By the time the ball went from Milburn to George to Joe Harvey, Newcastle United had surrendered possession. They'd won the toss and chosen to kick off. Now the Magpies were on the back foot and under siege. 'We can't play any worse than this,' George caught himself thinking during an early break in play and a let-up from Arsenal's determined assaults. Maybe Newcastle would be needing a certain amount of luck after all if they were going to win the cup?

The days, weeks and indeed months leading up to the FA Cup final of 1952 were eventful ones, not just for Newcastle United as a club but the United Kingdom as a whole. On the morning of 6 February, King George VI had been found dead in bed at Sandringham House, the royal residency in Norfolk, aged just fifty-six. Straightaway the UK went into mourning, with his eldest daughter, who'd been in Kenya at the time, immediately assuming the title of Queen Elizabeth II. In the week leading up to the cup final, it was announced that her coronation would take place at Westminster Abbey, London, on 2 June 1953. The news wiped every other story off the front pages of the national and regional press. Which was probably just as well, given some of the unwanted attention Newcastle's players were starting to attract.

In the early 1950s, clubs competing in the FA Cup final were each given 12,000 tickets to sell to supporters. The remaining 76,000 tickets were distributed by the Football Association across what, even today, is sometimes called the 'football family', consisting of people employed in various capacities within the wider game.

Clearly, the demand for tickets always far outstripped the supply. And that's where the black market kicked in.

This, by and large, is how it worked. As a perk for reaching the final, players from both teams would be given tickets for the match, ostensibly to pass on to family members or close friends. These were players, it should be remembered, with little job security and who earned good wages for the time rather than substantial sums of money. The opportunity to make a little on the side by selling any unwanted cup final tickets was, therefore, tempting. Usually, one face in the dressing room would know a tout. The face would collect any tickets being made available by his teammates, do business with the tout, then the proceeds would be divided as appropriate between the players involved. The process was risky, not to mention illegal, but that didn't stop it happening every year. The secret was not to get caught.

The rumours started abounding almost as soon as the boxes of tickets arrived at St James' Park from the FA. In time, those rumours began appearing on the pages of the north-east's daily papers, with journalists being tasked by their news desks to ask players outright whether or not they were supplying cup final tickets to the black market for personal gain. Much of the heat came to focus on Newcastle captain Joe Harvey, although in reality nobody was above suspicion, not even Jackie Milburn (who insisted all his tickets, bar two reserved for family, would be staying at home in Ashington). When the spotlight briefly fell on him, George, taciturn as ever, simply replied with a shake of the head.

Then, almost by some kind of divine intervention, Buckingham Palace revealed the date of the coronation and the story waned, swamped by a tidal wave of pageantry. By Friday, all eyes were on Wembley and the build-up to the big game the following day. Thanks to the young Queen, the alleged ticket scandal went from being front-page news to inside filler. And, in light of the result that Saturday, there it stayed.

Cheers, Liz.

• • •

Newcastle United's preparations for facing Arsenal at Wembley on Saturday 3 May began almost as soon as they'd seen off Blackburn Rovers in the semi-finals. During the weeks that fell in between, several first-team regulars were rested in a bid to keep players fresh for the big day, including George, who took no part in the league fixtures against Derby County and Aston Villa. In truth, his prolific exploits over the course of the 1951–52 campaign had left George dangerously close to running on empty. Or, as one newspaper put it, 'slow, out of form, and suffering the tortures of frustration'. With just one goal to show from seven appearances leading into the final, it was an assessment George could hardly argue with.

Reading the press on the morning of the match, as he sometimes liked to do before big games, George nevertheless noticed that at least *The Times* had faith in his abilities. 'While Arsenal are making their sixth appearance at Wembley, this in fact will be Newcastle's ninth final, five of them achieved at the old Crystal Palace between the years 1905 and 1911, their golden era,' wrote the paper's designated yet anonymous Association Football Correspondent.

Though they [Newcastle] never once won at Crystal Palace, they have never yet lost at Wembley. On quality alone, Newcastle should win, and it is to their attack that we shall look to bring life and colour into what promises to be a thrilling afternoon. [Tommy] Walker and [Billy] Foulkes, direct in approach on the right, [Bobby] Mitchell of the fluttering left foot and ball control down the left, with an inside partner, Robledo, who now shares over sixty goals this season with Milburn. We shall look for his [George's] long, low cross-passes that stretch opposing defences outwards, leaving the middle vulnerable for the flying Milburn, who of all centre-forwards possesses the spark that can suddenly spurt up and destroy.

Back on Tyneside, *The Journal* also continued to champion George despite his lean spell in front of goal. 'Strong and resourceful, he is always in the thick of the fray,' declared the paper in its 'pen pics' cup final preview section, which also heralded brother Ted as 'probably the most improved player on the club's books'. Much, however, would 'depend on whether George Robledo and Foulkes, restored to inside-forward, lump into the game at full speed'.

George wanted to lump into the game at full speed, Lord knows he did. But in order to lump in, he needed to get hold of the ball. Which, during the early exchanges, wasn't something Newcastle saw much of. And yet, right up until kick-off, everything about the day had felt swell. The morning brought with it rain, which George believed would suit Newcastle's attacking style of play, making the surface slippery but also conducive to their quicksilver passing game. The journey to the stadium, so often subject to delays with the huge crowds bound for Wembley, had gone according to plan, while the mood in United's dressing room leaned firmly on the right side of confident. No arrogance, no cockiness, no crippling nerves. There'd been the quick-fire adrenalin rush of the walk out onto the pitch, followed by a stirring rendition of 'Abide With Me' (the traditional FA Cup final hymn and one of George's favourite pieces of music) prior to shaking hands with Winston Churchill, there to present the cup as well as in his capacity as Prime Minister. He'd felt ready and, looking around at his teammates as they took up their positions, George sensed they were ready too.

But then there'd been that blasted wait, during which the wind seemed to pass out of Newcastle's sails straight into those of their opponents. When the referee's whistle finally came, United found themselves not only dead in the water but in danger of being submerged.

Until, that is, the game entered its eighteenth minute, at which point fortune chose to walk right out on Arsenal.

It seems ludicrous, in these days of multiple replacements in football matches, that the concept of substitutes not only took so long to arrive in the UK but was initially met with hostility from within the game. What began in August 1965 as a way of replacing injured players came to be regarded by some as a form of cheating, the overriding concern being that managers would use substitutes tactically in order to withdraw underperformers. 'A more likely form of abuse would be the substitution of a forward by a defender when a team want to retain the lead in the closing stages, or are struggling to hang on to a point,' wrote no less of an authority than the *Daily Telegraph*'s respected football correspondent Donald Saunders.

> This would be a clear case of twelve men competing against eleven. A lesser crime, but one I hope we shall not see committed, would be the withdrawal, after victory or defeat had become more or less certain, of a star player whose talents may be in greater demand a day or two hence.

In the immediate post-war years, if a team lost a player due to injury at any point in a game, then there was diddly-squat they could do about it other than continue one man down. It didn't matter if it was the FA Cup final, aka the biggest annual football spectacle in the country, if not the world – the disadvantaged side just had to soldier on as best as possible.

This was the scenario Arsenal faced after Walley Barnes, their Welsh international defender, twisted his knee during the first half of the 1952 final and, despite trying to play on, had to leave the field. Reduced to ten men for virtually three-quarters of the match, the Londoners immediately went into defensive mode as Newcastle finally started to get their act together. The pendulum had swung in the Magpies' favour. It was now just a matter of whether George and his teammates could capitalise on their numerical advantage.

For almost the entire second half, Newcastle hammered away at Arsenal's rearguard. Milburn, himself nursing a knock, went close, as did George, as did Walker, as did Mitchell, the latter slaloming his way past four defenders before having a shot charged down.

Still, the scoreline remained goalless, and the longer it did so the more tired and frustrated George became. He'd spurned one chance to score a thirty-ninth goal of the season and he wasn't altogether sure another would present itself. George later confessed that, with fifteen minutes to go, given the chance to trade twenty of his goals in the league that season for one in the FA Cup final, he'd have taken it 'at the drop of a hat'.

And it was around that point, as the match entered its closing stages, that 'Pancho' had his eureka moment.

There's a story Paul Newman, one of the greatest actors of his or any generation, used to tell about the making of *Hombre*, the 1967 western in which he plays the character of John Russell, an Apache-raised white man facing prejudice in nineteenth-century Arizona. Newman had been struggling with how best to portray the tough, alienated Russell, admitting in his memoir that 'it just wouldn't come together for me'. One morning, while on location in New Mexico, Newman happened to pass a small general store where a man stood on one foot outside on the porch, arms folded, his other heel hooked over a windowsill. A couple of hours later, he passed by the store again and noticed the man hadn't moved an inch. 'I ended up taking my whole character from that man,' said Newman. 'The sense that there was no reason for him to move, so he didn't.'

During those last fifteen minutes, George became the footballing equivalent of the man outside that general store. Rather than charging around the field trying to be all things to all men (and failing, what with his rapidly depleting energy levels), he resolved to slow things right down by lying in wait, in whatever attacking holes he could find. That way, should an opportunity present itself, he'd be well placed to get a shot or a header off towards the Arsenal goal. He knew Mitchell would be looking for him at the far post – the two men had discussed it in the dressing room at the interval, conscious of the gaps that could well open up in Arsenal's overworked defence late on. The time had come for George to deliver on his side of the bargain. Adopting a 'less is more' approach would, he reckoned, help him do that.

By the eighty-fourth minute, Arsenal were to all intents and purposes down to nine men, with winger Don Roper (who'd spent most of the game covering in defence for the injured Barnes) reduced to the role of a hobbling on-field spectator. It was then that Ted Robledo gained possession on the Newcastle left. Rather than advancing into the space in front of him, the younger Robledo chose instead to sweep the ball out to Mitchell, standing parallel with the Arsenal penalty area completely unmarked.

This, both Mitchell and George instinctively knew, was it. The cross, when it came, couldn't have been more inviting for an attacking player who loved scoring goals with his head. Mitchell had done his bit. Now it was all down to George, stationed at the back post just as he'd said he would be.

'When I saw [Arsenal defender] Lionel Smith moving towards the middle of the goal, I closed in hopefully to the far post,' George recalled after the game. 'The ball came very sharp over the heads of several players, and with Smith racing back at me and [goalkeeper] Swindin taking position, I daren't even delay in drawing my head back to really hit it. I nearly passed out as the ball hit the post and went into the net.'

'Mitchell centred into the packed goalmouth, as he had unsuccessfully done so many times before on this day of agony and heroism for the Gunners,' reported the *Evening Chronicle*. 'On this occasion the unmistakable mahogany skin of Robledo reacted with the reflexes of a cat. First a move that was an odd combination of spring and crouch, then a quick stab of the head. The ball struck the inside of the post and glanced into history.'

For George, what remained of the match passed by in a haze. On a physical level he was drained. However, the emotional rush of scoring also seemed to have a peculiar effect on his body. Years later, George would hear of Ipswich Town player Roger Osborne, who on scoring the winner in the 1978 FA Cup final, ironically against Arsenal, very nearly passed out and had to be substituted. 'I know that feeling,' George told a journalist in 1981, 'but of course there were no substitutes then, so we just had to carry on. Fortunately there wasn't long to go. I think we were all dead on our feet by then.'

He wasn't wrong. At the final whistle, the majority of the players on the field either sank to the turf or slowly went in search of the nearest man to shake hands. Two figures did, though, make a beeline for one another. They were George and Ted, who on coming together shared a knowing, wordless embrace. Once again, Newcastle United had carried off the FA Cup, becoming the first team since Blackburn Rovers some sixty years previously to win the trophy in successive seasons. Yet on the field there were surprisingly few signs of jubilation among their players. They'd done enough, just, but they hadn't played well. What's more, they knew it.

Even so, the general consensus in the north-east of England was that the gentlemen of the press (and they were all men in 1952) could have been a little more magnanimous in the Sunday and Monday editions when it came to how they reported Newcastle's achievement:

The *Sunday Times* said, 'Arsenal might easily have won this match even with ten men had they been able to finish off their attacks as well as they built them up.'

The *Times* said, 'Saturday, in truth, belonged to the vanquished. Newcastle won the cup. Arsenal won the glory.'

The *News of the World* said, 'So long as they were at full strength, Arsenal were the dominant force. But for Barnes' injury, I feel confident they would have won.'

And the *Sunday Express* said, 'This victory was as hollow as a kettle drum.'

'Personally, I would not have expected anything less from the London-based titles, especially when it comes to a cup final involving a London-based team,' complained one Tynesider in a letter submitted to the *Evening Chronicle*. Which, much like its sister papers based at Kemsley House in Newcastle, had in fact been surprisingly measured in its reporting of the Mapgies' performance.

'Fortune had stacked the cards for Newcastle to win at a canter, but they were lucky to snatch a short head verdict over a luckless Arsenal,' wrote the correspondent from *The Journal*, adding that 'Robledo's goal did much to make up for an indifferent [team] display'. Speaking to Ken McKenzie from the same newspaper, Arsenal manager Tom Whittaker went as far as publicly calling for the introduction of replacements in high-profile football matches. 'This cup final was ruined as a game and as a spectacle by the retirement of Barnes,' he complained. 'Substitutes should be allowed for players totally incapacitated in such showpiece games of classical importance.' Whittaker did, nonetheless, graciously admit, 'No one can begrudge the Geordies their amazing honour, in view of the fearsome programme of cup obstacles they have surmounted this season.'

Exhilarated. That, once he'd recaptured his breath and got some fluids into his body, was how George felt on Saturday 3 May as the late afternoon light began to dim over Wembley Stadium. Vindicated as well. His decision to put football ahead of engineering or any other potential career path had paid off in spades in terms of glory, if not riches. He was the First Division's leading marksman and he'd scored the winner in the FA Cup final. His brother, who he adored, had played a part in the move leading up to that winning goal, witnessed in the flesh by their mother, not to mention Winston Churchill – statesman, soldier, writer, two-time Prime Minister of the UK, the epitome of Britain's bulldog spirit in its darkest hour.

And, according to working-class folklore, the enemy of the miners. Of which George had once been one.

In November 1910, Churchill, then Home Secretary, had agreed to the use of military force to quell unrest in the Welsh town of Tonypandy, where miners were on strike over pay. The presence of the 18th Hussars and a detachment from the Metropolitan Police in South Wales that winter caused anger and resentment in local communities. It also made mud of Churchill's name among those who worked underground, not just in Wales but throughout the UK. And mud has a habit of sticking for an awful long time.

Thirty years on, it didn't matter that Churchill, as Prime Minister of a coalition government, epitomised Britain's opposition to Nazi

Germany. To many people in pit communities such as West Melton, he was still the guy who sent the troops in on the miners.

Churchill's presence at the 1952 FA Cup final hadn't really registered with George until the time came for the Prime Minister to meet the two teams prior to kick-off. To be honest, he'd been too wrapped up in the forthcoming game to give it a second thought. Climbing those thirty-nine steps to Wembley's royal box behind captain Joe Harvey to receive the trophy, George couldn't help but wonder what his former colleagues at Wath Main Colliery would have to say about him shaking hands with the man who sent the soldiers into Tonypandy.

Should he, in fact, even shake his hand?

Of course he should. George was too much of a gentleman to disrespect a figure who, since the Second World War, had come to represent the global face of his adopted homeland. He played for Chile now, but George was still proud of having been largely raised in England.

'Well done,' said Churchill as George received his winner's medal.

'Thank you,' replied Newcastle's goalscorer.

That evening, and indeed for much of the next forty-eight hours, George's reserved demeanour took a bit of a holiday. Post-match interviews were freely given, as indeed were cigarettes to anyone who happened to come into his orbit. Whether he jumped partially clothed into the pool at the team's hotel in London or simply went for a post-match swim to wind down is a matter of conjecture, but either way, he certainly got wet. George couldn't sing, but that didn't stop him keeping teammates and supporters entertained on the train back to Newcastle with an abridged version of 'The Blaydon

Races', a song composed in 1862 by Tynesider George Ridley and regarded for many years as Newcastle United's anthem.

> Oh, me lads!
> Ye shudda seen w'us gannin'
> Passin' the folks alang the road
> Just as they wor' stannin'
> Aal the lads and lasses there
> Aal wi' smilin' faces
> Gannin' alang the Scotswood Road
> To see the Blaydon Races

'I never knew what it meant, but it always sounded terrific when sung by the supporters,' George confided of 'The Blaydon Races' in the same 1981 interview in which he'd spoken about Roger Osborne of Ipswich Town.

> They used to sing it before and during the matches. In fact I'm pretty sure they sung it before the [1952] final. When you heard it you always knew it was our supporters singing it just for us, because there was no other song like it, with a tune like that. You couldn't mistake it for anything else.

Back home in Fenham, both George and Ted's FA Cup winners' medals took pride of place on the table in the dining room for visitors to see. Over the days that followed, they were joined by enough congratulatory mail to fill a small sorting office, including telegrams from the Mayor of Barnsley and Ambassador Bianchi, who George had come to regard as a friend. Newspaper cuttings also arrived courtesy of friends and admirers in faraway places, enabling him to read some of his own headlines in Yorkshire and South America (including 'Our Wembley Winner' from the *Barnsley Chronicle* and 'El Principito' from Chile's *Las Últimas Noticias*, the latter translating as 'the little prince'). And they say you can only ever be a local hero in one place.

'It was indeed an honour to be on the winning side again, but I think the lads who derived the biggest thrill and greatest satisfaction were the four for who it was their first Wembley appearance,' wrote George of Newcastle's 1952 FA Cup win in an article commissioned later that year by the *Soccer Fanfare* annual.

They were Ron Simpson, Alf McMichael, Bill Foulkes and my brother Ted. Yes, there is something about a cup final at Wembley that makes it stand out above all else in a player's memory. The pageantry, the tense atmosphere, the crowd singing 'Abide With Me', the presentation ceremonial before that start – and, if you are fortunate, the winners' medal at the end – all make it a real day, or days, that will live with all who experience it for the whole of their years.

They may have lived with him all his years, but that's not to say George ever crowed about his starring roles in the FA Cup finals of 1951 and 1952. In fact, over time, he barely talked about them at all. 'I knew he was a hero in England, particularly when it came to the FA Cup, but you would never have known it,' says Elizabeth Robledo.

I saw his medals and I knew those games meant a lot to him, but he was such a low-profile kind of person that he kept his memories to himself. It was actually my mother who used to talk more about him playing at Wembley and getting to meet King George VI and Winston Churchill. I was only young and I probably didn't realise just what a big deal that was. And it was a big deal – I get that, now I know more about it. But it took me a long, long time to understand.

10

(JUST LIKE) STARTING OVER

'I was trained to be an actor, not a star.'
– GENE HACKMAN

Britain has, it's fair to say, seen better years than 1952. The feel-good factor of the new Elizabethan age, with its conquering of Mount Everest and the breaking of the four-minute mile by Roger Bannister, had yet to come. Post-war austerity remained, as did rationing. It was almost impossible for many families to borrow money. Decent housing was at a premium. Thousands died from smog during December as pollutants conspired with cold, windless conditions to form a lethal, airborne cocktail. 'Threadbare, bombed-out, financially and morally exhausted,' is how historian Dominic Sandbrook has since described the cultural and economic lie of the land. Great, Britain was not.

Elsewhere, however, the world was moving on apace. New roads, railways and buildings were transforming the face of a mainland Europe ravaged by years of occupation and hostilities. In the US, Chuck Yeager's breaking of the sound barrier in 1947 had opened the door for Projects Mercury and Apollo, space programmes that would ultimately lead to twelve men walking on the Moon between 1969 and 1972, the first being Neil Armstrong and the last Eugene Cernan. 'It's tough to find an encore,' Cernan once confessed of the anti-climax that followed his lunar mission. Words that could just as easily have come from George Robledo's mouth during the latter half of 1952.

He'd starred for his country at a World Cup. He'd won an FA Cup winner's medal. He'd scored more league goals in a season than any other player in English football's top flight. He'd won a second FA Cup winner's medal. He'd scored the winning goal in an FA Cup final... all in the space of just two years.

Within the confines of the game as it was known in the early 1950s, other than winning the World Cup with Chile or the First Division title with Newcastle United, there really wasn't all that much left for George, at the age of twenty-six, to achieve.

All of which begged the question, 'What should he do next?'

Besides going fishing on the River Tweed with his angling mates from Fenham (which George did indeed do the week after the 1952 FA Cup final), the short-term answer lay in yet another of Newcastle's gruelling foreign tours, this time to South Africa to play sixteen matches in seventy days spanning May to July. With the cup itself in tow (valued at £200, according to the necessary export licence granted by the Board of Trade), United's players were hailed as heroes wherever they went. In fact, the hospitality became so excessive that Stan Seymour asked the organisers to cancel any cocktail parties scheduled to take place within twenty-four hours of a game.

On the field, the competition proved to be somewhat stiffer

than Newcastle's trek around North America three years previously, though George did manage to find the net seven times at the
expense of Border Province in a 10–0 mauling. They even lost a
game this time, going down 5–3 to the South African national side
in Johannesburg, having won a previous test match 3–0 in Durban.
Off the field, the players let their hair down whenever possible and
received gifts aplenty, with George taking ownership of a large decorative drum featuring paintings of traditional South African rural
scenes.

'Dad wasn't a real party person, but when he felt comfortable,
he would relax around people and the drum would come out,' says
Elizabeth Robledo, in whose home the drum now resides. 'It was
the only musical instrument Dad could play and he was very talented at it. People loved to watch him as he played, me included and
my mother of course. It's a very special memory that I have of him.'

Sure, South Africa was enjoyable, but it was also exhausting. Once
again, Newcastle United's hierarchy had put financial gain above
player welfare. The length of the tour left the team with little time to
wind down on returning to England or prepare for the forthcoming
1952–53 season.

Fail to prepare, prepare to fail, as they say. United's opening five
league matches saw them take just three points from a possible
ten under the old two-points-for-a-win system. The first victory
of the campaign, at home to Preston North End on 13 September,
brought some respite, but only after George managed to score two
late goals to overturn a 3–2 deficit. In short, the players were knackered. Injuries picked up on or exacerbated by the hard grounds of
South Africa left the side depleted. Loss of form dogged other key

members of the dressing room, including Jackie Milburn (who scored just five goals throughout the entire season while, admittedly, suffering from cartilage trouble). Given proper rest, there's no reason why Newcastle couldn't have built on their cup successes of 1951 and 1952 and gone full-tilt at capturing the 1952–53 First Division title. Instead, a side boasting such talents as George, Bobby Mitchell and Milburn was left staring up at the rest of the table from in or around the relegation zone. It was a scenario which made little sense to anyone other than Newcastle United's board of directors, seemingly intent on having their cake and eating it.

● ● ●

They say people who live in ports or places associated with the sea often tend to feel more of a connection with the outside world than they do their own country. That certainly used to be the case with cities such as Liverpool, Glasgow and Newcastle, major centres of trade, commerce, shipbuilding and/or passenger traffic, where the population sat on the water's edge rather than being surrounded by land. The pull of the sea and the lure of foreign shores was always there even if, as in the case of thousands of men from Newcastle and its suburbs, they only ever got to build the ships that served such exotic climes.

'On Sunday mornings my dad would take my brother and me down to the quayside to look at the boats,' recalled Gordon Sumner, better known as the musician Sting, born and raised four miles east of Newcastle city centre in Wallsend.

The Leda was a Norwegian steamer that would sail weekly from Oslo to Newcastle and back again across the cold North Sea, plying the same route as the old Vikings. I remember my father gazing dreamily up at the wheelhouse and the ropes securing the bows of the ships to the quay. 'Go to sea!' my father would always tell me, but I know now he was really speaking to himself as a younger man.

George Robledo may have spent his formative years in landlocked West Melton, but he was only too familiar with the call of the sea and the portal that it (along with foreign travel in general) afforded in terms of opportunity. That call had never sounded louder than it did as 1952 made way for 1953.

For all Newcastle United's on-field problems and general disheartenment in the dressing room, George still thoroughly enjoyed living in the area. He fished. He played table tennis in the Second Division of the Northumberland County League. He was a member of Fenham Tennis Club. He coached youth club football teams and ran gym classes two or three evenings a week on behalf of the local education authority, something he'd gladly taken on with no strings attached, working free of charge. He loved exploring Northumberland and all its beauty. Even so, if ever there was a time for him to leave St James' Park in search of a fresh challenge, then it was now. The seed that had been planted during Newcastle's tour of North America in 1949 was at the point of flowering. What's more, Colo-Colo of Santiago, still closely monitoring George's progress from the other side of the world not to mention United's tussle with relegation, seemed to sense this.

In common with several other key members of Newcastle's team, George missed almost as many games as he played over the course of the 1952–53 season due to niggles, as opposed to outright injuries, brought on by too much football. When he was fit enough to start, at least United had a fighting chance of getting a positive result. Never more was this the case than when Newcastle, without a win in eleven games stretching back to Christmas Day, travelled to face Derby County on 21 March. To say Derby battered the visitors in terms of dominating play would be an understatement, yet they didn't have anybody who could put the ball in the net. Newcastle did, and he converted twice in the last seven minutes to seal a crucial 2–0 win. As it turned out, they'd be the last goals George would ever score for the Magpies.

The previous month, George had claimed another brace in a match of huge significance for Newcastle United – one that, nonetheless, you won't find in the record books. The dawning of the 1950s saw several Football League clubs, including Arsenal and Southampton, install floodlights at their grounds, primarily to allow matches to be played at night. At first, the powers that be refused to sanction the use of such lighting for anything other than friendlies. That, though, didn't dissuade more clubs from installing them.

At the start of 1953, Newcastle set to work positioning eighty lights along the West Stand roof and on poles amid the Leazes Terrace. On Wednesday 25 February, a crowd of nearly 42,000 saw George become the first player ever to score under floodlights at St James' Park, claiming both goals in a 2–0 win over Celtic. As it was, another three years would pass before floodlights were officially sanctioned for use in the Football League, with Newcastle's match at Portsmouth on 22 February 1956 going down in history as the first of its kind in England. A new era had dawned, easing the congestion which existed in the fixtures schedule and ending the tradition of playing games on Christmas Day, while, somewhat illogically, ushering in football every single night of the week.

Two days after the Celtic game, on Friday 27 February, Manuel Bianchi paid another visit to the Robledo household in Fenham. Had anyone asked, he was there merely as a friend of the family. In reality, Chile's ambassador to Britain travelled north by train from London on a mission. Between them, Colo-Colo and the Federación de Fútbol de Chile had formulated a package which they believed George and his family would be unable to resist. Over tea and cake (of the homemade variety, baked by Elsie), Bianchi went through the extensive list of what was on offer. Colo-Colo wanted George and were willing to sign Ted as well in order to get him. They would be paid £30 each per week – that at a time when the maximum weekly wage for a player in the Football League stood at £14. In addition, there would be the equivalent of a £20 bonus for a win and £10 for a draw. On signing, George would receive £4,000 and Ted £3,000 in hard cash. They'd be given private tutors to help with the language, a personal bodyguard and a spacious fully furnished club house at the foot of the Andes in which to live with Elsie and Walter – providing, of course, they wanted to go to Santiago too. George and Ted would also hold official appointments as 'football consult-ants' to the Chilean government, whatever exactly that meant.

Off the scale – that's what the offer was, quite unlike anything ever seen before in the British game. Colo-Colo and the Federación de Fútbol de Chile really had thought of pretty much everything.

The Robledos asked Bianchi for a few days to think it over, though in reality, as much as they enjoyed living in Newcastle, there wasn't that much to think about. The opportunity for George and Ted to explore new horizons and earn enough money to live comfortably while playing for Chile's premier football club was just too good to turn down. Both men were single at the time, their only family obligations being to Elsie and Walter, who by now was old enough to make his own way in the world. Nonetheless, with the Robledos it remained a case of all for one and one for all. They would either go as a unit or not at all.

'I absolutely loved my time in Newcastle,' recalled Walter in his 2019 interview with Chris Waugh of *The Athletic*. 'People used to know me as the brother of the footballing Robledos. Once they heard my surname, they'd say "Any relation to George and Ted?" Then they'd immediately be my best friend. I've never been so popular as I was then!' Still, Walter had no hesitation in saying yes, treating the whole thing, in typical Robledo fashion, 'as though it was an adventure'.

As for Elsie? Determined as ever to do the best by her sons, and familiar as she was with South America, the grande dame of our story was never going to say no.

Twenty-one years after sailing from Iquique on the *Reina del Pacifico*, the Robledos were going back to Chile.

On Saturday 28 March, George walked onto the St James' Park turf to play for Newcastle's first XI for the last time – not that his teammates, nor the crowd, knew it. The opposition, appropriately enough, was Blackpool, a club that had featured so often in his career while playing for both Barnsley and the Magpies. In keeping with recent form, Newcastle lost 1–0. At the end, there was no wave to the crowd, no lap of honour, no theatrical throwing of his shirt into the stands. He simply left the pitch, showered, changed and made his way back to Fenham. After four years of unimaginable highs, during which he scored ninety-one goals over the course of 166 league and FA Cup appearances, so the Newcastle United chapter of George's life ended on a forgettable low. That's the thing about sport – you can't always choose how or when you say goodbye.

The following week, negotiations began between Colo-Colo and Newcastle United over the transfer of both George and Ted. A fee amounting to the equivalent of £15,000 was mentioned and duly accepted. Finally, in the week leading up to United's vital match at Portsmouth on 18 April, the press got wind of the story. On 19 April, with Newcastle licking their wounds after being hammered 5–1 on England's south coast, the *Sunday Sun* went to print with their story:

> Colo-Colo Club Santiago yesterday announced they had signed the Robledo brothers from Newcastle United and, without actually confirming the deal was completed, Newcastle officials admitted negotiations had been in progress for some time. The fee mentioned is £15,000–£11,000 less than that paid for the two players when they moved from Barnsley to Newcastle in 1949. It is reported from Santiago that the brothers, George and Ted, will arrive there on 5 May and that they will play in the Chilean [league] championships which begin on 9 May. According to the Santiago report, Newcastle United have confirmed their acceptance by cable.

The general feeling among Newcastle's supporters, not to mention

George's teammates, on hearing the news wasn't so much shock as resignation. Anyone with the slightest connection to St James' Park knew he'd been courted by various South American clubs. 'Pancho' was going to leave eventually, that much seemed apparent. However, the timing couldn't have been worse. 'It should have been ten [goals],' fumed Stan Seymour after Newcastle's capitulation to Portsmouth, a defeat that appeared at the time to have condemned the Magpies to relegation from the First Division. In the event they managed to just stay up, thanks largely to George's return of eighteen goals from twenty-four league appearances, allied with the inadequacies of other clubs towards the foot of the table. To agree to sell George with half-a-dozen games remaining, especially with Milburn out of form and blighted by injury, seemed tantamount to giving up the ghost.

By the time the *Sunday Sun* piece appeared, the Robledos had already vacated their club house in Fenham. Journalists visiting 5 Ridgeway looking for exclusives were met with nothing but the sound of their own knock. Which is just the way George, never one for fuss, probably wanted it. This time, the press were left to pick up the pieces of a story that had already set sail. On the other hand, an interview with, say, *The Journal* would've given George a platform to say thank you and goodbye to the fans who idolised him. It also meant sports writers and broadcasters were scuppered when it came to filing tributes to the Robledos featuring quotes or audio. OK, so a transfer in the offing for months finally came together at speed, but was there really not enough time to say adios?

'The Robledos, especially George, made the kind of footballing contribution to the post-war years that would later be held up as trademarks of the best foreign players,' Nick Harris would write fifty years after their departure in his book *England, Their England*.

> Their professionalism was unquestioned, on or off the pitch. They trained well and looked after themselves as full-time athletes, not twice-weekly entertainers who could spend five nights a week in the pub. They sought new experiences, and ultimately better money, befitting their talents. And George, while adapting to whatever system of play he was asked to be part of, also liked innovation. Players who could execute the 'bicycle kick' were a rarity and he was one of them. Above all, through their looks, style and George's flair, they compelled people to pay good money to walk through the turnstiles and watch them play. And on numerous occasions those same people would leave two hours later having seen something just a little bit different, a little bit magical.

Beautiful words, lovingly crafted. It's just a shame few scribes, if any, had the chance to pen equally fitting homages half a century earlier, such was the haste with which George and Ted departed north-east England.

It seems only fitting, not to mention supremely ironic, that some of the last people to spend time with George on Tyneside prior to his departure for Santiago were from Chile. Towards the end of April, a 11,400-tonne, Chilean-registered tanker called the *Sonap* put into Smith's Dock in North Shields for repairs. In search of something to do, around a dozen of the ship's crew made for St James' Park to catch a glimpse of the place where George Robledo, hero of Chile's 1950 World Cup side, plied his trade. By sheer chance, a reserve team game against Sheffield United was scheduled for later that day with George making a surprise appearance, given his transfer to Colo-Colo had already gone through. In they went to witness what would be his last outing of any description in a Newcastle shirt. After the match they also got to meet George, who joined them on board the *Sonap* the following afternoon for a slap-up meal.

Unlike many professional football players, George wasn't a superstitious person. He didn't believe in omens. And yet as signs go, his encounter with the men of the *Sonap* was, so he figured, a pretty positive one.

• • •

Like it or lump it, there are certain football clubs which, for all manner of reasons, tend to be associated with their respective countries more than others. Asked to name a French football team, you're probably more likely to cite Paris Saint-Germain than, say, Nantes. Likewise, Bayern Munich when it comes to Germany or Juventus when it comes to Italy and so on. There was a time when two of the most recognisable words in the English language were 'Bobby' and 'Charlton', such was Manchester United's appeal around the globe. Fans of the likes of Marseilles, Borussia Dortmund, Inter Milan and Liverpool may quibble, but that's just the way history has declared it.

So it goes with Colo-Colo when it comes to Chile.

Formed in 1925, Club Social y Deportivo Colo-Colo, for that is their full and proper name, have won more titles in Chile's Primera División than any other side (thirty-four, to date). They've won more Copa Chile titles, the annual cup competition open to every club in the Chilean football league system, than any other club. They were the first Chilean club to win a continental tournament, scooping the Copa Libertadores in 1991. They have more supporters than any other club in Chile. Along the way, they've survived internal mismanagement, bankruptcy and tragedy. In 1927, Colo-Colo founder and captain David Arellano died after accidentally colliding with an opponent during a friendly match in Valladolid, Spain, where the club was on tour. Five years later, three people were killed and over 130 injured when a stand collapsed while a fixture against Audax Italiano was in progress. Through it all, the name Colo-Colo garnered a certain cachet and romance in the same way that Manchester United did in the wake of the 1958 Munich air disaster, both in terms of the way the club handled itself in times of adversity and the calibre of the players it attracted.

And of the hundreds of players to have worn its famous white shirt (complete with black stripe, in memory of Arellano), the heavyweight champion of them all remains George Robledo.

First the Robledos went from Newcastle to West Melton to spend time with family and friends in Yorkshire. Then, at the beginning of May, they travelled to London, staying there while the more cumbersome elements of their latest adventure, such as visas and work permits, were prepared at the Chilean embassy. Elsie and Walter departed first, in order to pave the way and prepare the house that Colo-Colo had arranged for them. One week later, on Thursday 14 May, George and Ted took off from London Airport bound for Santiago. George, of course, had charted this course before – the seemingly never-ending flight via Paris, Lisbon, Dakar and other cities, picking up passengers, dropping off passengers, refuelling the plane, replenishing the galley and changing the crew. For Ted, though, this was a new experience. When last on Chilean soil, he'd been three years old. He had no memories of the place, no familiar points of reference, no real expectations other than what he'd been told by his elder brother and Manuel Bianchi.

Nevertheless, one thing Ted did have in common with George was neither of them had any idea of the scale of the welcome that awaited them at Santiago's Los Cerrillos Airport.

In May 1950, George had arrived in Santiago as a potential star in the making. He'd done well for Barnsley. He'd done well for Newcastle United. That much the people of Chile knew. Maybe, just maybe, he'd do well for them at the forthcoming World Cup in Brazil?

Three years on, George was now a superstar in the land of his birth – not that he knew it yet. He'd done more than well for Chile in Brazil. He'd scored the winning goal in the final of the most famous club cup competition on the planet. He'd scored more goals in one season than anyone else in the top tier in England, the country that had given the game of football to the rest of the world. The stuff of legends – that's what George had become, and he hadn't even kicked a ball for his new club yet. What's more, this time he was bringing his footballing brother with him.

The first inkling George had that something was afoot came shortly after their plane landed on the tarmac at Santiago. Asked by a stewardess to remain seated until all the other passengers had disembarked, George, courteous as ever, enquired, 'Yes, but why?'

'You'll see,' replied the stewardess.

In 1953, the benchmark for all airport welcomes – the Beatles arriving at New York City's John F. Kennedy Airport ahead of a two-week US promotional tour – was still eleven years away. On that occasion, the 'Fab Four' had around 100 police officers to protect them from the screaming hordes. George and Ted, to all intents and purposes, were left to fend for themselves, with only a handful of security guards present to control in excess of 2,000 people who converged on Los Cerrillos Airport to witness their arrival. Santiago had never seen anything quite like it, Chile had never seen anything quite like it and George and Ted had certainly never seen anything like it, not even after Newcastle United's victorious FA Cup homecomings of 1951 and 1952. This time, everyone had turned up *just for them*. As a child, George had left Chile feeling confused and abandoned. Now, he and Ted were returning to a red carpet of love and affection. No wonder both men embraced the experience, taking time to shake as many hands as possible while moving through the vast, good-natured crowds.

In a perfect world, the following days would have been a slightly calmer extension of everything that had happened at the airport. Instead, 'Jorge' and to a lesser extent 'Eduardo', as he would become known in Chile, were to learn that Colo-Colo and the Federación de Fútbol de Chile weren't necessarily on the same page about everything. By sheer coincidence, England had arranged to tour North and South America during May and June of 1953, with fixtures lined up against the US, Argentina, Uruguay and, you've guessed it, Chile. That meant George, if selected, would play for the national team before making his Colo-Colo debut, something his new club weren't especially enamoured about.

On the other hand, the Federación de Fútbol de Chile, along with fans of the national side, were desperate for him to appear against the tourists. 'Why go to such lengths to bring the man over here if you're not going to play him in showpiece matches such as this?' went the argument in the cafes and bars of Santiago in the build-up to the game, scheduled for Sunday 24 May.

In the end, some kind of common sense prevailed. Having only been in the country a matter of days, George barely had enough time to meet the Chilean team, let alone train with them. Parachuting him straight into the national side before he'd sufficiently acclimatised or played for Colo-Colo seemed at best premature, at worst irresponsible. The Wednesday before the match, Chile's team manager Luis Tirado declared that neither George nor Ted would be selected to face England.

Five days later, an own goal by Sergio Livingstone, Chile's long-serving goalkeeper, together with a second-half strike by Nat Lofthouse gave the visitors a 2–1 win in Santiago. In some ways, it was the worst possible result for Tirado, who inevitably faced questions from the media as to why he hadn't fielded George, given the narrow margin of England's victory. 'Many people here are still saying that George Robledo, at least, should have been included in the Chilean forward line because of his knowledge of England's team,' wrote Clifford Webb of the *Daily Herald*, one of the British journalists covering the tour. 'Critics said after the match that if he and his brother Ted had been in the Chilean team, then England might not have secured their victory.'

On the other hand, Tirado's decision to go without them gave George and Ted, along with the rest of the Robledo family, some valuable breathing space in their new surroundings. Ted, in particular, found this extremely beneficial, taking the time to explore Santiago and pick up on some of the little things which George had noticed three years previously – the Carabineros in their green and white uniforms directing traffic with sweeping theatrical gestures, those tempting little coffee and empanadas bars that attracted city workers on their breaks like bees to nectar, the free and easy way Santiaguinos conducted their lives in the years before Augusto Pinochet seized power in a military coup and freedom of speech became a thing of the past. In 1953, nearly a quarter of Chile's population of 7 million people lived in Santiago. By the end of his first week in the city, Ted – always the more gregarious of the two older Robledo brothers – was convinced he'd met most of them.

'Ted and Jorge became the most famous football players in Chile up to that point without having played a match,' says the Chilean sports writer and author Néstor Flores.

It was enough for them just to arrive and to be here. Everyone, no matter which team they supported, wanted to see the so-called gringos – in Chile, Anglo-Saxons in general are called gringos – who came with all the English technique and strategy to play here. People used to wait for them in hotels, outside training, everywhere. You had this pair of gringos who dressed elegantly and walked elegantly, living their very English life in Santiago de Chile.

For George, the brief respite from playing football allowed him time to do one of the things he loved most in life – write to people. Over the weeks that followed, untold letters, telegrams and postcards started dropping through the letterboxes of homes across York-shire and north-east England courtesy of 'Geo Robledo', as George usually signed his name. 'We're safe and well, a few people came to the airport to meet us, the weather's warm, I'm looking forward to starting training with Colo-Colo, here's our new address, please write to us' – those were the common threads among the first wave of correspondence from South America. In an attempt to keep pace with what became known as 'Robledo Mania' in Chile, Colo-Colo also had thousands of postcards produced featuring a picture of George in his first-team kit, many of which found their way back to friends and acquaintances in England. Anyone contacting the club seeking an autograph would receive a postcard signed by George, more often than not bearing the inscription 'With the best of wishes, Geo Robledo' accompanied by the date. It must have taken him ages, but it was something he was determined to do. So long as they were written down, words came easily to George.

'I grew up in Fenham in a house with my mum, my dad and two brothers,' says Sheila Gray, now resident in North Yorkshire.

I didn't really like football, but my dad and my brothers were mad keen on it. To this day, I can probably only name a hand-ful of footballers and one of them is George Robledo, who my dad got to know a bit when he was playing for Newcastle United. The reason I remember George Robledo so clearly is because he wrote to us at our house from Chile where he'd gone to play. Even I know that's not the kind of thing most footballers do. What's more, my dad wrote back! My dad never used to write to people, but he wrote to George Robledo.

'I'd first met George all those years before when I was a lad look-ing for autographs outside Oakwell,' says Barnsley supporter Don Wearmouth.

> I liked all the players, but he was special. He became a mate – as much as someone like that, a proper football star, can be your mate. When George went to Newcastle he would write to me, and I'd occasionally send him copies of the *Green 'Un* so he knew what was going on locally. When he went to America with Newcastle United in 1949, he sent me all the match programmes and lots of books about sport, as well as postcards from places where they'd been. The sound those parcels made when they came through the letterbox onto the floor – wumpf! When he went to Chile, it was the same thing. In fact, he wrote very quickly after he'd got there. 'Here's our address where you can contact me' and what have you. Can you imagine that! And it wasn't just me, clearly, because I know now that a lot of other people used to write to him, and he'd always write back to them. To receive mail from someone like him, from the other side of the world, when you're a teenager living in Barnsley… well, I can't tell you how much that meant to me.

There would, however, be a slight sting in the tail for the teenage Wearmouth – not, it should be said, through any fault of George's.

'When I was eighteen, I went off to do my National Service in the RAF,' adds Wearmouth.

> I was based over in Driffield on the other side of Yorkshire, but on

weekends I used to come home to Barnsley. One time I was back and my mother, almost as an aside, said, 'Oh, you know all those old books and programmes? Well I've let a little lad up the street have them as he collects things like that. He were thrilled to bits.' And I thought, 'I bet he flipping was!' What could I do? I couldn't really go up there and ask for them back. Anyway, years later, after my mum and dad died, we were clearing out the house when I came across all the old postcards and letters that George had sent, including the ones from Chile. I'd presumed she'd given them away too, but there they were, hidden in a drawer. When I got to meet Elizabeth Robledo a few years ago, I decided it made more sense for her to have them. You know, as something to remember her dad by. But I did keep one signed photograph and one of his old postcards from Chile back for myself, just for keepsakes. He meant such a lot to me that I felt I owed that to myself.

11

LOVE

*'She was so extraordinarily beautiful that I nearly laughed
out loud ... She was unquestionably gorgeous.'*
– RICHARD BURTON, ON FIRST ENCOUNTERING
ELIZABETH TAYLOR

On 31 May 1953, a fortnight after arriving in Chile, George made his Colo-Colo debut in front of around 40,000 people at the Estadio Nacional in Santiago, scoring twice in the 4–0 thrashing of mid-table Ferrobadminton. Six weeks later, he won a fourth international cap, albeit his first in a little over three years, as Chile narrowly lost 2–1 to Spain in a friendly inside the same venue. Two weeks on, George snatched a late winner for 'La Roja' as Peru were beaten 2–1 in Lima in the first ever Copa del Pacífico match between the two countries. (Chile and Peru have continued to play one another ad hoc over the years in this neighbourly competition for two, which has zilch to do with the club tournament of the same name.) On 15 November he scored not one, not two, not three, not four but five times in the 8–3 demolition of Magallanes, a result that saw Colo-Colo crowned champions of the Primera División for the sixth time in the club's history. All told, George would finish the 1953 season (which ran from May to December) on twenty-six league goals, more than any other player in the top flight of Chilean football, despite missing the opening weeks of the campaign while relocating from England to South America.

Not bad, as debut seasons go. Not bad at all.

For George, however, the defining moment of 1953 had nothing to do with silverware or goals or headlines or victory parades. A few weeks after making his Colo-Colo debut, George and his teammates had travelled to Viña del Mar on the Pacific coast to face Everton, the reigning Primera División champions christened after the English club of the same name (who themselves had toured South America in 1909). While tucking into his lunch at the city's plush Hotel Alcazar, George was approached by an attractive dark-haired woman flashing a smile seemingly as wide as Chile is long. Gladys Nissim, for that was her name, just wanted to welcome George to her homeland and wish him all the best in his new surroundings, having broken away from her own lunch with friends to say as much. The exchange was brief, but some kind of connection seems to have been made.

Months later, with Colo-Colo having been crowned as the new Primera División champions, Gladys took it upon herself to invite the club's directors, along with the Robledo brothers, to her residence for dinner. As up front, if borderline deranged, as this may at first sound, it should be said that Gladys worked as an executive secretary at the American embassy in Santiago. Organising functions and making people feel at home were, in other words, her forte. The dinner, held on Tuesday 8 December, was a roaring success, with food and wine and music and dancing. Towards the end of the evening, George and Gladys found themselves dancing together. One by one, everybody else melted away until only Gladys and George were left, still dancing.

'And they were never apart again,' says Elizabeth Robledo, their daughter.

By the time the couple came to be married in September 1959, Colo-Colo had won another Primera División title in 1956, having also finished runners-up in 1954, 1955 and 1958. Given the more traditional, conservative attitudes surrounding relationships and marriage that were prevalent, why wait so long to tie the knot? In short, that's a question which can be answered in two words – Elsie Robledo.

Ever since Inés Suárez, the Spanish conquistadora, travelled to Chile in the sixteenth century, becoming a contemporary role model to those at risk of persecution or mistreatment, so the influence of women in Chilean society has far outweighed that of just about every other South American country. The times, relatively speaking, may have been more traditional and conservative, but that didn't prevent women in Chile from becoming doctors, judges, politicians, economists or, in the case of schoolteacher and poet Gabriela Mistral, a Nobel Prize winner (for literature in 1945). Chile was progressive, a place where sisters had been doing it for themselves for years, and it was that kind of progression which had opened doors for people like Gladys Nissim, working in exciting, sometimes high-powered positions.

None of which cut the slightest bit of ice with Ma Robledo.

'With Grandma Elsie around, it was tough for them,' says Elizabeth Robledo.

She didn't want anyone for her sons. Mum and Dad wanted to get married, but they couldn't. She made it hard for them by not being very welcoming. In some ways, I get that. She had looked after her three boys for so long. She'd protected them since she was a young mother, and they had been through so much together as a family. They say Chilean mothers never really let go of their sons, and Elsie was very much like that, even though she was from England. That part of her was so, so Chilean.

Be that as it may, there might have been another reason why Elsie struggled to accept Gladys.

'At the time when my mum and dad met, she was a widow,' adds Elizabeth.

When Mum first went to work at the American embassy, she had been married to a carabinero, a policeman, and he'd died in an aeroplane accident in Ecuador. He had gone to the United States on some kind of mission, and when they were on their way back to Chile the aeroplane went down in the middle of the Ecuadorean jungle and they vanished. They never found them. Everybody knew she was a widow – it wasn't the kind of thing she kept secret – but obviously she was still young and needed to rebuild her life afterwards. I don't know whether that had anything to do with the way Grandma Elsie was. I just think she was reluctant to accept any woman for her sons.

• • •

'For the love of money is the root of all evil: which while some coveted after, they have erred from the faith, and pierced themselves through with many sorrows.' So goes 1 Timothy 6:10 of the King James' Bible published in 1611, some 350 years before Johnny Haynes became the first footballer in the English game to earn £100 per week following the abolition of the maximum wage. Prior to 1961, when players were on no more than £20 per week, money still had the power to destroy a dressing room. Once word got round that someone was on better readies than his teammates, unity and camaraderie could go out of the window faster than it takes a penalty kick to reach the back of a net.

When George Robledo signed for Colo-Colo, there was no maximum wage in Chile. Football players were, on paper, free to pocket whatever they were being offered financially. In reality, there really wasn't that much money in the game beyond the Andes, which hadn't long turned professional. Initially, the league consisted of just eight clubs – all based in or around Santiago – simply because they were the only ones with the pulling power to make a go of it. In the days before television and sponsorship deals, football club income streams relied almost entirely on attendances. The bigger your crowds, the more you could afford to pay in wages. By 1953, the Primera División had expanded to fourteen clubs with the addition of provincial sides such as Everton, yet still the average attendance across the league throughout the season remained just below 9,000. Consequently, player wages had to remain moderate, even at clubs such as Colo-Colo which traditionally drew the bigger crowds.

With that in mind, it's easy to see how George's arrival might have caused resentment, not only within the wider game in Chile but inside his own dressing room. The relative success of 'La Roja' at the 1950 World Cup led to a number of other high-profile overseas players being signed by Chilean clubs, including the Argentine stars José Manuel Moreno and Roberto Coll who joined Universidad Católica and Palestino respectively. Some imports met with success, others less so. With his handsome salary, win or draw bonuses and spacious club house – not to mention that hefty £4,000 signing-on fee – George could potentially have become a divisive figure, especially if things hadn't gone according to plan on the field. As it was, he hit the ground running, scoring and creating goals seemingly on repeat.

But there was more to it than that. Three years previously, George had been Chile's talisman at the World Cup in Brazil. He'd galvanised their young side, encouraging and cajoling them through an endearing combination of hand gestures and pidgin Spanish. He'd scored the opening goal in their 5–2 thrashing of the US. He'd hit an upright against England. He'd become 'Jorge', the unassuming star of the dressing room who had helped transform 'La Roja' from also-rans into competitors. And his teammates loved him for it. 'Hasta luego, muchachos. Ya estaré en Chile con ustedes', George had pledged at Rio's Galeão Airport before returning to England – 'See you later, boys. I will be back in Chile with you.' True to his word, here he was. Now the rest of the country was seeing first-hand what only a privileged few had witnessed in Brazil.

Cue the dawning of 'Robledo Mania'.

It helped, of course, that football was far less tribal in the 1950s than it is today. People supported their favourite clubs, of course they did, but they also tended to be followers of the game in general. In the same way that Fulham fans used to alternate between Craven Cottage in west London one week and neighbouring Stamford Bridge, home of Chelsea, the next, so supporters of, say, Audax Italiano might venture out to watch another team from the Santiago area in action. With his reputation as a star of the 1950 World Cup preceding him, George brought glamour to the domestic game. People wanted to see 'Jorge' play, regardless of where their club loyalties lay, and attendances at Colo-Colo matches both home and away soared accordingly. They also warmed to his character and personality. George's reputation for being 'a gentleman on the field, a gentleman off the field', as Chileans often described him, chimed with the familiar national traits of being reserved, respectful and modest, as well as friendly and laid back. He wasn't hot-headed. He didn't cheat. He wasn't prone to temper tantrums. He wasn't dirty. He didn't kick the ball away or pull other players' shirts when things went against him. He didn't argue with referees. He just played the game his way, to great effect.

In the sepia days before social media and merchandising, fan worship of footballers could manifest itself in all sorts of unusual, quirky and somewhat endearing ways, as George and indeed Ted would discover after arriving in Santiago. One hospital reported a marked increase in the number of newborns called 'Jorge'. A popular city centre bar changed its name to 'Robledos' for a week in honour of George's goalscoring debut against Ferrobadminton. Unsolicited deliveries to the family home of bread, cakes, cigarettes, wine, seafood and, rather touchingly, English tea became a daily occurrence.

One newly formed amateur football club in Santiago chose to call itself 'Robledo Hermanos' ('Robledo Brothers') while also adopting the black and white of Newcastle United for its colours. Considering how self-effacing he was, it's a wonder George didn't find the attention horribly overwhelming. Instead, he chose to roll with it in his own retiring way. 'Look, I'm not a star,' he told one newspaper reporter as the 1953 season unfolded. 'I'm just one more player who is doing his best to make everyone else shine.'

'I don't think it was ever something that he found disturbing,' says Elizabeth Robledo.

He dealt with everyone in his own natural way, which was to be polite and friendly to them. There's a photograph taken when he first arrived at the airport with my Uncle Ted and they are surrounded by I don't know how many people trying to touch him and shake his hand. Even then, if you look at his face, he is smiling. That's how he was, even though it could sometimes get a little crazy. And that never changed, even after he'd retired from playing. The attention never went away, but he always had time for everyone. Every Christmas, he would go out and give the guys who emptied the trash whole chickens and champagne or wine and cakes. The gardener, the plumber, they'd always get something. He was so adored, but little things like that made people adore him even more. Whenever we went out, every single door would open for him. He got triple VIP treatment everywhere without even requesting it. It would always be 'Mr Robledo, here, please join us!' or 'Mr Robledo, Mr Robledo, be our guest!' That's how I grew up, with a father who was a true idol to so many people but who always managed to remain so humble.

For George, 1953 was almost like watching a fast-motion film of a flower blossoming. Everything happened so quickly, just about all of it good – the goals, the assists, the public adulation, winning the league title, feeling the love from his own teammates not to mention the wider game in Chile, meeting Gladys, waking up in the mornings to the sight of the towering Andes in their majestic glory, satisfying that long-held desire of his to explore new horizons and cultures. Complaints? You had to be joking.

Well, except one. In the days and weeks after Manuel Bianchi visited Fenham conveying details of the offer to go to Chile, George had spent time weighing up the pluses and minuses that a move to the other side of the world might entail. Ultimately, the pluses won out, but if there was one nagging doubt in the back of his mind, it went something along these lines: 'Am I too young to be doing this?'

For all Newcastle United's on-field struggles, the 1952–53 season had seen George at the peak of his powers. He was twenty-six years old, the First Division's top scorer the previous season, still averaging not far short of a goal every game. Physically, he was in tip-top condition, with (injuries allowing) at least another couple of years ahead of him playing alongside or against the best players in the world. Which is what George believed Stanley Matthews, Tom Finney, Jackie Milburn, Bobby Mitchell, Stan Mortensen, Joe Harvey, Nat Lofthouse and their like were. Could the Primera División compete with that? Would it satisfy his competitive juices?

Would his Colo-Colo teammates be on the same wavelength as him or more akin to what you might find in the Second or Third Divisions in England and Wales? George had his suspicions, based on what he'd seen of the Chilean team at the 1950 World Cup – fit, keen, young, eager, yet tactically naive and limited in ability when held up against the best of British. Alas, those were questions which could only really be answered once he was there, by which time it would be too late.

Within the opening quarter of an hour of his Colo-Colo debut against Ferrobadminton, George knew exactly where he stood. And it wasn't good news. As intense, physically demanding and, yes, enjoyable as the experience was, the skill levels around him weren't anything like those found at St James' Park, Old Trafford or any of the citadels of the Football League. At first George thought it might be the inferior quality of the opposition or perhaps his teammates fathoming how best to accommodate him in their ranks. But as the weeks went by, so he came to realise that's just the way it was in the Primera División. 'Robledo's typically English style did not fully harmonise with the rest of the side in the first half, but after the interval he achieved better understanding with the rest of the forwards and the line functioned smoothly,' wrote one reporter covering the Ferrobadminton match. Truth be told, it was more a case of George deliberately 'playing down' in order for him to function alongside those around him.

Instead of moaning, sulking or slapping in a transfer request, George resolved to make the best of the situation. He would try his darnedest to score and create as many goals as he could, while also looking to improve the skill sets of his teammates, educating,

encouraging and, in effect, coaching them to become better players. Much as he'd done while at Barnsley, George would often stay
behind after training to work with younger players, including Colo-
Colo's goalkeepers. 'Forwards and goalkeepers, and defenders for
that matter, can learn a lot from each other,' he once said. 'We're
trying to score goals and they're trying to stop us. It helps to know
your enemy!'

'The arrival of the Robledo brothers saw strategies and forms
of training being incorporated into the Chilean game that were
common in England but had, up until then, been ignored in this
part of the world,' says Néstor Flores.

In Chile, we were very distant from Europe. The immediacy of
today, with its live news and social media, did not exist. Therefore, everything the Robledo brothers brought to Chile, even the
frequency that players trained, was different and innovative. For
example, they imported new methods of heading the ball, using
headers offensively and as a way of passing the ball, which had
never been done here before. Players also started passing the ball
over distances of thirty or forty metres which, again, was something no one had previously attempted on Chilean fields. The
way they did things benefitted not only Colo-Colo, but also the
development of the Chilean national team and soccer at all levels.

Nevertheless, as 1953 made way for 1954, so the nagging doubt started to find a voice. He'd scored twenty-six league goals in his first
season in Chilean football. The following year George notched another twenty-five as Colo-Colo finished runners-up to Universidad

Católica, missing out on the title by one point. He still had plenty to give, in other words, even allowing for the inferior standard of the Primera División. 'Did I leave England too early?' he found himself wondering – not to the extent that it kept him awake at night but more out of curiosity. Paradoxically, George's age (twenty-eight as of April 1954) made him one of the grand old men of the Primera División where few of the more talented outfield players seemed to last much beyond twenty-five, due largely to a combination of the pitches (hard), the weather (humid) and the style of play (abrasive). It was, George couldn't help but think, almost as if he was caught between two contrasting football worlds.

Needless to say, it wasn't long before rumours of George's supposed transience reached boardrooms 8,000 miles away in the UK. Not that the man himself was behind such gossip – that wasn't George's style. Maybe, just maybe, a journalist received a tip-off or word slipped out of some mail bound for England. Whatever the source, as 1954 progressed, so the number of enquiries heading Colo-Colo's way regarding George's reputed availability steadily increased, fanned by Chile's failure to qualify for the World Cup finals in Switzerland that year. Tottenham Hotspur were interested, as were Arsenal, as were Cardiff City. Newcastle United, almost inevitably, threw their hat in the ring. Lincoln City of the Second Division, where George had made one solitary appearance during the Wartime League, made a firm offer via cable, still the standard way of transmitting messages overseas. 'If they want to make the signing, then they may have to take both brothers or none at all,' commented the *Daily Mirror* on the growing speculation involving, so the newspaper reckoned, as many as eight British clubs. 'The Robledos have always kept together in their varied football careers.'

On the final day of November, with the race for the 1954 Primera División title coming nicely to the boil, Colo-Colo at last went public with some kind of response. 'We are not selling the Robledo brothers at any price,' insisted Antonio Labán, the club's president. 'They are happy to stay here, and we are happy to have them.' Still, the speculation refused to go away. Two days before Christmas, the *Daily Mirror* muddied the waters further by reporting that George 'and his brother Ted would return to England if the Colo-Colo club, for whom they play, gave its approval'. However, it transpired that the source of the story in Chile and the reporter who wrote it up in London had lost something in translation, and the sentence should have read, 'If the Colo-Colo club, for whom they play, don't want them.' An entirely different meaning, in other words. Newspapers occasionally get stuff wrong – shocker – even back in 1954.

So, for the second time in less than two years, George found himself weighing up the pros and cons of whether to stay put or join another team in another country. This time, he chose to stay where he was, much to the disappointment of the many clubs hoping to lure him back to the UK. Even accounting for the skill gap between the upper echelons of the Football League and the Primera División, there were just too many reasons for George to remain in Chile. He was, after all, doing well for both club and country, as was Ted, who'd made his international debut that February in an otherwise forgettable 4–0 defeat to Paraguay (the first leg of a World Cup qualifier which Chile ultimately lost 7–1 on aggregate, with George scoring their consolation). The fan worship was fervent but bearable. The lifestyle was terrific. The wages were better than anything George could ever hope to command in the UK. He didn't have an agent in his ear, as might be the case today, angling for a lucrative transfer and any resulting commission. He was in love with a beautiful woman working in a sought-after job, the kind she'd be unlikely to secure in the UK. More to the point, she was also in love with him. Walter had landed a position as head chemist with the Anaconda Copper Company, an American firm with mines in Chile. Elsie, God only knows, could be overbearing, but by and large she was happy because her sons were happy. Why put all that at risk for another spell in the English First Division, which could conceivably last no more than a single season, the typical length of a contract in the Football League?

Plus, he still had some exploring to do.

In the Atacama Desert, the average daytime temperature points towards thirty degrees Celsius, falling to two degrees Celsius at night. It hardly ever rains, meaning it's impossible for anything to grow (evidence suggests some parts of the Atacama received no rainfall at all between 1570 and 1971). The oldest desert in the world, it may just be. The driest desert in the world, it most definitely is. When scientists and researchers want to replicate the look and feel of Mars, they head for the Atacama Desert in the far north of Chile. When moviemakers want to create the look and feel of Mars, they too head for the Atacama Desert.

It was here, in the desert outpost of Oficina Alianza, that George was born in April 1926. And it was here, in April 1955, where George returned, setting eyes for the first time as an adult on the place 'where not a single blade of grass can grow in the nitrate soil', as Che Guevara wrote of the Atacama in his travel memoirs.

In its bustling, gnarled, wild, menacing heyday, Oficina Alianza was one of more than 200 settlements (or 'company towns', as they became known) fanned out across the Atacama and built on the profits of sodium nitrate, otherwise known in Chile as saltpetre. Over the nine decades spanning the 1870s to the 1950s, thousands of people came to the Atacama to extract nitrate from the ground for export to Europe and North America, where it was used mainly in the production of gunpowder or as fertiliser. These settlements were financed largely by private companies based in the UK who, in turn, paid high export taxes to the Chilean government, generating great wealth for some built on the toil of others. The hours were long, the conditions poor and the pay quite literally non-existent, with employees receiving tokens rather than money for their labour (exchangeable for goods at the local general store), in effect tethering them indeterminately to the Atacama and the sodium nitrate economy. There were schools, though in reality the children of employees received little or no formal education, busy as they were working alongside their fathers in the mines to help make ends meet.

Think Mos Eisley Spaceport in Star Wars, only without the spaceships (or the cantina). Welcome to Oficina Alianza.

By the time George, accompanied by Ted, returned in 1955, Oficina Alianza had long since been abandoned to the desert, a victim – along with virtually every other saltpetre settlement on the Atacama – of the development of artificial sodium nitrate during the 1920s, compounded by the Great Depression in the 1930s. Some company towns struggled on, underpinned by private investment and government help from within Chile, only to throw in the towel during the 1950s. Oficina Alianza wasn't one of them. When the British owners upped sticks and left in 1932, so too did the employees, joining the exodus of men and their families heading to central and southern Chile from the Atacama in search of work. Twenty-three years on, much of the infrastructure remained intact despite the effects of weathering and the attention of looters. The shell of the hospital where George and Ted had both been born was still there. The shell of the school was still there. The grid pattern of the roads was still there, even if the rudimentary homes which once lined them were gone. The office where Arístides, their father, had worked as the mining company's accountant was still there.

Twenty-three years, in the grand scheme of things, isn't long. And yet so much had changed. Oficina Alianza, a hive of activity at the time of their birth, lay in ruins. Arístides, the ghost in their lives, was dead. They'd become local heroes in Barnsley and the Dearne Valley, local heroes in north-east England, and national heroes in Chile. There wasn't a football team on Earth that wouldn't have wanted George in its starting XI. Returning to Oficina Alianza was a sobering experience for both men, but it also served as a salutary reminder of just how far they had come.

Today, Oficina Alianza – or at least what is left of it – stands on private land, out of bounds to the public. All that remained in 1955, bar the odd lump of concrete embedded in the ground, has now vanished completely. In September 2023, Elizabeth Robledo, never backwards in coming forwards regarding her father's legacy, asked if she could visit the site. Permission granted, she spent a few hours exploring the area in the company of local historian Patricio Díaz, who was able to point out where certain key buildings once stood, including the hospital.

'People are right when they say it looks like the Moon or Mars,' says Elizabeth.

When you're walking around, you do feel as if you're on another planet. To think my father and Uncle Ted came from there and went on to play at Wembley is almost crazy. There is no place on Earth that is more unlike Wembley than Oficina Alianza, so to make that journey is incredible. I know there's nothing to see anymore, but I still cried. Then, when I finally managed to stop, I cried some more. But I'm so glad I went. There might be nothing to see but, when you're there, you can feel something. You can really feel something

12

IN MY LIFE

'Oh, to be in England / Now that April's there'
– ROBERT BROWNING

'It's a place defined by absence, or at least extreme sparseness,' said travel writer Maggie Shipstead after visiting the Atacama Desert on assignment for the *New York Times*. 'Of water, of life. Whatever is determined enough to exist there – people, plants, animals, even microbes – must be hardy, resilient and well adapted.'

You can take the boy out of the Atacama, but you can't take the Atacama out of the boy. Hardy, resilient, well adapted – George needed all those qualities to survive and thrive in the often brutal surroundings of the Football League, not to mention the Primera División where, come 1955 and aged twenty-nine, time wasn't necessarily on his side. For now, at least, he was still managing to hit the right notes despite an escalating nicotine habit that Colo-Colo had initially tried to curb, insisting on his arrival from Newcastle that George smoke no more than five cigarettes a day to help his body function in the humid conditions. It was a rule he struggled and ultimately failed to stick to, one Colo-Colo had no real way of enforcing during his downtime away from the club. George could still make goals, score goals and stay on the move in much the same way as he had in his physical prime with Barnsley and Newcastle United. The old strength, vision and awareness prevailed, even if the speed wasn't quite what it once was. Somehow, despite a habit of between twenty to thirty cigarettes a day, George remained a force to be reckoned with.

'At that time Colo-Colo used to play all their home games in the Estadio Nacional, and as a boy I would always sit in the same place with my father and sometimes his father, my grandfather,' says Lucas Moreno, now resident in Granada, Spain.

In those days George, or 'Jorge', was the star of the team. He created a lot of goals for the other players, but he scored a lot of goals too. I always remember one in a game against Magallanes, a team from just outside Santiago. The ball was loose inside the penalty area, and it came to him no more than five or six yards out. All he had to do was roll the ball into the goal to score, but instead he hit it with such force that you thought the net was going to burst. You could hear the sound of boot on ball all around the ground – boom! A lot of his goals were from close in like that, sometimes with his feet – his left foot was as strong as his right – and sometimes with his head. I believe you have a word in Great Britain for that type of player – poacher. I think in Chile, and Spain, it would probably translate as something like 'rabbit-catcher'. It's the same thing though – a player who gets into great positions to score what seem like easy goals, but there's an art to making them look that easy.

All told, George made fifty-five league appearances over the course of the 1953 and 1954 seasons combined, chalking up fifty-one goals in the process. The 1955 campaign saw him come out of the blocks in equally devastating fashion, scoring eight times in Colo-Colo's opening seven fixtures, including a hat-trick in the 6–1 thrashing of Universidad Católica.

During late February and March, George was the jewel in the free-scoring 'La Roja' side that finished runners-up in the South American Championship staged entirely in Santiago, scoring three goals and creating several more throughout the tournament (besides beating Ecuador 7–1, Peru 5–4 and Paraguay 5–0, Chile also drew 2–2 against Uruguay before narrowly losing 1–0 to competition winners Argentina). Later that year, he took to the field in Rio de Janeiro as Chile did the unthinkable by drawing 1–1 in a friendly with glorious, flamboyant, all-singing, all-dancing Brazil. George's steady supply of goals and star turns ensured that the equally steady supply of bread, cakes, cigarettes, wine, seafood, tea and other assorted goodies to the Robledos' door continued, albeit perhaps not in the same quantities as two years previously. The steady supply of goals and star turns also meant transfer speculation linking George to any number of British clubs continued unabated.

In late October, with Colo-Colo some way off the pace in the Primera División title race, club president Antonio Labán met with both George and Ted in a Santiago restaurant for dinner and an informal chat, which he hoped might provide him with the answer to a question. Of course he was happy the Robledos had come to play for Colo-Colo, Labán said. Of course he wanted them to stay at the club. But did *they* want to stay? On this occasion Ted, only too aware of his role as a pawn in a much wider game, let George do the talking. Yes, he was happy to stay, George replied. There were probably more reasons to stay than to go, he added. But he was also torn. Labán told him not to worry – no matter what the future held, 'Jorge' was assured his place as a Colo-Colo hero. If he wanted to leave, then that was OK with him. 'But the terms have to be good,' Labán insisted. If another club wanted to sign George, they would have to pay handsomely for his signature, in other words.

Three weeks later, Labán received a letter postmarked England, which had nonetheless been translated into Spanish. The correspondence was from Joe Richards, chairman of Barnsley Football Club, and he was interested in knowing whether George Robledo was for sale. Labán cabled Richards straightaway – yes, 'Jorge' was available to buy with, inevitably, 'Eduardo' in tow. The final decision, though, would be down to George himself, with a transfer fee in the region of £15,000 being acceptable to Colo-Colo. This amount, even by 1955 standards, was a colossal sum for a club such as Barnsley, especially considering George's age (five months shy of turning thirty). Even so, Richards told Labán he was serious about doing a deal and would be approaching George in the coming days to gauge his feelings.

Of all the offers that came George's way throughout 1954 and 1955 to return to the UK, the one from Barnsley unquestionably tugged at his heartstrings the most. It didn't matter that the wages on offer paled in comparison to what he was earning at Colo-Colo. It didn't matter that Barnsley were, by that time, a struggling Second Division side. It didn't matter that the Pennines and not the Andes would've greeted him in the mornings. None of that mattered because Barnsley and its surroundings were the nearest thing he'd ever had in his life to a home. It was Yorkshire that had taken him and his family in when circumstances started working against them in the Atacama Desert of the 1930s. It was where he'd spent his formative years. The roots of so much of what was good in his adult life stemmed from Barnsley and the Dearne Valley. It was a place that had always called to him. Now, thanks to Richards, he'd been given the opportunity to answer that call.

As Christmas presents go, George's return to Oakwell would've been up there with the best of them, as far as Barnsley fans of all ages were concerned. 'First we must come to terms with Colo-Colo, and then the brothers,' Richards declared on 1 December 1955 to a group of journalists who'd got wind of the story. 'Perhaps nothing will be done this side of Christmas, but the issue is still alive.' Barnsley's chairman was confident he could find the money but wanted some kind of assurance from George before setting the financial wheels in motion. With Colo-Colo reiterating that £15,000 would be enough to do a deal, all heads duly turned in George's direction for an answer either way.

Never one to be rushed, unless on a football field, George thought long and hard. Once he'd done that, he thought long and hard some more, right the way through the Christmas period into the new year.

The answer, when it finally came, wasn't what Barnsley fans wanted to hear. George would be staying in Chile with Colo-Colo.

Once again, having weighed everything up, there were just too many reasons to stay put in South America, not least of all the love of a good woman who George increasingly believed may just be *the* one. If moving back to Britain risked jeopardising his relationship with Gladys in any way, then he wasn't prepared to do it. Thanks but no thanks, Mr Richards.

And with that, so the drawbridge went up between George and the UK. It wasn't that the enquiries ceased, more that they never got past first base. He was fine where he was, so there really wasn't much to discuss. As far as anyone is aware, George never again came remotely close to moving away from Chile, continuing to live there until the day he died. Not that he ever forgot Britain. On the contrary, in fact.

'Dad had this big collection of vinyl records which he would listen to,' says Elizabeth Robledo.

A lot of them featured the music of British regimental marching bands playing the kind of music they have on Trooping the Colour – you know, the ceremonial event that takes place in London every year to mark what, then, was always the Queen's birthday. Dad used to get up for it early in the morning in Chile so he could watch it on television. He could get emotional very easily, and while he listened to those records, I could see him crying. When the FA Cup final came around at the end of April or in early May, again he would get up early to watch it on television and quite often become emotional. He also had a very British sense of humour. We used to watch the *Benny Hill Show* in Chile when it was shown on television and we would laugh and laugh. For Dad, England and Britain never went away. It was always in his heart. I think there's a part of him that would have gone back to live there, even though he never actually came right out and said so. He was happy in Chile, definitely, but a bit of him never really left England.

Over time, slightly more contemporary records would start to appear alongside George's collection of marching band music, including albums by the Beatles. In the 1960s, at the very height of 'Beatlemania', everyone from Southport to Santiago seemed to be in love with the four Liverpudlians, often for their looks, sense of humour, accents and haircuts as much as the music itself. For George, though, there was something else about them. Part of the attraction was that they were from Liverpool, the city that had been his gateway from the Atacama to a more fulfilling life in the UK. But most of all, the Beatles reminded him of Britain, of people and things that had gone before, to paraphrase the group's 1965 song 'In My Life'. Years later, Arthur Ellis, who'd refereed the Newcastle versus Arsenal FA Cup final of 1952, recalled visiting George and Gladys at their home in Chile and being tickled by his choice of music while the trio enjoyed lunch. 'I don't know why but I was expecting something classical or maybe a bit of Spanish guitar, but instead he put on a record by the Beatles,' said Ellis, who died in 1999. 'Looking back, I don't know why I expected anything else, but at the time I remember thinking how funny it seemed going all the way to Chile and hearing the Beatles, a group that until then I'd always thought of as being very British.'

The longer a person lives somewhere, the more they tend to become attached to it. As much as George was in love with Gladys and as much as he occasionally yearned for Britain, by 1956 he'd also developed a deep affection for Chile and Santiago in particular. In the same way as John Lennon had been moved to write about Liverpool's urban environment in his original drafts of 'In My Life' (including St Columba's Church, Penny Lane and the Abbey

Cinema, before switching course to make the song more universally palatable), so George became drawn to the people and the places of his adopted home city: the Avenida O'Higgins with its pristine flower beds and statues of presidents, scholars and generals; the relative peace and tranquillity of the Plaza de Armas, Santiago's main square; and the hustle and bustle of the Estadio Nacional on match days. Over time, strangers became acquaintances. Some of those acquaintances went on to become good friends, among them Luis Ayala, the formidable Chilean tennis player and two-time French Open runner-up (in 1958 and 1960), with whose family George, Gladys and Elizabeth would often holiday in the years to come.

To his amazement, George also came to realise that his privileged position as one of the most recognisable faces in Chile was in fact largely down to the kindness of complete strangers. During the 1950s, football clubs in many parts of the world would often rely on the generosity of supporters to help keep their finances ticking over. If, for example, a manager wanted to buy a new player, then it wasn't unusual for a supporters' group to raise at least some of the required capital, which would in turn be donated to the board of directors. Sometimes the money raised exceeded the sums contributed by directors, leading to all sorts of animosity and resentment (no matter how much supporters helped swell the coffers, they were rarely, if ever, given a say in how their favourite clubs were run).

Two or three years after arriving in Chile, George was astonished to learn that his and Ted's transfer from Newcastle United had in part been funded by an increase in the club membership fees paid every month by Colo-Colo supporters. Rather than being angry, George felt flattered, bordering on humbled. In the cold light of day, his South American adventure had only been made possible through the benevolence of thousands of supporters, who, at the start of 1953, hadn't even seen him kick a ball. If he'd ever needed confirmation about the virtues of moving to Chile and staying there, that was it.

And then, bless them, there were the *Barrabases*.

Shoot. Striker. Roy of the Rovers. Match! Charles Buchan's Football Monthly. Goal. Tiger. Football Handbook. Scorcher. The list of football magazines and comics from the pre-digital age aimed at children goes on and on (and those are just some of the British titles). History has it that *Charles Buchan's Football Monthly*, carrying analysis from current and former professionals alongside full-page pictures of players, predated the lot of them, published, as it was, for the first time in 1951. Even so, the honour of being the first sports comic in the world goes, supposedly, to *Barrabases*, created by the Chilean cartoonist Guido Vallejos. Officially launched in 1954, it featured the eponymous children's football team (named after the biblical character Barabbas) from the fictional city of Villa Feliz. The underlying message in the stories was always the same – never give up, always display great sportsmanship and no matter what the result, you'll be a winner. *Barrabases* sold well from the get-go and continued doing so for the next three decades, with Vallejos (who died in 2016) overseeing special one-off commemorative editions well into the twenty-first century, including to mark Chile's participation in the 2010 World Cup.

In 1955, *Barrabases* ran a competition asking readers to name their favourite football player. Over 10,000 people responded, and of that number, one name polled more votes than all the others put together – Jorge Robledo. The trophy he received from the magazine would come to mean as much to him as his FA Cup winner's medals and all the plaudits he'd received for topping the goalscoring charts once in England (1951–52) and twice in Chile (1953 and 1954). Indeed, it remains in the family to this day, a reminder of the high esteem in which thousands of young Chileans held George during the 1950s.

'Dad was very good with children,' says Elizabeth Robledo.

Although he was a man of few words, he would always have the right ones for them – words of advice, words of encouragement, words that spoke to them on their level. He was never, ever patronising. The kids used to show him so much respect, and he would show them respect in return. He was so proud of that trophy because of what it stood for – young people throughout the country had taken the time to go out and chose him as their favourite player. The inscription on it says, 'From the kids of *Barrabases* to Jorge Robledo.' For a man who always chose his words carefully, that said it all. To him, winning that trophy was up there with anything he achieved in his entire career.

John Lennon was twenty-four years old when he wrote 'In My Life'. George Robledo was twenty-nine years old when he decided his future lay not in England but in Chile.

No matter how much of a rock 'n' roller or superstar footballer you are, you're never too young to be reflective.

• • •

Boxers, so they say, are the first to know when the time is right to quit and the last to admit it. Ditto footballers. No matter how many times an ageing defender gets beaten for pace by a younger attacker or a goalkeeper concedes the sort of goal they once would've saved in their sleep, the urge to keep on playing, to rage against the dying of the light, remains. Until, finally, reality bites in the form of injury, abuse from a section of supporters or that last professional contract which fails to materialise.

For George, there never were any injuries. There was certainly never any abuse. As long as he kept scoring, Colo-Colo seemed happy to give him a new contract. And yet, with every passing season, so the statistics began to speak for themselves. Forwards were, and always will be, judged on the number of goals they score. Forget about all the chasing, harrying and unseen legwork carried out over ninety minutes – it's the goals-scored tally that ultimately counts. Even inside-forwards like George, who were expected to do much of the heavy lifting for the benefit of others around them, stood or fell by how many times they found the back of the net.

Having started the 1955 Primera División season with eight goals in seven matches, George went on to score a further eleven over the course of the campaign as Colo-Colo finished runners-up to Palestino. Nineteen goals to show from thirty-one appearances – a far from terrible return yet still something of a disappointment by his own high standards. The following season, George weighed in with twelve goals from twenty-five appearances as 'Los Albos' ('the white ones', as Colo-Colo are nicknamed) won the league title for the second time since his arrival from Newcastle, with one perfor-mance in particular against Magallanes (when George scored twice in a 3–2 home win in front of over 40,000 spectators) regarded by many supporters as among his finest in a Colo-Colo shirt.

But then came 1957, the year Colo-Colo finished eighth in the table, tantamount to disastrous for a club of their pedigree. The year George scored just twice in seventeen appearances at club level, tantamount to disastrous for a player of his stature. The year George made his thirty-first and final appearance for Chile, losing 2–0 to Argentina in a World Cup qualifier on 13 October, the eighth consecutive match in which he'd failed to score for 'La Roja'. The year his age and that smoking habit finally started to catch up with him.

The following season, Colo-Colo regained their dignity by finishing runners-up in the Primera División to Santiago Wanderers, with George enjoying something of an Indian summer by appearing in twenty-four of their twenty-six fixtures. Of his ten goals that campaign, six arrived like buses during a three-game purple patch spanning late August and early September, including a hat-trick within the space of eighteen second-half minutes against Audax Italiano inside the Estadio Nacional. The wizardry was still there – on occasion. The dry periods were, however, becoming more frequent.

Needless to say, when negotiations surrounding a new contract came around, Colo-Colo declared that although they wanted to keep George, the pay rise being granted to other players would not be coming his way. George wasn't the kind of man who was easily riled, but that raised his hackles. In fact, it irked him so much he threatened not to play for the team during the closing weeks of the 1958 season. When Colo-Colo called his bluff, George stood his ground and made himself unavailable for the latter stages of the Copa Chile, the curtain call of the campaign. It was, he would insist, a 'matter of principle' and nothing to do with histrionics.

Nevertheless, Colo-Colo still went and won the trophy without him. Nobody is indispensable, as the old adage goes.

'There was stubbornness on both sides,' says Néstor Flores of the spat that failed to dent George's status as a Colo-Colo legend but which spelled the end of his time at the club after 154 appearances and ninety-six goals. With neither party prepared to budge, a parting of the ways became inevitable. No shots were fired – at least not in public – but that didn't change the fact that George felt let down. Worse still, as of January 1959, for the first time in his adult life, he was also technically unemployed.

By that time, Ted Robledo had long since departed Chile, having won his eighth and final international cap as far back as March 1955 before becoming surplus to requirements at Colo-Colo. Like his elder brother, he had also fallen in love. The marriage, to a flamenco dancer called Carmen Calé, was a troubled one, however, and in 1957 he decided to return to England to try his luck playing for Notts County, then in the Second Division of the Football League. Having criss-crossed the world seemingly joined at the hip in search of domestic contentment and sporting glory, the Robledos were no longer all for one and one for all. Soon Walter would also return to England, settling in London in his new role as head of exports for Thomas Bolton, another copper company, followed eventually by Elsie, who retreated to the Suffolk coastal town of Lowestoft. After living in each other's shoes for twenty-five years, George, Ted, Walter and Elsie would never again be together in the same country, let alone the same room.

Today, footballers with CVs bearing league titles, domestic cup triumphs and international caps would never have to work again for a living on retiring from the game (providing, of course, they'd been responsible with their earnings). In the late 1950s, that wasn't quite how the world turned. One minute you're entertaining forty or fifty thousand people, the next you're running a pub or driving a truck. Or, in Ted's case, working as an electrician for NASA, as in the National Aeronautics and Space Administration, which is where he ended up after Notts County said no siree to his fading talents off the back of just two games.

As for George, he had to settle for something a little more grounded. Fifty or so miles south of Santiago lies the city of Rancagua, home to the O'Higgins Football Club and, in the neighbouring hills, the Braden Copper Company, owners of what was once the largest underground copper mine in the world. It was here that George, along with Gladys, came in 1959 to take up new jobs – Gladys as executive secretary to the firm's boss and George as manager of industrial relations between Braden's top brass and its employees. If the position sounded dour and starchy, then it was anything but.

'Dad was in charge of all the sports and social events within the company,' says Elizabeth Robledo.

Any big celebration or event, he was the one who organised everything, from putting up the stands to sorting out the music. A lot of people worked for the Braden Company and a lot of them had children. So at Christmas, Dad was the person who made sure they all received presents. It was a big job and he had a lot of people working under him throughout the year, but it was something nice for him to do. And given who he was, it was a great piece of public relations by the company as well.

On 12 September 1959, almost six years after they'd first met, George and Gladys finally got married in a relatively small ceremony held at the mayor's residence in Rancagua. He wore a black suit, white shirt and a pastel-coloured tie, while she stole the show in an unconventional, slightly risqué, knee-length white dress. Elsie attended, a somewhat peripheral figure captured standing off to the sides in a couple of wedding photographs, as did the Everton forward René Meléndez, one of George's closest friends in Chile, along with the politician, industrialist and sports fanatic Patricio Mekis, who would later become Mayor of Rancagua.

An ex-firefighter educated at an English school in Santiago and in the US, Mekis also happened to be one of the founding fathers of the O'Higgins Football Club, formed in 1955 as an amalgamation of two local clubs (O'Higgins Braden and América de Rancagua) and admitted to the Primera División the following year. As president of O'Higgins from 1958 to 1965, Mekis and his board of directors set out to challenge the traditional hierarchy of Chilean club football, dominated by the likes of Colo-Colo and Universidad de Chile. In part, they did so by bringing in several star names who, despite being past their best, added experience and a certain pizzazz to the club. There was Jaime Ramírez, the Chilean forward brought back from Spain after a couple of successful seasons playing for Granada. There was Federico Vairo, the Argentine defensive war horse drafted in from River Plate (who, while working as a scout many years later back in Argentina, would unearth none other than Lionel Messi). There was George's friend René Meléndez whose eleven goals made him the club's top scorer during the 1960 campaign. And in defiance of his age (thirty-three) and that spiralling smoking habit, there was

George himself, who returned after almost a year out of the game to make a few cameo appearances as 1959 made way for 1960.

It wasn't, however, for his contributions on the field that George came to be best remembered by those connected to O'Higgins. After finally hanging up his playing boots for good, 'Jorge' was asked if he'd take charge of the club's under-14 ('infantil'), under-16 ('cadete') and under-18 ('juvenil') football teams. For the better part of the next twenty years, in conjunction with his day job at the copper company, George and his coaches oversaw the development of hundreds of young hopefuls from Rancagua and the surrounding O'Higgins district, many of whom went on to appear in the first team. In a 1999 poll, Vairo was chosen by supporters as the club's outstanding player of all time, but it's easy to see why Mekis once described George as their most important signing.

Ultimately, O'Higgins FC never quite managed to scale the heights of their more illustrious rivals from up the road in Santiago, but 'Jorge' as much as anyone ensured they at least remained competitive throughout the lion's share of the 1960s, 1970s and early 1980s. 'I had my own things going on, as you do as a teenager, but I used to love going with Dad to watch the boys at O'Higgins play in their games right up until I went away to university in 1978,' says Elizabeth Robledo.

As I said, he was very good with children and young people. Coaching was something he loved to do. He guided them so well – never shouting, always encouraging, not saying too much, only the right things whenever necessary. That was his approach. And because of that, they all loved and respected him in return.

13

BORROWED TIME

'It's like everything in life. You bring something out of nothing,
and it always goes back to nothing again.'

– GEORGE MARTIN (RECORD PRODUCER AND ARRANGER)

In 1989, Billy Joel, the American singer and pianist, released a song called 'We Didn't Start the Fire' listing 119 key cultural, political, scientific, social and sporting events spanning the forty years since his birth in 1949. You name it, it's in there – North Korea, South Korea, Joe McCarthy, Marilyn Monroe, the Communist Bloc, James Dean, 'Rock Around the Clock', the Suez Crisis, Elvis Presley, Vietnam, Cuba, the Congo, John F. Kennedy's assassination, Beatlemania, birth control, Sonny Liston beating Floyd Patterson, the Profumo Scandal, Woodstock, Watergate, Palestine, going to the Moon, terrorist hijackings, punk rock, Ronald Reagan, Russia invading Afghanistan – and much, much more, all neatly packaged into a four-minute pop song. With one significant, often forgotten, exception.

At 3.11 p.m. on Sunday 22 May 1960, an earthquake registering

9.5 on the Richter scale struck about 100 miles off the coast of Chile, roughly parallel with the city of Valdivia. In the ten to fifteen minutes that followed, thousands of people were either killed or injured, with approximately 2 million left homeless. Much of what survived the initial quake along the south Chilean seaboard was subsequently wiped out by tsunami waves measuring up to twenty-five metres high, which engulfed entire communities (besides Chile, countries as far away as New Zealand, Japan and the Philippines were also severely affected, with the Hawaiian city of Hilo being devastated). Estimates put the damage in Chile alone at around $550 million, coming in at something like $5 billion in today's money. At the time of writing, the Valdivia earthquake (sometimes referred to as the Great Chilean Earthquake) remains the most powerful on Earth since records began.

George Robledo was at home in Rancagua, about 300 miles north of the epicentre, when the ground began to shake. He'd experienced earthquakes before in Chile, but this, he immediately sensed, was something literally off the scale. 'It really was quite frightening, but we had it nothing like as bad as some places further south,' he told English journalist Willie Graydon (who wrote under the name John Graydon) the following year. After Gladys, George's immediate concerns were for the workers of the Braden Copper Company and their families. Having established that Rancagua and its surroundings had got off relatively lightly, he and other members of the firm's senior management took the decision to send men south to help with the rescue and relief efforts. If there's one thing miners are good at, it's digging, so their rationale went.

After that came the burials, followed by the mourning. And then, bit by bit, came the rebuilding.

Getting on for four years prior to the Valdivia quake, in June 1956, the FIFA Congress had met in the Portuguese capital of Lisbon, tasked with determining where the 1962 World Cup would take place. Germany had been in the running, but with Europe having staged the tournament in both 1954 (Switzerland) and 1958 (Sweden), so the onus gradually fell on South America to do the honours. On 10 June, Raúl Colombo, president of the Argentine Football Association, put forward his country's bid. 'We can do the World Cup tomorrow,' he boasted at the climax of his speech. 'We have it all.'

The following day, Carlos Dittborn, highly regarded throughout Chile for his work as a football administrator, presented the case for his homeland. '*Porque no tenemos nada, queremos hacerlo todo*,' Dittborn declared ('Because we have nothing, we want to do it all'), deftly spinning Colombo's words and, in the process, playing on FIFA's commitment to promote football in countries deemed to be 'underdeveloped'. When the counting was done, Chile polled thirty-two votes compared to ten for Argentina, with fourteen members abstaining. The World Cup was heading over the Andes.

Or was it? In the aftermath of the Valdivia earthquake, serious questions were asked as to whether Chile could, and indeed should, stage the 1962 competition. So much of the country's infrastructure south of Santiago lay in ruins. Was it right for money to be spent on football when homes, hospitals, schools, offices, roads, factories and ports needed reconstructing? Chile's government countered by reiterating Dittborn's memorable quote from Lisbon. The country needed the World Cup more than ever as part of its rebuilding process and as a way of raising morale.

In the twenty-four months between the earthquake and the World Cup, Chile went hell for leather reworking a tournament that had initially been mapped across eight different cities. Out went Talca, Concepción and Talcahuano as venues along with Valdivia, defeated by a combination of time, location and common sense. Instead, all games would be focused on Arica in the far north of the country along with Santiago, Viña del Mar and Rancagua (or 'seedy, broken-down Rancagua' as Brian Glanville, who covered the 1962 World Cup on behalf of the *Sunday Times*, described it). Sixteen teams, four groups, four cities – that would be the format. Simple, practical, economical.

In theory, England – the only one of the UK home nations to qualify – could have ended up playing in any of the four host cities. It just so happened, however, that in Rancagua there lived a man who spoke perfect English, knew the English game inside out and was in charge of industrial relations for the city's biggest employer.

And so in May 1962, England travelled to Rancagua where they set up camp at the Braden Copper Company compound in the nearby mountain retreat of Coya, with George Robledo acting as their liaison officer, attaché, interpreter and all-round fixer. It was, in all honesty, part of a make-do-and-mend solution to the wider earthquake-shaped hole which Chile found itself in, with England's living quarters consisting of two accommodation blocks separated by a ravine. Besides talking, reading or playing interminable games of head tennis, to the dismay of certain members of the squad, there really wasn't anything to do.

'The only way to reach it [Coya] was by railcar or a narrow mountain path,' striker Jimmy Greaves recalled some years later of his first experience of being at a World Cup.

> To have our meals we had to walk from our barrack-style quarters across a narrow, rickety wooden bridge with a 500-foot drop either side. It was great for building up an appetite. Bobby Moore and I shared a miner's shack that had a corrugated roof, and when it rained, which was often, it sounded as if the Grenadier Guards were marching above us. It was Walter [Winterbottom, serving out his final months as England's team manager] who had recommended the training camp after a reconnoitring trip to Chile, and I said to him after my first view, 'Well done Walter, you've really hit the jackpot. Even the dogs here run round with their tails between their legs.'

With plenty of time to kill before their opening Group Four match against Hungary on 31 May, a friendly against a local grassroots team – facilitated by George and agreed to by Walter Winterbottom – took place involving some members of England's team. For one of those who played, the game would prove to be the end not only of his World Cup campaign but also his international career.

'Walter asked us what we thought, and again we signalled our approval,' Bobby Robson, a future England team manager in his own right, recounted in his 2005 autobiography.

Why not? Sure, we'd give them a game. We were bored. We knew the World Cup was edging closer, but surely this was only training in a different form. Walter asked for volunteers. My hand went up – big mistake. My role in this Anglo-Chilean diplomatic exercise ended painfully and prematurely when one of the local players nicked me in a tackle and caused me to go over awkwardly. I had chipped a bone in my ankle. That's how Bobby Moore was promoted to the England team.

Sure enough, Robson's misfortune did indeed open the door for Moore, England's World Cup-winning captain of 1966, to play in all four of his country's matches at the 1962 competition (a 2–1 defeat to Hungary, a 3–1 win over Argentina and a 0–0 draw versus Bulgaria in the group games in Rancagua, prior to losing 3–1 to eventual champions Brazil in the quarter-finals in Viña del Mar). 'I never played for England again, and Bobby Moore never looked back,' added Robson ruefully.

Mind, as crumbs of comfort go, Robson did manage to land a big one while in Chile.

'I got to meet George Robledo,' he said proudly in a 1999 radio interview shortly after taking over the managerial reins at Newcastle United, his last job in football.

We'd never really met before. I'd stood close by him when I was a supporter and he was a player, but now things were different. I was the player and he'd retired. It was lovely to meet him as something of an equal. And he was everything I hoped he would be – kind, considerate, thoughtful, very gentlemanly. Which is something a lot of people always said about him – what a gentle-man he was. My luck ran out on me during those few weeks [in Chile], but it was marvellous to be able to spend a little time with him. They always say never meet your heroes. They can be wrong.

Twenty-two years later, the two men got the opportunity to meet again when England, with Robson now in charge as manager, conducted a three-match tour of South America during June 1984, facing Brazil, Uruguay and Chile in the space of seven days. This time, though, it wasn't just Robson who got to exchange pleasant-ries with George but the entire England team. Prior to the match at the Estadio Nacional, at the instigation of Robson and Ted Croker, secretary of the Football Association, a gathering took place in one of the conference rooms at the Sheraton Hotel in Santiago. 'It was more like a homage to my dad,' recalls Elizabeth Robledo, who ac-companied her father along with Gladys Robledo.

Each member of the England team came forward, one by one, even the reserves, to greet him and shake his hand. It was all very simple but very emotional, and they presented my mum with flowers. Then, after the game, everyone went back to the Sheraton where they closed the bar and made it a private party for us. I think there were about forty-two men and three women there – my mum, myself and a friend of mine. But we had an unforgettable time. All night long, I was dancing with the guys – Bryan Robson, John Barnes, Ray Wilkins, Chris Woods. I met everybody. Every time I hear Daryl Hall and John Oates, I think of that night, because they played their music constantly. It was a wonderful gesture by the bar manager to do that and it was a wonderful thing for Bobby to organise. That was when I saw the connection between Dad and him for myself. People always said Dad was the perfect gentleman on the field and off it, and they used to say that about Bobby too. When he [Robson] passed away in 2009, I was in Australia writing for a Spanish-language newspaper, and I wrote a piece in his honour saying how proud I was to have had the chance to meet him and how proud I was that he knew Dad.

All things considered, the 1962 finals are regarded now by those in the know as a triumph over adversity. Sure, violence marred several games, not least of all when Chile and Italy met at the Estadio Nacional in what became known as the 'Battle of Santiago', the fires having been stoked by a series of unflattering articles penned by two Italian journalists in the run-up to the game, one of which described Santiago as a 'backwards and poverty-stricken dump full of prostitution and crime'. On the other hand, the relative success of the Chilean team, progressing as far as the semi-finals before succumbing to Brazil, set the tone of the whole competition, with thousands of people throughout the country watching on televisions located on street corners. Bars stayed open late, musicians wrote and performed songs inspired by events on the field, and George got a welcome fix of all things English courtesy of Walter Winterbottom and his squad. Brazil may have retained the trophy, beating Czechoslovakia 3–1 in the final, but there was little doubt that Chile – the place, as much as the team – was the real hero of 1962.

'That long, thin, impoverished Chile should put it on at all was remarkable,' Brian Glanville reflected in 2001.

Criticisms of the country, of the organisation, were often unfair. If there was corruption over tickets, at least an official was hauled off to jail. When there were similar stories four years later in England, the dirt was swept quickly under the carpet. If there were tales of overcharging for accommodation, then the police quickly made indictments. The two Italian journalists who indicted Chile as a backward country, and thereby exposed their own team to the calvary of the Battle of Santiago, were not even justified in their criticism. It was a country at once squalid and sophisticated, backwards yet subtle, but for the visitor Chile left more congenial memories than either Sweden [in 1958] or Mexico [1970 and 1986].

• • •

The rest of the 1960s saw George content to play the role of 'Mr Rancagua', overseeing industrial relations at the Braden Copper Company, running the junior teams at the O'Higgins Football Club and being a family man to Gladys and daughter Elizabeth, born in April 1961. Conscious perhaps that his own father had missed out on the majority of his childhood, George resolved to be there for Elizabeth, no matter what the sacrifice. When 'La Roja' qualified for the 1966 World Cup finals in England, the Federación de Fútbol de Chile asked if he would travel to his former homeland in an administrative role, responsible for pretty much everything from logistics to translating. George turned them down for the simple reason that he didn't want to be away from his family for several months, which is what the job would have entailed.

Brother Ted, however, having split from his wife, had no qualms about roaming the globe performing a veritable A to Z of occupations. There was the NASA role, which took him to the US. There was a brief coaching position in El Salvador for a now defunct football team called Club Deportivo Once Municipal. He worked on oil rigs and for an American shipping firm specialising in transporting petroleum, based in the Persian Gulf. Which, having just returned from a few days' leave in England, is how Ted came to be in Dubai on Saturday 5 December 1970 in the company of Heinz Bessenich, a thirty-year-old German merchant navy captain employed by the Delmon Navigation Company, a subsidiary of the Gray Mackenzie shipping agents.

The circumstances surrounding Ted Robledo's last twenty-four hours on Earth are shrouded in heartache, mystery, lies and deception. This much, we do know. On 5 December, Bessenich invited Ted aboard his ship, a tanker called the *Al Sahn*, for a few days' steaming up the Gulf coast. The following morning, Ted was found to be missing. The finger of suspicion pointed towards Bessenich, and Dubai's police force, led by a Lancastrian called Jack Briggs, set to work building a case against him.

The rest, sad to say, is conjecture, born largely out of Bessenich's high-profile trial held in Dubai in April 1971, just months before the territory became part of the United Arab Emirates.

'The news burst like a small bomb among the western media,' wrote Andrew Trimbee of the Bahrain-based English-language newspaper the *Gulf Mirror*, who broke the story.

Their troubleshooters were on the next plane out to Dubai. Hotel rooms, already limited, became at a premium. The news desks of a dozen leading newspapers not only in Britain but across Europe kept my phone permanently engaged. I flew down to Dubai to interview the sheikhdom's chief of police, Jack Briggs, a tiny bundle of energy. Briggs, from Blackpool, had made a career out of police work in the Gulf, serving in Qatar then moving further south to become the trusted security aide to Dubai's ruler, Sheikh Rashid Al-Makhtoum. He [Briggs] was fluent in Arabic, having taken a degree course in Britain in addition to fitting in his work policing the dynamic, bustling state. Sitting in his tiny office in the old police fort, barely changed in fifty years, he told me what he could. Robledo, it was believed, had embarked on a drinking session with the well-built Bessenich. This, said Briggs, was believed to have got out of hand. He was killed and it was thought that the German skipper had thrown him overboard. That was the police case. The body was never found.

'I remember our backyard at home in Rancagua being full of journalists asking Dad about the news and he couldn't speak at all. He just couldn't stop crying,' says Elizabeth Robledo.

I can't remember now how he heard about it, whether it was on the news, or someone came to the house or Uncle Walter called on the phone, but I do remember seeing all of these people and dad crying and crying. I can't imagine how hard it was for him, because he'd been a brother and a father to Uncle Ted after their own father left them on board the *Reina del Pacifico* when they were coming to England as boys. It was Dad who had done so much to raise him and Walter while Grandma Elsie was busy working in the shop. He'd been a role model to them while they were growing up. Ted was his young brother, his partner in football through Barnsley, through Newcastle United, through Colo-Colo and through Chile… and now he was gone in the most horrible of ways. You know when they say that real men don't cry? Well, I'm sorry, but that's not true.

Charged with 'wilfully and unlawfully causing the death of Ted Robledo in a brutal and savage manner', Heinz Bessenich stood trial in front of a British judge together with three independent assessors from Dubai, pleading not guilty. 'Speaking in good English, he insisted that the disappearance of Robledo was "just a tragic happening"', wrote Trimbee.

At a preliminary hearing, the court was told that the skipper had made no report of a missing passenger. The skipper's Indian steward testified that Bessenich had told him, on the return leg from Muscat to Dubai, 'If anybody asks, you are to say there were no passengers.' He had earlier seen two knives hanging in Bessenich's cabin. A day later, he noticed that only one was there.

Bessenich, so the prosecution claimed, had told 'a web of lies'. He hadn't reported Ted Robledo as missing. He hadn't turned the *Al Sahn* around and mounted a search. He hadn't sent out a radio alert. He'd flatly denied that Robledo had been on the ship. He'd destroyed all material evidence of Robledo being aboard. Why? Because he'd killed him.

In his defence, Bessenich claimed Ted must have committed suicide. Edwin Robinson, appearing for Bessenich on behalf of the ship's owners, also outlined how death could have been accidental. 'It is possible for a man to lose balance leaning over the vessel's rail and fall into the sea,' he told the court. 'This possibility is heightened if a man had drunk a couple of whiskies and had one foot on the pipe running beside the rail. A stranger could fall into the sea through an open gate.'

On the other side of the world, George followed reports of the trial while also receiving updates from Walter, who sat in the Dubai courtroom throughout proceedings. On Monday 12 April, the verdict came in – not guilty. While the judge had been unimpressed with Bessenich's defence, there was insufficient evidence to find him guilty. 'The blond skipper, who never once lost his composure during his two-and-a-half-months behind bars, walked out into the sun a free man,' reported Trimbee. 'The mystery was never solved.'

Not, it should be said, for lack of trying. Ted Robledo's affable nature made him a well-connected man in England, in Chile, in football and in the oil industry. Rewards were offered for information. Appeals were made within the merchant navy community. Walter himself travelled to Dubai on three separate occasions, engaging a solicitor to try and unravel the chain of events and bring justice for Ted. None of it came to anything.

'I think it's almost certain that it was murder,' says Elizabeth Robledo.

They say Uncle Ted met this German captain at a bar and that he invited him onto the ship. Maybe they had some drinks. And then Uncle Ted disappeared. The only thing they could see as evidence was that one of the sabres in the captain's room went missing, so they say he might have killed him with the sabre and thrown his body into the ocean. That's the story I was told and how I remember it.

'He was undoubtedly murdered,' says Néstor Flores, who documented Ted's fate extensively in his book *La Misteriosa Desaparición de Ted Robledo* (*The Mysterious Disappearance of Ted Robledo*). It was, so Flores maintains, 'impossible for him to jump into the sea on his own'. He adds that had Ted fallen into the water accidentally, he would have easily been able to swim to the coast. In other words, he was thrown dead or wounded into the Persian Gulf. 'Don't forget that one of the knives disappeared from the ship and no one could explain how or why,' adds Flores, who believes the knife in question probably ended up in the sea, quite possibly 'embedded in Ted's body'.

Ted Robledo was just forty-two years old at the time of his death, disappearance, murder – call it what you will. The nature of his demise did his legacy few favours. There was no burial, since there was nothing to bury. There were no ashes to scatter, since there was nothing to cremate. Those left behind found it difficult to talk about him due to the circumstances surrounding his final hours. In 1981, George told *The Journal* he believed Ted's death had taken years off their mother's life, while Walter confessed in his 2019 interview with Chris Waugh of *The Athletic* that 'it's not something I talk about too often'. There was also the underlying sense that justice had been denied.

He played for Barnsley. He played for Newcastle United. He played for Colo-Colo. He played for Chile. He won an FA Cup winner's medal in 1952. He was part of the Colo-Colo side that finished top of the Primera División in 1953 and 1956. Ted Robledo deserves to be so much more than a footnote in the life of his more prolific older brother. And yet that, sadly, is what he has become – the steady, honest, hardworking and ultimately tragic sibling. Would the opportunities which came Ted's way have presented themselves had it not been for George's talent? Perhaps not. Be that as it may, when they did, Ted rarely let those around him down.

Unfortunately, when justice needed to be served, many of those around him, through no fault of their own, were unable to repay the compliment. Which is why, over half a century later, to quote Walter Robledo, 'it's still raw'.

14

REVOLUTION 9

'Our job as Americans and as Republicans is to dislodge the traitors from every place where they've been sent to do their traitorous work.'
– JOSEPH McCARTHY

You were either with them or against them. At least that's what they had you thinking. If the United States of America, the world's self-appointed post-Second World War policeman, liked the cut of your jib – individually, collectively, politically, culturally, intellectually – then you were on safe ground. If it didn't, then you could be alienated, blacklisted, demonised, disgraced, humiliated, spied on, imprisoned, bombed, invaded or overthrown. No matter where you were, the land of the free had your number listed under friend or foe. And as the curtain went up on the 1970s, it was Chile's turn to get the call.

In September of 1970, Salvador Allende was elected as Chile's first socialist president. His majority was a narrow one. While half of the country rejoiced in the hope of improved living standards and a fairer society, the other half feared the prospect of communism.

Within a year, nearly 100 major firms had been nationalised (including the Braden Copper Company, expropriated from its American owners without compensation), duly followed by agrarian reform and the redistribution of land among local workers. As popular as some of Allende's policies were, government expenditure was soon outstripping income, creating an enormous budget deficit exacerbated by a global fall in the price of copper. As inflation went up and wages stagnated, so Chile began sliding into political chaos, stirred by the country's right-wing press and with the US covertly pulling strings from afar (the CIA, it would emerge, had an $8 million pot set aside specifically to bankroll efforts to destabilise Allende).

By 1973, the strikes of the previous year had given way to widespread civil disorder. On 11 September, as tanks surrounded the presidential palace in Santiago, Allende supposedly took his own life in the face of a military coup led by a junta that included General Augusto Pinochet, chief of the army.

In the days and weeks that followed, death squads travelled the length of the country executing anyone deemed to be a threat to the new regime. The Estadio Nacional, home to some of George Robledo's finest moments playing for Colo-Colo, became a detention centre in which thousands of people (including political opponents, trade union leaders, journalists and socialists) were incarcerated, threatened with torture, tortured and, in some cases, killed. Curfews were imposed, strict controls put on the press and military personnel sent into factories, universities or anywhere else that socialists might just be residing. Before long, Congress had been dissolved, opposition parties and trade unions banned and a dictatorship led by Pinochet was in place – a dictatorship that would, over the years, be actively (if clandestinely) supported by the US through the CIA, right down to the elimination of so-called dissidents. A land built on freedom of expression had fallen into the hands of a tyrant, albeit one supported by a sizeable portion of the Chilean population, won over by Pinochet's commitment to liberate them from the political and economic mess into which the country had, admittedly, fallen.

God bless America.

'When Allende came up, things changed a lot,' says one London-based Chilean with connections to Rancagua who would prefer to remain nameless (even now, the early 1970s is a subject that remains sensitive).

People who worked at the Braden Copper Company used to be paid in US dollars because it was an American firm. When Allende came, the gringos were kicked out and they started being paid in Chilean pesos instead. The staff at Braden [including George and Gladys Robledo] stayed in their positions. They were professionals, not politicians, so they were secure at work. But then the situation across the country began to get hard. There was money, but there was nothing to buy. There were queues everywhere – to buy gasoline, to buy bread, to buy milk. The country couldn't handle that situation any longer. Then Pinochet took over... and not in a very nice way. There were a lot of mixed feelings about that time in our history. There still are a lot of mixed feelings about that time in our history.

'Because he was loved by all sorts of people from all sectors of society and politics, my dad never had any problems getting hold of anything,' says Elizabeth Robledo.

> But he would then feel bad about that. He'd queue up like everyone else but then it would be, 'No, Mr Robledo, you can buy this, you can have that.' He was being offered more than other people because of who he was and he didn't like it. Of course he was grateful, but it would also make him sad because a lot of people were having trouble getting hold of things.

Meanwhile, 5,000 or so miles north of Santiago, another left-leaning figure was having issues of his own with the US government, only on American soil. On Friday 3 September 1971, John Lennon – now aged thirty and in the early stages of his divorce from the Beatles – had arrived in New York City with his wife Yoko Ono on a six-month B-2 visitor visa issued by the US Immigration and Naturalization Service. Despite the temporary visas, it was always their intention to stay long-term. 'Yoko and I were forever coming and going to New York, so finally we decided it would be cheaper and more functional to actually live here, so that's what we did,' Lennon once said. 'We love it, and it's the centre of our world. America is the Roman Empire and New York is Rome itself. New York is at my speed. They're like me – they don't believe in wasting time.'

Being in New York City did, however, present Lennon with a problem. President Richard Nixon, the man who had authorised the opening of a Federal Bureau of Investigation file on Lennon in 1969, was up for re-election in 1972. Worried that the outspoken former Beatle might do or say something to turn the youth vote against him, Nixon was growing increasingly edgy. 'We can use the available political machinery to screw our political enemies,' John Dean, counsel to the President, had proposed to Nixon in a memo dated August 1971. 'If Lennon's visa is terminated, it would be a strategy [sic] counter-measure,' Nixon loyalist and senate representative Strom Thurmond recommended in 1972, on the topic of the 'political machinery' which might just be available to 'screw' Lennon (who, along with Ono, had already been granted two- and four-week extensions to his visa on 29 February and 16 March 1972 respectively).

'I felt followed everywhere by government agents,' Lennon told TV talk show host Dick Cavett of the FBI's increasingly blatant efforts to unsettle and undermine him.

Every time I picked up the phone, there was a lot of noise. I'd open the door and there'd be guys standing on the other side of the street. I'd get in the car and they'd be following me, and not hiding. They wanted me to see that I was being followed.

Throughout 1972, Lennon and Ono continued to contest efforts by the US government to have them removed, with immigration hearings being bumped back as the election drew nearer. Testimonials from a string of luminaries including Norman Mailer, Fred Astaire and actor Tony Curtis helped keep the wolf from the door. 'He has improved this town just by showing up,' declared the *New York Post*.

On 7 November, to the couple's dismay, Nixon defeated the Democratic Party presidential nominee George McGovern in a landslide, sealing four more years in the White House. Conversely, in light of Lennon's 'inactivity in revolutionary activities', New York City's FBI office informed headquarters that it was closing its case against him. Within a month of Nixon being re-elected, Lennon's FBI file was closed full stop.

Nevertheless, his visa issues continued, which meant he couldn't, in theory, leave the US because if he did, he probably wouldn't be allowed back in. Whether Lennon liked it or not, he was stuck. Still, there are worse places to be stuck than New York City.

Despite that, 1973 saw Lennon go well and truly off the rails. He drank excessively, started an affair with his in-house assistant May Pang (at Yoko Ono's instigation, according to Pang), split with Ono and went on what amounted to a fifteen-month-long bender stretching into 1974, which has since become known as his 'lost weekend'. There was an album of rock 'n' roll cover versions that ran into trouble, due in part to the antics of legendary yet eccentric record producer Phil Spector (who not only brought a pistol to one recording session but also fired it before disappearing with the tapes). 'I just fell apart, and the only thing I knew was go to the bar, and drink,' Lennon would tell the BBC's Andy Peebles in 1980. 'It was a pretty hectic period, pretty wild, and it sounds funny in retrospect, but it was pretty miserable.'

When the booze-induced clouds finally began to part, Lennon strapped on his guitar and went back to work, writing songs for an album that would be released under the title *Walls and Bridges*. All told, twelve tracks made the final cut, recorded in New York City during July and August of 1974, among them the perennial Lennon gems 'Whatever Gets You thru the Night' (featuring Elton John on piano and vocals) and '#9 Dream', the latter inspired by a dream he'd had in which two women could be heard saying his Christian name.

Initially, '#9 Dream' had been called 'So Long' after the opening words of the song, but at some point during the recording process Lennon decided to change it. He'd been born on 9 October 1940. His mother had lived at 9 Newcastle Road in Liverpool. Brian Epstein, who managed the Beatles, had first heard them play on the ninth of the month. The band signed their first recording contract on the ninth of the month. One of his earliest songwriting efforts from 1957 had been 'One After 909' (which ultimately saw the light of day in 1970 with the release of the album *Let It Be*). Arguably his most adventurous Beatles song had been 'Revolution 9'. Over the years Lennon had, for whatever reason, locked onto the number nine, seeing it as being especially important in his life. So out went 'So Long', and in came '#9 Dream'.

Then there was the picture he'd painted as an eleven-year-old schoolboy, the one showing the football player sporting a black and white kit heading a ball, with a teammate standing beside him wearing a shirt with the number nine clearly visible on the back.

John Lennon had been born in Liverpool at a time when the city was being bombed almost on a nightly basis by the Luftwaffe. His father Fred, a seaman, was rarely if ever around, while his mother, Julia, soon found herself another partner and started a new family. Consequently, John was taken in from the age of five by his Aunt Mimi, sister of his mother, who lived in the relatively quiet middle-class suburb of Woolton to the south of the city. It was Mimi who arranged for him to be transferred from Mosspits School in

Wavertree to Dovedale Road Primary School in Mossley Hill, close to Penny Lane, which he started attending as of May 1946.

'My first class in 1950 contained forty boys, one of whom was John Lennon,' Harry Holmes, who taught at Dovedale Road and later became the school's deputy headmaster, recalled in 2006.

> He was a pleasant boy, with only a trace of a Scouse accent. I be-
> lieve he cultivated a lapse in this respect later in his professional
> life for reasons unknown to me. I saw no evidence of musical
> ability, but there was not the opportunity to display such ability at
> Dovedale, if it existed. He was, however, very well spoken, polite,
> self-confident with a twinkle in his eye and an unusual, mature
> sense of humour. His academic rating would be good average.

Whatever Lennon may have lacked at that stage in the musical department he more than made up for in other areas. Inspired by reading books such as *Alice in Wonderland* and *Just William*, he'd had a go at writing some of his own while attending Dovedale Road. Featuring jokes, drawings and pasted-in photographs of well-known public figures, these 'books' particularly evolved during his final year at the school. 'If you liked this, come again next week, it'll be even better,' became his signature sign-off when it came to one regular serialised story.

In the summer of 1952, aged eleven, Lennon sat what was known as the eleven-plus exam, which every child in the UK did in those days to determine which school they would go to next. He passed and started attending Quarry Bank Grammar School as of September that year. He also busied himself drawing and painting more pictures, including one featuring Native Americans riding horses and another of a football match between two teams, one in black and white, the other wearing red. Lennon's football painting was based on a still photograph taken at the FA Cup final on Saturday 3 May 1952 and reproduced in the majority of England's national and regional newspapers over the ensuing days. Despite not being much of a football fan, Lennon felt drawn enough to the image to want to reproduce it.

Did he realise the two teams in the photograph were Newcastle United and Arsenal? We will never know. Did he realise the man heading the ball was George Robledo? We will never know.

Did he realise the other man in the picture wearing a black and white shirt, the one with the number nine on his back, was Jackie Milburn? We will never know. Did he feel compelled to paint the picture because of the number nine on the player's back? We will never know.

Did he paint the picture because the player wearing the number nine shirt also played for Newcastle United (his mother's home had been 9 Newcastle Road, Liverpool, where John lived until he was five years old)? Again, we will never know.

What we can say with some certainty is that Lennon would have seen the photograph in a newspaper at either 251 Menlove Avenue, Mimi's pre-Second World War semi-detached house in Woolton, or at school. He had access to coloured pencils and paints both at home and at Dovedale Road, so the picture could have taken shape at either location. He clearly liked the finished result enough not only to put his name, age, the date and a title on it ('John Lennon, June 1952, AGE 11, football') but also to keep it for posterity. Indeed, the picture remained stashed away for the next twenty-two years, until the time came for Lennon to choose the artwork for *Walls and Bridges*. At which point, unable to return to England and retrieve it himself due to his immigration issues in the US, he asked Mimi to dig it out and send it to him in New York City, along with several other pictures of his dating from around the same time.

Why did Lennon select his football painting as the main image for the front cover of the album's elaborate outer jacket (which divided into three separate parts, with two fold-out sections featuring other pictures produced by Lennon)? Once again, we will never know. While Roy Kohara, the in-house designer at Capitol Records (the label responsible for distributing *Walls and Bridges*) oversaw the album's art direction, it was the former Beatle who supplied him with those images from his childhood and had final sign-off on the designs.

Granted US resident's status in July 1976 with the promise of full citizenship by 1981, Lennon was fatally shot by Mark David Chapman outside his apartment block in New York City late on 8 December 1980 (by which time, ironically, the date had become the ninth in the UK), so we can't ask him.

Released on 26 September 1974 in the US and 4 October 1974 in the UK, *Walls and Bridges* became a certified gold record as of 22 October 1974 (for sales reaching 500,000 copies), with the single 'Whatever Gets You thru the Night' claiming the number-one spot in the US Billboard chart three weeks later. On 28 November 1974, Lennon joined Elton John on stage at Madison Square Garden in New York City to perform 'Whatever Gets You thru the Night' – if the song topped the charts, so Elton had challenged, then Lennon should repay the favour of asking him to guest on it by appearing at one of his live shows.

In a case of bittersweet irony, that concert – which also saw the pair perform 'Lucy in the Sky With Diamonds' and 'I Saw Her Standing There' – would be Lennon's last on a public stage. Almost everyone who heard *Walls and Bridges* loved the album – except, it seems, for Lennon himself. 'The only thing about it is it's new,' he said at one point, the memory of its conception perhaps having been tainted by his split, albeit of a temporary nature, with Yoko Ono (who has since called it 'one of the best albums that he made'). As the English music journalist and author Paul Du Noyer wrote of *Walls and Bridges*, 'Whatever pain he was in, it inspired a great album.'

A great album, featuring great songs, with a great guest turn by Elton John, wrapped in a great jacket with a great front cover. It's just a shame that with Lennon so reluctant to sing its praises at the time, the truth about who was on that front cover took another thirty-six years to emerge.

'At the beginning of 2010, I'd already been researching my book about the disappearance of Ted Robledo for a couple of years,' says Néstor Flores, who besides being a Colo-Colo supporter also happens to be a lifelong fan of the Beatles and their music.

I wanted to know at what point Ted had come to hug Jorge after he scored the goal against Arsenal in the 1952 FA Cup final. For that, I asked some people in England to send me photos or press clippings from the final, because there was only one video on YouTube and that failed to clarify when Ted and Jorge had hugged. Two or three months later, I came to look at these photos, comparing and observing them to see if I could get some answers. It was close to midnight and suddenly, my vision was drawn to one of them. It was a very curious feeling. I thought, 'I've seen this photo somewhere. I know this photo.' I felt a strange sense of déjà vu about this image. But it was getting late and I went to bed, falling asleep with this vague, ghostly idea in my head that I'd seen it somewhere before.

At around 3 a.m., I woke up and suddenly thought, 'Wow, that photo is the same as the cover of *Walls and Bridges*, Lennon's album from 1974.' I had the album in my house, along with many other albums by Lennon and the Beatles. I got up almost immediately, turned on my computer, made some coffee and went to look for the LP. Then I held it next to the photo I had been sent which, by now, was visible on the computer screen. And that's when I realised – it was exactly the same image. After that, I questioned how I, a Beatles fan who has devoured at least twenty books about the band, had never read that there was a Chilean football player on the cover of a Lennon album. And effectively, that was down to the fact that no one had ever made the connection before. Nobody had noticed that Jorge Robledo was on the cover of Lennon's album, drawn by the hand of this genius boy from Liverpool.

Having had his eureka moment, Flores contacted the Robledo family to tell them of his discovery. 'I was actually in Australia at the time and I remember Mum calling to tell me,' says Elizabeth Robledo.

At first I was like, 'I'm sorry, what? Dad is on the front of a John Lennon album? How can that be?' I really couldn't take it in. I think I was more surprised than anything. It was only when I got back to Chile that it really began to sink in. That's when I met Néstor and he was able to explain it to me himself.

There are so many different stories about why John Lennon might have drawn that picture. Some say it's because he liked the number nine and some say other things. But at the end of the day, it's my dad's goal that he decided to draw. What an honour that is for such a magnificent musician to have done that. And it's not just any goal – it's the goal from the 1952 FA Cup final. He could have drawn so many other things, but something made him keep that newspaper clipping and then make a painting of it. It's such an unusual story, but it's such a beautiful story. Knowing John Lennon drew that picture when he was growing up in Liverpool, the place where my dad arrived in England from Chile as a boy, makes it even more special to me. I'm very proud of my dad, but I'm also very proud of John Lennon.

'Newcastle United have plenty of celebrity fans, and while John Lennon could never really be said to be a supporter, it's certainly wonderful that such an icon was at one time enchanted by the black and white stripes as a young lad,' says Paul Joannou, the club's historian.

When he sketched the drawing used on his solo *Walls and Bridges* album cover, perhaps the young Lennon was caught up in the magic of the FA Cup, just like any other football-mad youth, especially as United lifted the famous trophy twice in consecutive seasons – a rarity back then – and made it three times in five years soon afterwards. He must have been. It shows how big Newcastle United were then, and that every young lad in the country associated the Magpies with the FA Cup. Lennon's coloured portrayal of George Robledo's winning goal captures the moment at Wembley in 1952. He also includes United's number nine, Jackie Milburn, in the picture, just like the newspaper photograph. His fixation with 'nine' lived with him – born on 9 October, spent his early years living at 9 Newcastle Road in Liverpool and so on. Maybe he was a bit of a Newcastle fan after all?

George Robledo and John Lennon never met. But besides being closely associated with port cities on opposite sides of northern England, they had plenty in common. Both knew what it was like at different points in their lives to be strangers in a strange land – aliens, for want of a better word. Both suffered what might be described as disturbed childhoods, having been abandoned at an early age by their fathers (and in Lennon's case, losing his mother Julia in a road traffic accident when he was seventeen). Both loved writing letters and postcards. As Beatles biographer Hunter Davies once noted, 'John Lennon lived and died in an era before computers, emails, twits, tweets and twitters, hence he handwrote or typed letters and postcards to his family, friends, fans, strangers, newspapers, organisations, lawyers and the laundry.'

Of the two, George emerges as the more stable personality. For all his talent, warmth and kindness, Lennon could also be moody, selfish, domineering, hurtful and cutting, traits that simply didn't reside in George's DNA. Both came to be raised by strong women for whom the word 'uncompromising' could have been invented. According to Julia Baird, John Lennon's half-sister, Aunt Mimi possessed an 'obsessive need to control the lives and actions of those around her'. Everyone, including Lennon's erstwhile friend and songwriting partner Paul McCartney, seems to agree that Mimi was a snob, an accusation which, for all her faults, can't be levelled at Elsie Robledo. Other similarities in their respective personalities suggest, however, that Mini and Elsie would've got along pretty well with one another.

They may never have met in person. And yet one day in June 1952, George Robledo and John Lennon crossed paths in a painting drawn by the latter, featuring the former. A painting which shows George scoring his sixth goal in Newcastle United's victorious FA Cup campaign of that year, his thirty-ninth overall of the 1951–52 season. A painting that lives on to this day in the record and CD collections of thousands of people around the world. A painting which unites two men, talented in the extreme in their respective fields, whose premature deaths would bookend the 1980s.

15

WATCHING THE WHEELS

'Death is the sound of distant thunder at a picnic.'
– W. H. Auden

They were called the DINA, which stood for the Dirección de Inteligencia Nacional (the National Intelligence Directorate). Established in November 1973 by Augusto Pinochet as his very own secret police, the DINA carried out surveillance on all walks of civilian society in Chile. If there was opposition, they silenced it, often in the most brutal of ways. People disappeared. People were tortured. People were executed. 'There is not a leaf that stirs in Chile without my knowing about it,' boasted Pinochet at his height of his purge against the left, when the absence of any organised political opposition enabled him to do pretty much whatever he liked. At the time, only the Catholic Church spoke out against the government's human rights record, providing help and sanctuary to many who suffered while also documenting reports of abuse. Men and women who'd sought refuge in Chile from other South American dictatorships found themselves caught up in Pinochet's merciless drive to reverse the policies of Salvador Allende and restructure the country's government, economy and society. No wonder the vast majority of the population, George Robledo included, chose to keep their heads down.

'Jorge was not a political person, he was not outspoken and so he wouldn't have come to the attention of the government,' says one Chilean ex-pat, now resident in England, who lived through the repression of the 1970s.

> Even if he had spoken out in any way, the government might not have done anything because of who he was. He had a very high public profile. He was probably Chile's most famous football player ever. If he went missing, many people would know about it, so it would not put the government in a good light for something to happen to him. But, back then, you never knew. Many thinkers, many artists, many talented people suffered in the most terrible of ways because of their politics, because of their beliefs, because of who they were associated with. If you stuck to the path, you were probably going to be OK. If you didn't, then things could get very difficult.

Throughout the 1970s, George stuck to the path. When he wasn't working for the copper company, he was overseeing the junior football teams at O'Higgins FC. When he wasn't overseeing the junior football teams at O'Higgins FC, he was busy being a family man. His regular supply of letters and postcards back to the UK contained no mention of the political situation in Chile. If anything even vaguely political cropped up in conversation, then George would carefully steer the talk onto safer ground – usually football. Or, thanks to his daughter, swimming.

'In February 1974, I became a national swimming champion in Chile, winning gold in the 100 and 200 metres breaststroke,' says Elizabeth Robledo.

Of course, you can imagine what it was like with all the media. They didn't care if the other swimmers won five gold medals. I won just two, but I was George Robledo's daughter, so all the attention was on me and my dad. I get that, but it must have been hard on some of the other girls. That's the way it was because of our name. But Dad was so proud, and it was lovely to have him there, encouraging and supporting me.

The widespread abuse of human rights under Pinochet's rule meant Chile found itself politically isolated from the rest of the world throughout much of the 1970s and 1980s. However, unlike the Eastern Bloc countries of central and eastern Europe, which found themselves economically, politically and militarily aligned with the Soviet Union after the Second World War, Chilean citizens remained free and able to journey abroad. Not that George did any long-haul travelling in the years after his international career as a footballer came to an end in October 1957, after thirty-one caps and eight goals. He simply had too much going on in Rancagua.

But then, late in 1980, word reached him that plans were afoot to reunite Newcastle United's team of 1951 to mark the thirtieth anniversary of their FA Cup final victory over Blackpool. Would he be interested in attending, the organisers wanted to know? George didn't have to think twice, booking a return flight to the UK out of his own pocket (although the cost would later be reimbursed by Metro Radio, a radio station in north-east England, which helped underwrite the event). For the first time in twenty-eight years, he was going back to Tyneside.

On Sunday 26 April 1981, George flew out of Santiago bound for London's Gatwick Airport, with two stops along the way to change planes. Over the next twenty-four hours, almost everything that could possibly go wrong did go wrong (except perhaps for one of the planes falling out of the sky). There were delays and a ground strike, leading to connections being missed. By the time George eventually touched down in London he'd missed the main thirtieth anniversary dinner in Newcastle, with every member of the victorious 1951 team present except himself and winger Bobby Mitchell. 'He ended up getting a taxi up, which Metro had to fund as well!' recalled Malcolm Dix, former chairman of the Newcastle Sports Council, which helped arrange the reunion.

Still, all was far from lost. During the days that followed, George attended several other dinners and gatherings in and around Newcastle organised as part of the thirtieth anniversary celebrations, getting to meet most of his old teammates, including Jackie Milburn, in the process. 'George had a magic knack of hitting the back of the net,' Milburn declared at one such event. 'I couldn't have wished for a better partner and it's wonderful to see him after twenty-eight years.' The feeling was clearly mutual. 'I am quite overwhelmed but so happy to be back among old friends because the best years of my life were spent in Newcastle,' George replied, touched by how much affection there remained for him as well as the team.

'We had photos of every player who had scored more than twenty goals for Newcastle up on the wall,' said Dix of another dinner held at the Gallowgate Club (now the Tyneside Irish Centre) close to St James' Park. 'George wanted his photo. Then, in the spot where it used to be, he signed his autograph on to the wall!'

There was, though, a hint of melancholy about George's trip down memory lane. Twenty-eight years after last setting foot on Tyneside, he was shocked to discover just how much the landscape had changed. Gone were the vast majority of the mines, shipyards and steel works that had provided Newcastle United with generations of supporters from across the region. The Tyne itself had, in reality, ceased to be a working river. Entire streets along which he'd once walked had disappeared completely, bulldozed in the name of urban regeneration. At times, George struggled to recognise the place, if not the people. That accent, that sense of humour, the way strangers greeted one another as if they were old friends, to his immense relief, remained very much intact.

Then there was the horror of what had happened to Newcastle United. On the final day of the 1980–81 season, the Magpies entertained Orient (as Leyton Orient were then known) at St James' Park in the second tier of English football, or the Championship in today's money. Only 11,639 people turned up to see it – one of them being George, invited along as a special guest – a pale shadow of the huge crowds that had watched United during the post-war years. Take a struggling team located in an area of mass unemployment, then add the spectre of football hooliganism prevalent throughout the UK during the 1970s and 1980s. In hindsight, it's a wonder the attendance reached five figures.

'Perhaps it was the Robledo influence which prompted United to go crazy and score three goals that day, bringing their final tally for the season to a humble, if not embarrassing, thirty,' wrote Paul Joannou, the club's official historian, somewhat sardonically of 'a match that echoed with emptiness'. Thirty goals to show from a season comprising of forty-two league games, three fewer than George had managed to score single-handedly during the 1951–52 campaign. Pity poor Bobby Shinton who finished the 1980–81 season as top scorer with a paltry seven goals – the same number George had netted in the space of just ten days during September 1951. Still, despite the travails of Tyneside and Newcastle United, George returned to Chile 'made up and possibly the happiest I'd seen him in a long time' according to Elizabeth Robledo.

Seven days after attending the Orient game at St James' Park, George sat down in front of his television in Rancagua to watch Tottenham Hotspur take on Manchester City in the FA Cup final. Thirty years previously, he'd become the first South American player to appear in an FA Cup final. The following year, brother Ted had become the second, with George making history as the first South American to score in the final. Now, in 1981, Osvaldo Ardiles and Ricardo Villa, both of Tottenham Hotspur and Argentina, were about to become the third and fourth. The match finished 1–1 and five days later, Villa scored twice in the replay, the second a marvellous solo effort in which the bearded midfielder danced his way around several outfield players before slotting the ball beneath Joe Corrigan in the Manchester City goal. What's more, like George's header against Arsenal all those years before, Villa's wonder strike proved to be the winner.

In 1983, with daughter Elizabeth having fled the nest to go to university, George and Gladys decided to kiss goodbye to Rancagua, along with its copper mine and O'Higgins FC, and move to Viña del Mar, the beach resort where they'd first met back in 1953. The plan was that George would retire, but plans have a habit of changing. Spotting an advertisement in the local newspaper for the position of sports director at Saint Peter's, the local British school, he applied for and got the job. And so began the Indian summer of George's life – living in contentment by the sea, imparting his sporting knowledge to the pupils at Saint Peter's and entertaining guests at their apartment on Avenida Marina overlooking the Pacific, including many old friends and pen pals from the UK.

Just as Chilean citizens were free to travel abroad during Pinochet's reign, so foreign nationals were also able to visit Chile. It was at George and Gladys's apartment that Arthur Ellis, the referee from the 1952 FA Cup final, enjoyed lunch while listening to the Beatles. It was here where journalist Willie Graydon came while on a return visit to South America, not so much for a story as to shoot the breeze with a chum who'd kept in touch via postcard for over thirty years. And it was here that Barbara Fox – or Barbara Gofton as she was then – took a break from her backpacking trip around Chile to sip pisco sour, a favourite Chilean cocktail, with George and Gladys on the balcony of their apartment.

'I used to live in Newcastle and my dad well remembered George from his time as a footballer in England,' says Fox, now a successful author.

I'd been in a jewellers in Newcastle and for some reason, I

mentioned that I was going travelling in Chile with a friend. And the jeweller, who was clearly a football fan, said, 'Why don't you visit George Robledo while you're out there?' So I wrote to him and, incredibly, he wrote back straightaway saying, 'Sure, that's no problem, I'll be around, looking forward to seeing you, yours sincerely, Geo Robledo.' I ended up going to see him twice while I was out there and on the second occasion I did an interview with him, even though he was in the middle of giving a football lesson while we were talking. I can still hear his voice in my head, sounding very English despite all the years he'd spent in Chile. I think he even did an imitation of a Geordie accent for me!

'All in all, my years in Newcastle were the best of my life,' George told Fox during that interview, which appeared in the Newcastle United fanzine *The Mag*. 'If there was a part of my life I could live again, it would be then. Northumberland is such a beautiful county. I spent nearly five years on Tyneside with the team and I have only very happy memories of that period. The other players were very special and the fans were wonderful. I always thought the Gallowgate crowd was the best in the country with its support.' George also took the opportunity to thank everyone who'd corresponded with him during his time in Chile. 'I have never met some of these people and yet they write to me faithfully,' he said.

Peter Donaghy, the Newcastle United season-ticket holder whose mother had fielded phone calls for the Robledos during their years living in Fenham, never quite made it to Viña del Mar. But he did manage to reach Santiago and meet up with George in the process.

'I used to publish dictionaries about financial terminology, and my work took me to Chile where I interviewed people at an accounting company with offices in Santiago,' says Donaghy.

> I happened to mention to them that the only Chilean person I knew by name was George Robledo and they said, 'Oh, yeah, of course, Jorge!' and hunted down his phone number for me. George was coming up to Santiago and he very kindly agreed to meet me. Santiago wasn't a particularly nice place at that time. There had been some hostilities and one or two explosions to do with resistance to Pinochet. You had soldiers on the street corners and tanks parked in various places, so it was nice to meet George in the calm atmosphere of a nice hotel. And he was wonderful, the perfect gentleman. I'd worked as an interpreter for Newcastle United when they'd played Real Zaragoza in the 1969 Fairs Cup [the forerunner to the UEFA Cup or what is now the Europa League] and had been lucky enough to travel with the team for that match, so we had a lot to talk about. He said, 'The next time you come to Chile, you will have to come to Viña del Mar and stay with us.' But of course there never was a next time.

At the end of November 1988, when George came to write his Christmas cards bound for the UK, there was one significant name missing from the list. On 9 October, Jackie Milburn had died at home in Ashington, Northumberland, surrounded by family and with the bedroom curtains open so he could see the sky. He'd been diagnosed with lung cancer (refusing chemotherapy as, in his words, he 'wanted to die with dignity'). His diagnosis was something George had been unaware of, making the news of his death at the age of sixty-four all the more shocking. 'They're coming for us now,' George observed ruefully to Benny Hill, his old Yorkshire-based sports writer friend, in a letter accompanying that year's card. He was, clearly, aware of his own mortality yet still he continued to chain-smoke. And with every cigarette, the cough he'd developed seemed to get worse.

George's first heart attack came at home on Saturday 1 April 1989. He survived that one – just – and was rushed to hospital. Later the same day, he suffered a second cardiac arrest, which proved to be fatal.

Elizabeth Robledo was in Sydney, Australia, at the time, having finished her university studies in Chile. She was staying at the Young Women's Christian Association (YWCA) in the Hyde Park area of the city. 'They had really strict rules about receiving phone calls at night, so what with the time difference, I didn't get to hear about it until the next day,' she recalls.

That's when Mum called and explained to the security guy on duty that my father had passed away and could she please speak to me. At first, I really didn't understand what she meant. She said, 'I wanted to let you know that Dad had a heart attack and he is in the church now.' I said something like, 'OK, so how is he doing?' I thought she meant Dad had gone to church to pray. You know, to say, 'Thank you, God, for saving my life.' I asked if I could talk to him when he got back, but then Mum started to get confused as well. Then I understood what she was saying – Dad was lying at rest inside the church. In Chile, that's what happens the day after someone dies. Then the day after that, the person is buried. It's not like in Australia, or the US or the UK, where you might have two or three weeks before the funeral. And so I couldn't go. There was no way I could make it back in time from Australia. That was hard for me, very hard indeed.

In Chile, George's death was greeted with an immense outpouring of grief. Every television news bulletin, every radio news bulletin and every national newspaper led on the story for days. 'I'm old enough to remember the assassination of President Kennedy in Dallas, and I always think of it as being a bit like that,' says Colo-Colo supporter Lucas Moreno.

With Kennedy, they say people remember where they were when they heard the news. With Jorge, I had been out with some friends, and when I got home my girlfriend of the time said, 'Have you heard?' I said, 'Heard what?' and she told me. Apparently, it had just been announced on the radio. I could not believe it because to me he was still a young man. I can still see it all – where my girlfriend was standing, where I was standing, the look on her face, the colours in the room. I haven't been in that room for more than thirty years, not since I moved from Chile to Spain, but I can remember it like it was yesterday.

In those pre-digital days, when there was no internet or social media, it took a little time for word of George's death to filter into the outside world. Even then, national newspaper editors in the UK chose largely to ignore it as a story. George had been born in Chile. He'd played international football for Chile. He hadn't lived in England for thirty-six years. The connection with John Lennon had yet to be made. His record for scoring more goals in a single season than any other overseas registered, foreign-born player didn't really bear scrutiny because, at that time, there were so few overseas players in the UK. As far as Fleet Street was concerned, George's passing didn't exactly scream front-page news.

Fortunately, that wasn't the case in Yorkshire and north-east England, where George's name continued to carry weight. On the afternoon of Sunday 2 April, with Newcastle United having lost 1–0 at Southampton the previous day, the *Evening Chronicle*'s sports writer John Gibson stepped away from his back-page duties to compose a few words for the newspaper's front page. This is what he wrote, under the headline 'Cup Hero Robledo Dies In Chile':

George Robledo, Newcastle United's great goalscoring star of the 1950s, has died suddenly at his home in Chile. Robledo, who played in the 1951 and 1952 FA Cup triumphs at Wembley, suffered a heart attack at his home. He was 62. George is the third member of United's glory sides of the early fifties to die recently following his fine striking partner Jackie Milburn and skipper Joe Harvey. George's younger brother Walter, who lives near Richmond (London), told me 'I received a phone call earlier today to say that George had died. The funeral is tomorrow. He hadn't been in bad health and this is something of a shock. He wasn't drinking but was smoking a lot and was dreadfully missing his daughter who had just gone to live in Australia.' Robledo, who was teaching at the local English school, was a fabulous goalscorer and a great partner for 'wor' Jackie. He played in the 1951 side that beat Blackpool 2–0 at Wembley – Milburn got both the goals – and the following year Robledo got the only one of the match against Arsenal to give United the trophy again. The Robledo family emigrated to England in 1932 and he joined United from Barnsley along with his brother Ted in January 1949 in a £26,500 deal. After his two Wembley appearances – Ted played in the second cup final with him – the pair went home to join Colo-Colo in Santiago in May of 1953. George, a bustling goalscorer, scored ninety-one goals in 164 appearances and was capped by Chile in the 1950 World Cup. He paid a nostalgic trip back to Tyneside in 1981 when he met a lot of his old teammates including Milburn and Harvey. Brother Ted died in 1970 in mysterious circumstances when he went missing from the tanker Al Sahn in the Persian Gulf. The captain was later charged with his murder but acquitted.

It was through reading newspapers such as the *Evening Chronicle*, *The Journal*, the *Yorkshire Post* and the *Barnsley Chronicle* that the vast majority of those in the UK who remembered George found out about his death. 'It did come as a real shock,' recalls Peter Donaghy.

It was probably four or five years since I'd seen him, but as far as I was aware, his health was good. There were no signs of any illness at all. He'd been thoroughly enjoying his work – obviously you have to be relatively fit to teach physical education, as he did. Afterwards I sent a letter of condolence to Gladys and that started quite a long line of correspondence between us. It was nice to keep in touch.

'I remember hearing the news and, I think, reading about it in the *Barnsley Chronicle*,' says Don Wearmouth.

Sixty-two – that's no age, is it? In those days, when celebrities died, it didn't tend to be all across the TV screens or newspapers, not to the extent that it is today. I know George was a footballer, but he was still a celebrity in my eyes. I must admit, I didn't know he smoked. That came as a bit of a shock. We tend to think of football players leading clean, healthy lives these days, so it's easy to forget how people sometimes lived back then. You'd think he'd have known better, wouldn't you, being an athlete? But then I suppose there's so much more that we know now about smoking which we didn't know then.

George's funeral service took place on Monday 3 April at the Iglesia Las Carmelitas in Viña del Mar. En route to the church, the hearse paused outside Saint Peter's so staff and pupils could pay their respects. Prior to the service beginning, a group of St Peter's students laid the school's flag across his coffin. Afterwards, in scenes reminiscent of those witnessed at Jackie Milburn's funeral in Newcastle seven months previously, George's body was driven through streets lined with people on its way to the Chilean capital before being laid to rest in the Mausoleo de Colo-Colo, the club's own dedicated mausoleum (reserved for a select group of distinguished ex-players and administrators, including Colo-Colo founder and captain David Arellano) at the Cementerio General in Santiago. Which is where it remains to this day, should you ever feel the desire to pay your respects.

Less than two weeks later, the Hillsborough disaster happened. Hillsborough was where George had watched his first ever professional football match as a child. He'd always loved the look of the place, the feel of the place, the humour of the crowds and that wonderfully manicured pitch on which, it should be said, he nearly always seemed to score. On Saturday 15 April 1989, viewers to the BBC's *Grandstand* programme watched in horror as live pictures showed hundreds of people seeking refuge from the carnage at the Leppings Lane end of the ground on that very same pitch. The vast majority appeared to be in a state of distress or disbelief. Some were injured. Others, it transpired, were either dying or already dead.

'The Hillsborough disaster was as inevitable as it was shocking,' Phil Scraton, the criminologist, academic and author, wrote ten years after the event in his pivotal book *Hillsborough: The Truth*.

The appalling terror of those pens which left 96 dead (later to become 97), hundreds injured and thousands traumatised could, and should, have been anticipated and avoided. Without doubt, the full responsibility for the disaster lay with those organisations which owned, ran, maintained, hired and managed the stadium. Each had a primary role in ensuring a safe venue. Put simply, both legally and morally, they owed a duty of care to the fans.

An appalling terror compounded, it should be said, by the ongoing torment of injustice for the survivors and bereaved, subjected for decades to flawed coronial procedures, inappropriate inquest verdicts, questionable police practices and the failure to prosecute or discipline those responsible.

Would justice have been better served thirty-seven years previously had the events of that day played out, as they could so easily have done, when Newcastle United took on Blackburn Rovers in the 1952 FA Cup semi-final with way too many people inside Hillsborough?

Quite possibly. Yet that still wouldn't have changed the fact that these things kept on happening at football matches throughout the 1940s, the 1950s, the 1960s and the 1970s into the 1980s. And, for every sizeable loss of life involving overcrowding or crushing – Burnden Park, Ibrox, Hillsborough – there were countless near misses and smaller tragedies involving fatalities in single-digit figures, including the incident at St James' Park in January 1951 when two people died at the Newcastle United versus Bolton Wanderers FA Cup tie. To reiterate what Barry Murphy – the boyhood Newcastle supporter turned Barnsley FC record appearance holder, who was at Hillsborough on 15 April 1989 in his capacity as a scout for Nottingham Forest – said earlier in these pages, 'You look back now at those huge crowds and you think "Really?" But we didn't know any better.'

Maybe not, but the authorities certainly should have.

April had always been a special month for George, Gladys and Elizabeth. The fourteenth day of the month was when George had been born. The thirtieth day of the month was when Elizabeth had been born. The twenty-third marks St George's Day, not traditionally celebrated in Catholic countries but recognised by many in Chile due to the country's old trade links with England. April was also when George had enjoyed some of the happiest moments of his playing career, including victorious FA Cup semi-finals – not to mention the 1951 final itself, staged on the twenty-eighth of the month.

April 1989, though, was different. For many people with ties to the world of football living at opposite ends of the globe, April 1989 was about mourning those who had died prematurely and unexpectedly.

16

YOU KNOW MY NAME

'Hasta la victoria, siempre.' (Until victory, always.)
– CHE GUEVARA

Gladys Robledo always knew she would make it to Newcastle one day. George had talked about the city and its surrounding areas so often that she felt as if she knew the place and its people intimately. She'd just always presumed, when the time came, that George would be there to show her around.

Sadly, it wasn't to be. Nevertheless, two years after George's death, in the company of their daughter Elizabeth, Gladys finally got to walk down bustling Northumberland Street, look out over the River Tyne and visit St James' Park. Where, in the presence of six of George's former teammates, she presented Newcastle United – or more specifically, the club's museum – with George's two FA Cup winner's medals from the 1951 and 1952 finals.

'The medals belong only in one place,' Gladys told the assembled gathering in word-perfect English.

I treasure them, especially since George's death, but I know that they should go on display for the people of Newcastle to see. George always talked about the happy times he had at Newcastle United and the special players he played with. They were names that meant so much to us. Now we are able to meet them and know them, which is a great honour. But there is sadness that Jack Milburn and Joe Harvey are not here today. George talked so much about them, and I remember how upset he was when he heard of Jack's death.

Several of those special players then took the opportunity to tell Gladys just how much her husband had meant to them. 'George Robledo was a first-class professional and a first-class person,' said defender Charlie Crowe. In his Lanarkshire brogue, centre-half Frank Brennan recalled how 'we were a match for any team in the land' with George in the side. 'We never knew George's wife, for they married after he had left Newcastle,' added Bobby Mitchell, whose wing-wizardry during the closing minutes of the 1952 final had paved the way for George's winning goal. 'It is very special to be able to meet his family like this after his death.'

'I was fortunate enough to be invited that day,' says Barbara Fox, who by then had returned to the UK from her backpacking trip to Chile.

It really was a wonderful, relaxed occasion. Peter Mallinger, Newcastle's vice-chairman at the time, played the role of host and the local BBC television news was there to record it. They interviewed Gladys and she spoke about George's very strong love of the club and the north-east. I also remember some of the players' wives were laughing about Ma Robledo and how she'd kept a beady eye on her son, especially where women were concerned!

A few days later, on Monday 10 June 1991, Gladys and Elizabeth visited Oakwell, where they met with some of George's teammates from his days as a relative stripling at Barnsley, including inside-forward Johnny Steele, defender Gordon Pallister and goalkeeper Norman Rimmington (who would work for the club well into the twenty-first century as a coach, physio, groundsman and, finally, kit man). Stops were also made at West Melton and Brampton, where George, Ted and Walter had gone to school, with headmaster Barry Sampson providing a tour of the rooms where the Robledo boys once studied. 'There were a few tears,' admitted Benny Hill, who helped organise the Oakwell get-together, in his piece for the local Saturday evening sports paper, the *Green 'Un*.

Decades later, there are still tears at the memory of what amounted to a pilgrimage of north-east England and Yorkshire, especially the Newcastle leg of the journey and the handing over of George's medals. 'That meant a lot to Mum and me,' says Elizabeth.

The way I remember it is that Newcastle United were looking to open their museum later that year and they approached us to see if we could perhaps donate something. We chose the FA Cup medals because… I'm sorry, but I get emotional about this… somehow it meant we were giving back to the city of Newcastle something that was so treasured by Dad. Newcastle had given him so much – now it was time to repay a little of that. Those years [at

Newcastle United] were the peak of his career in England, maybe of his entire career, and we felt that was the best thing to do.

Fast-forward a matter of weeks to Wednesday 17 July 1991. At a meeting attended by the chairmen of the twenty-two clubs in English football's First Division, it was decided that as of the following summer, a new league would be formed. Goodbye First Division, hello Premier League. In the years since, the Premier League has arguably become England's principal cultural export. From Sydney to Stockholm, its various twists and turns are followed with unswerving devotion by untold millions of people. Gone are the old-fashioned stadiums that once doubled as death traps. Training facilities are beyond compare, as are the wages. No matter where you are on Earth, the Premier League is almost impossible to ignore.

And yet, as the sports journalist Jim White wrote on the twentieth anniversary of the Premier League's inception, 'As with many a revolution, the collateral damage has been extensive.' Large numbers of traditional fans continue to be priced out of watching their teams play in the flesh. The atmosphere inside the reconfigured stadiums can be tepid. Local footballing talent tends to be overlooked in favour of foreign imports. The all-important element of jeopardy has largely been removed due to the financial skewing of the league in favour of the bigger clubs, reducing the likelihood of an underdog winning the title or a cup.

What's more, the tendency to airbrush all that occurred prior to 1992 from the history books has become irksome, misleading and downright disrespectful. Scroll through the records for the most goals scored by a player in English football's top flight, or the most clean sheets kept by a goalkeeper or the highest number of appearances and you won't find anything from the 1980s, the 1970s, the 1960s or beforehand. It's almost as if Dixie Dean, the man who still holds the record for the most league goals scored in a single season (sixty, for Everton during the 1927–28 campaign), and his peers from previous decades never existed. 'If you say that you can't compare eras, what's the point in having any records?' Dean's granddaughter, Melanie Prentice, commented in a 2023 interview. 'In boxing, it goes right back and you have these comparisons. The same in cricket. Why not football?'

There was a reason Prentice was speaking in 2023. In May of that year, Erling Haaland was championed far and wide for having broken the all-time record for the most league goals (thirty-six) scored in a single English top-flight season, despite him being well shy of Dean's tally. In doing so, Haaland supposedly set a new record for the most league goals scored by an 'overseas' player, surpassing the thirty-two notched by Egypt's Mohamed Salah during the 2017–18 season. From what your author has seen, only one UK media source came close to publishing the alternative truth. That, perhaps unsurprisingly, was the *Barnsley Chronicle*, which, on Friday 5 May 2023, ran the following story on its back page and accompanying website:

Erling Haaland broke a record held by a former Barnsley player this week. The Manchester City striker netted his thirty-fourth Premier League goal of the campaign in their 2–1 win at Fulham. That meant he has the most goals by a 'foreign' player in an English top flight season. The record had previously been held by George Robledo who set it with Newcastle United in 1951–52. Robledo began his career at Barnsley and grew up in nearby West Melton having been born in Chile, for whom he played.

Even then, the *Barnsley Chronicle* omitted to say that Haaland had actually been born just twenty-five miles up the road in Leeds, an unavoidable fact that blurs the lines as to who actually holds the record for the most goals scored in a single English top-flight season by a 'foreign' player. At the time of writing, logic suggests that if you're going with the most goals scored by an overseas registered player, then it's Erling Haaland. If you're going for the most goals scored by an overseas registered, foreign-born player, then it's George Robledo. Two men from two contrasting eras, both equally deserving of a place in the history books. Both equally deserving of being remembered. Except that George, by dint of having been born in 1926, largely isn't.

Unless, that is, you live in Chile, where Erling Haaland's goalscoring exploits during the 2022–23 season brought about more reasons to celebrate George's achievements from a bygone age on television, in print, digitally and on the radio. As Julio Martínez, the country's most famous football commentator, was fond of saying, 'In Chile, football is divided into before and after George Robledo.'

Or, as Don Wearmouth ventured, almost as an aside, during the research process for this book, 'Over there, they seem to want to celebrate their football heritage. We seem to want to bury ours.'

There are, admittedly, other reasons why George's light has dimmed over the years and had in fact begun to do so before the arrival of the all-singing, all-dancing Premier League. As with so many other great football heroes from the pre-*Match of the Day* and Sky TV eras, very little of his star pedigree was captured on film for posterity. What does exist is in black and white, which will always play second fiddle to colour when it comes to compiling montages of the game's great moments and characters. Perhaps if George had returned to live in, say, north-east England once he'd stopped playing in Chile then his legacy might have endured in much the same way as that of his great friend and attacking partner, Jackie Milburn.

Jackie got a stand named after him at St James' Park. Jackie got a statue on Northumberland Street (which has since been moved to Strawberry Place, just outside St James' Park and adjoining Shearer Place, named after Alan Shearer, another of Newcastle United's great goalscorers). There's even a train called Jackie Milburn. It's not a competition, but it would have been nice if George had got something.

But then, in the spring of 2022, thanks largely to the efforts of a former Yorkshire teacher by the name of Chris Brook, he did.

'For many years I've been involved in organising the Totty Cup, the competition for schools in the Don and Dearne areas of Yorkshire wedged between the towns of Barnsley, Doncaster and Rotherham,' says Brook.

Back in 1939, the Totty Cup had been won by Brampton Ellis School, with a certain George Robledo scoring four goals in the final. That name always struck me as unusual – you don't tend to get many Robledos in this part of the world. Decades ago, a guy called Jimmy Kelly, who'd gone on to become an England schoolboy international, said there'd been someone who had played in the final of the Totty Cup, the final of the Montagu Cup – a club competition which covers the same geographical area – and in the FA Cup final. That player turned out to be George. It took some verifying, but the more I searched for information, the more I became interested in George's story. In fact, the more I became interested in the whole Robledo family story. That's how it first started – the idea of putting a blue plaque on the wall of 97 Barnsley Road, West Melton, where they had once lived, as a way of keeping that story alive.

Having sought and received both funding and permission for a plaque, a date was arranged for the unveiling. All being well, Elizabeth Robledo would make the journey from Chile to witness proceedings (this time on her own, with Gladys having died in 2011 aged eighty-five). That date was 14 April 2020, on what would have been George's birthday.

At which point, the Covid-19 pandemic drove a coach and horses through the game plan.

By the time society felt ready to mingle again, Brook's idea had grown legs to include a second blue plaque on the wall of 5 Ridgeway, Fenham. On 14 April 2022, the West Melton plaque was finally unveiled in front of a large crowd bolstered by members of the local media. Elizabeth Robledo was there, as was Barnsley's record appearance holder Barry Murphy, as was Lucy Thorpe (whose great-grandmother had married Frank Oliver, George and Ted's uncle, the man who'd acted as co-signature on George's first professional contract with Barnsley due to his nephew being seventeen years old). Three weeks later, on Tuesday 3 May – the seventieth anniversary of Newcastle United's 1952 FA Cup win – the second blue plaque was unveiled in Newcastle's western suburbs.

'This is important in England but in Chile too,' Pavel Piña, the Colo-Colo club historian who travelled from South America to north-east England especially for the occasion, told *The Chronicle* (which, by now, had lost the *Evening* half of its title).

> George revolutionised football in Chile and was, is, so important to our club and our institution. He is one of the reasons why Colo-Colo is so popular in our country. For our club, this [unveiling] is so important. We are really happy to be able to share this moment with people from Newcastle.

Also present in Fenham that day, as indeed he had been in West Melton the month before, was Francisco Tello, a London-based Chilean diplomat who needed no second invitation to attend on behalf of his government. 'It's a privilege to be here, it really is,' he told the assembled crowd (which, besides Elizabeth Robledo, also included Peter Donaghy). 'They were two of the biggest sportsmen in Chilean history. They were also great ambassadors for Chile. They embodied very important values – friendship, sportsmanship and fair play, all the things you need to be a good person in life.'

'It was a tremendous surprise when Chris Brook contacted me about the blue plaques,' says Elizabeth.

> It was almost unreal. How come a teacher is going to these lengths to remember my father and his family? But then I came to real-ise that Chris thinks more like a historian. He appreciates today,

but he also understands the importance of yesterday, in sport as well as in life. The whole thing made me feel very proud, very excited and very emotional. My dad had stories, lots of stories, but somehow it was like we were creating new ones by bringing all these people together to unveil the plaques and remember the past. That was all Chris's idea.

'You might expect me to say this, but stories are important,' adds Ashley Ball of the *Barnsley Chronicle* who, somewhat appropriately given his lifelong admiration for the Robledo brothers, covered the West Melton unveiling on behalf of his newspaper.

Stories are what get handed down from generation to generation. They are how we tend to remember people and events. As a lad, growing up in nearby Wath, my dad talked to me about football quite a lot and he would speak of the Robledos. My dad was born in 1949, so he'd have seen the tail end of their careers or heard things through the grapevine. He talked about the Robledos as if they were ours. To anybody else the name Robledo sounds exotic, but I was so accustomed to hearing it I actually thought it was a local family name! That's because they were held in such high esteem and everyone was so proud of them. They might not necessarily know it, but there are probably Newcastle fans living in or around South Yorkshire who support Newcastle because of the Robledos.

'It's so important that these people aren't forgotten, because football is not just about the twenty-first century,' says Lucy Thorpe, who only discovered her own personal link to the Robledos following the death of her grandmother and the house clearance that ensued, during which George and Ted's first professional contracts resurfaced.

I'm a football fan myself, and people sometimes say to me, 'Barnsley have never won anything.' And I say, 'Yes, we have. Look at the records and tell me who won the FA Cup in 1912.' I like looking back through Barnsley's past to when Tiverton Preedy founded what was initially Barnsley St Peter's FC. Without him, I wouldn't have a football team to support and George wouldn't have become a Barnsley player. It's all linked through the generations. That, to me, is a nice feeling, knowing that we're all part of the same history.

For Elizabeth Robledo, 2022 marked the third time she'd visited her father's adopted homeland. It was also her longest stay in the UK, with a three-week gap between the unveiling of the two plaques – time enough to take in some of the cities and football landmarks that George had filled his daughter's head with over the years. She went to Glasgow, Manchester, Old Trafford and Liverpool. There, besides taking in Anfield, she gorged like there was no tomorrow on the Beatles, making three separate trips to the current incarnation of The Cavern, the club which became the band's adopted home during the early 1960s. Penny Lane, Strawberry Fields, Paul McCartney's house, John Lennon's house – Elizabeth savoured them all, along with Liverpool Docks, the place where her father's ship quite literally came in one Saturday morning in April 1932. 'And I cried all the way round because everything was so meaningful,' she recalls. 'Every place was a song, and every song was a memory, not just a memory of the Beatles and their music but of my dad.'

As word of Elizabeth's visit spread, so her diary began to fill with a combination of unlikely, random and frankly jaw-dropping engagements. The year 2022 just happened to be the 150th anniversary of the FA Cup. To mark the occasion, the Football Association selected a person to represent each decade of the trophy's glittering history. Incredibly – and even she's not exactly sure how this came to be – Elizabeth was chosen to represent the 1950s, with a VIP pass to the final between Chelsea and Liverpool thrown in. There she was, a few days before the match, attending a press event at Wembley Stadium alongside John Motson, one of Britain's favourite football commentators. There she was, the evening prior to the final, being interviewed about her dad on the *One Show*, the BBC's magazine-style current affairs television programme. There she was, standing on the pitch at half-time holding a Newcastle United shirt with the name 'Robledo' emblazoned across the back, flanked by some of the great and the good of the competition including former Leeds United striker Allan Clarke (representing the 1970s) and ex-Chelsea forward Gianfranco Zola (representing the 1990s). 'A lovely moment, there,' mused former player-turned-broadcaster Gary Lineker, anchoring the BBC's coverage of the final alongside, fittingly, Alan Shearer in his latter-day role as a football pundit.

Away from the FA Cup, Elizabeth got to meet Ben Brereton Díaz, then of Blackburn Rovers, born in Staffordshire with a Chilean mother, who had followed in George's footsteps and been capped internationally by 'La Roja'. There was also a trip to the Manchester

City versus Real Madrid Champions League semi-final, courtesy of UEFA. But, in all honesty, from a football perspective, nothing could compare to Wembley on FA Cup final day. 'That was something Dad and I used to watch on television in Chile,' says Elizabeth.

It was a tradition. I don't know how many finals we saw, but there were a lot. So for me to actually be there at Wembley, where he scored the winning goal all those years ago, was very hard to take in. It was such a special place for Dad and because of that, it's a special place for me. I know the ground has changed over the years, but the name is still the same. The occasion is still the same. If Chris Brook hadn't had the idea of the plaques, then I would never have been there. Everything that happened on the trip, I owe it all to Chris.

Before returning to Chile, Elizabeth took the opportunity to visit her Uncle Walter and his wife Helen, along with their daughters Mandy and Nicky, at their house in west London. It was the last time Elizabeth and Walter would ever speak in person. Seven months later, on 23 December, Walter died a couple of weeks after turning ninety-one. The funeral wasn't so much a funeral as a celebration of life, with Handel's 'The Arrival of the Queen of Sheba' and Stevie Wonder's 'I Just Called to Say I Love You' bookending readings and tributes along with the rousing hymns 'Lord of the Dance' and 'Jerusalem'. Walter may have been, in his own self-effacing words, 'the brother of the footballing Robledos', but unlike George, he made it into old age. Unlike Ted, his death had been peaceful, surrounded by family.

'There is a powerful impression that, irrespective of his feelings for the game [of football], he wanted to make his own independent mark on the world,' Richard Williams, the music and sports writer, had observed of Walter on interviewing him for *The Independent* in 1999. 'Which he was to do, with a resolve surely inherited from his remarkable mother.'

Which – with George, Ted and Walter now gone – brings us to Elsie, or rather Elsie's fate.

One Saturday morning during the late summer of 1970, a reporter from the *Sunday Express* newspaper doorstepped Elsie at her home in Lowestoft. Would Elsie be attending the wedding of her son Ian at St Andrew's Church in Chesterton, Cambridge, on 19 September? At first Elsie denied that she had a son called Ian, but when the reporter doggedly returned later the same morning, the truth began to emerge. And it went something along the following lines.

In January 1936, Arístides Robledo had travelled from Chile to England, or more specifically Hull, supposedly for a job interview. Unbeknown seemingly to anyone, least of all her three sons, Elsie went to Hull to meet him.

Shortly afterwards, with Arístides having returned to Chile, she discovered she was pregnant. Later that year, Elsie left West Melton to stay in Lancashire, where she gave birth to a son. The son, named Ian, was given up by Elsie and went on to be raised in a children's home.

Now, with Ian about to tie the knot, the banns of marriage were being read in public at St Andrew's Church and someone had put two and two together regarding the surname 'Robledo'. Word of this reached the *Sunday Express*, which ran with the story of how 'a quiet wedding, planned in a Cambridge church, has uncovered a secret kept for 34 years from the outside world by Mrs Elsie Robledo, mother of the famous footballing Robledo brothers of the 1950s'.

'Perhaps I was wrong, but times were difficult and different in those days,' Elsie was quoted as saying of her decision to give up Ian, who died in 2006.

When I returned in 1932 to England my husband, Arístides, remained managing his business interests in Chile. So I was on my own with George, Ted and my next youngest, Walter. We lived with my father and family at West Melton and later moved over a general store which he ran. There was very little money and I had to bring up three growing boys. Then my husband came over for a fortnight for an interview for a job in Hull. He returned to Chile, but shortly after that I found I was expecting Ian. It was a great shock. My father was a very strict man and said he was not going to have another child in the house. How would it look to you? A woman, nearly 40, expecting a child and no husband around. I did not know what to do for the best. After Ian was born he was put in a children's home. I sent money and clothes to the home but never wrote or contacted Ian. I thought it would upset him if he knew he had a real mother somewhere.

Over half a century later, the fallout from that piece in the *Sunday Express* is still being felt. Elizabeth only learned of the story's existence during her 2022 visit to England. Did George, Ted and Walter realise they had a younger brother prior to the story seeing the light of day in 1970? We're unlikely ever to know. Ted went to his watery grave just months after it was published. Whatever thoughts or emotions George and Walter harboured over Ian, they appear reluctant to have discussed them with anyone, even their respective children. It was, and indeed continues to be, a sensitive subject for all concerned, as well as a painful one. And nobody seems to have suffered more than Elsie herself, laid to rest in a Suffolk churchyard in 1976 having been judged by the British tabloid press.

She could be difficult, she could be obstinate, she made mistakes, but there can be no denying Elsie Robledo paid a heavy price for some of her character flaws.

• • •

'The past is a foreign country; they do things differently there.' The line may come from L. P. Hartley's novel *The Go-Between* but it could so easily have been found in the pages of George Robledo's autobiography, had he ever got around to writing it. Since 1953, when *The Go-Between* was published and George left Newcastle United for Colo-Colo, the world in which we live has changed almost beyond recognition, as indeed has the game of football. And yet our obsession with those who play it remains.

In the years since George's death, no end of local heroes and foreign imports have thrilled the masses at Oakwell, St James' Park and across Britain in general. Between 1996 and 2006, Tyneside native Alan Shearer scored more goals than any other Newcastle United player in history (although George's goals-per-game ratio of 0.55 remains superior). Dwight Yorke came from Trinidad and Tobago and, almost half a century after it was set, took George's record as the highest-scoring overseas player in the English leagues. Erling Haaland came from Norway and, no matter which way you look at it, scored more league and cup goals combined during the 2022–23 season than George did back in 1951–52. With every new kid on the block, so the 1950s recedes a little further in our rear-view mirror, to the point where it's almost out of sight altogether. Which, for all the game's faults in the UK at that time – low wages, restrictive contracts, scant medical treatment, poor spectator facilities – is also a colossal shame, given the thrills and spills of what took place on the field during those post-war years.

'If I were to be asked which era of football I preferred between the 1950s, when I began my career, and the 1970s, when it all came to an end for me, I would say the '50s every time,' the great Jimmy Greaves once commented of a decade in which 'teams were not too worried about shipping goals as long as they scored one more than the opposition'. When it came to Barnsley, or Newcastle United, or Colo-Colo, that one more goal was often scored by George Robledo. And if it wasn't George finding the back of the net, then there's a fair chance he would've supplied the ball to whoever did.

In 1973, Basil Easterbrook, one of the finest football and cricket writers in British regional journalism throughout the post-war decades, was tasked with penning a seven-part series of articles for the *Evening Chronicle* about Newcastle United's 'Stars of the Fifties'. Easterbrook – who, like so many others, had corresponded with George via letters and postcards since his departure from England for Chile – knew instinctively who his seventh and final star should be. A player who'd stood out for his skill, his speed, his strength, his awareness, his vision, his work rate, his goals and, yes, that incredible back story, the one about the boy from the Atacama Desert who, in Easterbrook's opinion, became the nearest thing to the complete footballer he had ever seen.

'Some shrewd observers of the game of soccer have expressed the opinion that, if it were possible to combine the skill and flair of a South American with the temperament and power of an Englishman, you would have one very fine player,' Easterbrook wrote by way of his introductory paragraph. 'Just after the Second World War, the Gods arranged it for us, and the result was outstanding.'

BIBLIOGRAPHY

BOOKS

Beckett, Francis and Hencke, David. *Marching to the Fault Line: The Miners' Strike and the Battle for Industrial Britain* (Constable, 2009)

Bedford, David. *Liddypool: Birthplace of the Beatles* (Dalton Watson Fine Books, 2011)

Bowen, J. David. *The Land and People of Chile* (J. B. Lippincott Company, 1966)

Brown, Craig. *One, Two, Three, Four: The Beatles in Time* (4th Estate, 2020)

Buchan, Charles. *A Lifetime in Football* (Mainstream, 2010)

Clavane, Anthony. *Moving the Goalposts: A Yorkshire Tragedy* (riverrun, 2016)

Davidson, Mark. *The Rough Guide to Chile & Easter Island* (Rough Guides, 2023)

Davies, Hunter. *The Quarrymen* (Omnibus Press, 2001)

Davies, Hunter. *The John Lennon Letters* (Weidenfeld & Nicolson, 2012)

Dennis, Brian, Daykin, John and Hyde, Derek. *Barnsley FC 1887–1998: The Official History* (Yore Publications, 1998)

Du Noyer, Paul. *The Complete John Lennon Songs* (Welbeck Publishing, 2020)

Firth, Grenville. *The Official History of Barnsley Football Club* (self-published, 1978)

Firth, Grenville and Wood, David. *The Who's Who of Barnsley FC* (Derby Books, 2011)

Glanville, Brian. *The Story of the World Cup* (Faber and Faber, 2001)

Grainger, Colin. *The Singing Winger* (deCoubertin Books, 2019)

Greaves, Jimmy. *The Heart of the Game* (Time Warner Books, 2005)

Greaves, Jimmy and Giller, Norman. *Don't Shoot the Manager* (Boxtree, 1993)

Green, Mark. *Barnsley at War, 1939 to 1945* (Pen and Sword, 2019)

Harris, Nick. *England, Their England: The Definitive Story of Foreign Footballers in the English Game Since 1888* (Pitch, 2003)

Hornby, Nick. *Fever Pitch* (Victor Gollancz Ltd, 1992)

Hutchings, Steve and Nawrat, Chris. *The Sunday Times Illustrated History of Football* (Ted Smart, 1994)

Joannou, Paul. *United: The First 100 Years* (ACL & Polar Publishing, 1991)

Jones, Ron. *The Beatles' Liverpool* (Ron Jones, 2008)

Lupson, Peter. *Thank God for Football!* (Azure, 2006)

Matthews, Stanley. *The Way it Was: My Autobiography* (Headline, 2001)

McKinstry, Leo. *Jack & Bobby* (HarperCollins, 2003)

Miller, David. *Stanley Matthews: The Authorised Biography* (Pavilion Books, 1989)

Moffat, Alistair and Rosie, George. *Tyneside: A History of Newcastle and Gateshead from Earliest Times* (Mainstream, 2006)

Noble, Graham. *Oakwell Heroes: A Who's Who of Barnsley Footballers 1945–1986* (Glenwood Publications, 1986)

Parkinson, Michael. *My Sporting Life* (Hodder & Stoughton, 2022)

Patterson, James. *The Last Days of John Lennon* (Century, 2020)

Pearson, Harry. *The Far Corner: A Mazy Dribble Through North-East Football* (Abacus, 2013)

Priestley, J. B. *English Journey* (Heinemann, 1934)

Reynolds, John E. *Stars of Soccer* (Michael Mason, 1948)

Robson, Bobby. *Farewell but not Goodbye* (Hodder & Stoughton, 2009)

Robson, Bobby. *Newcastle: My Kind of Toon* (Hodder & Stoughton, 2008)

Rollin, Jack. *Soccer at War* (Headline, 2005)

Scraton, Phil. *Hillsborough: The Truth* (Mainstream Publishing, 1999)

Soar, Phil. *The Illustrated Encyclopaedia of British Football* (Marshall Cavendish, 1989)

Taylor, Rogan and Ward, Andrew. *Kicking and Screaming: An Oral History of Football in England* (Robson Books, 1998)

Trimbee, Andrew. *The Inshallah Paper* (Quartet Books, 2009)

Vignes, Spencer. *Eric & Dave: A Lifetime of Football and Friendship* (Pitch, 2022)

ONLINE RESOURCES

www.as.com

www.bbc.co.uk

www.britannica.com

www.memoriachilena.gob.cl

www.nationalgeographic.org

www.robledobrothers.wordpress.com

www.womenfootballfans.org

www.youtube.com

ACKNOWLEDGEMENTS

Writing a book, I always maintain, is very much a team effort. You need good people around you to provide help, advice, information, quotes, statistics, pictures, designs, constructive criticism, mugs of tea and the occasional ale when the sun goes down and the creative juices run dry. If you haven't got that team, then there is no book.

First and foremost, thank you to Elizabeth Robledo, the midfield dynamo in my team and the source of so much information about her father, George Robledo. I am also hugely indebted to Ashley Ball at the *Barnsley Chronicle*, Chris Brook, Xavier Caseras, Peter Donaghy, Barry Erskine, Néstor Flores, Barbara Fox, Sheila Gray, Paul Joannou, David Kitchen, Nick Loughlin, Lucas Moreno, Barry Murphy, Pavel Piño, Professor Stacey Pope at Durham University, Dave Purcell, John Shearon, Lucy Thorpe, Chris Waugh of *The Athletic*, Don Wearmouth, Richard Williams and David Wood.

A big tip of my hat goes to Alastair Hignell and the late Bobby Robson who, in their own small ways, started the ball rolling, and to those who spoke to me on condition of anonymity regarding Chile's political climate of the 1970s and 1980s.

Thank you to the journalists who went before me in terms of producing match reports and features that proved helpful in telling George Robledo's story, especially those tied to the *Barnsley Chronicle*, *The Journal*, the *Evening Chronicle* and the *Yorkshire Post*. To access much of that information, time was spent at Cathays Library in Cardiff, Experience Barnsley, the Lightbox in Barnsley and City Library, Newcastle. The National Archives in Kew, Liverpool's Maritime Museum and the National Coal Mining Museum near Wakefield were treasure troves when it came to researching other parts of George's life, while the Anglo Chilean Society went above and beyond in their support by providing a grant to help fund my research. *Muchas gracias, amigos!*

Closer to home, thank you to my partner Jane and children Rhiannon and Luca for their enduring love and patience. Thank you to my mother Sally for always being there. Last but not least, here's to James Stephens, Olivia Beattie and Catriona Allon at Biteback Publishing for sharing in my enthusiasm for George and wanting to bring his remarkable story to the attention of the wider world.

INDEX